THE RUSSIAN-ORTHODOX TRADITION AND MODERNITY

NUMEN BOOK SERIES

STUDIES IN THE HISTORY
OF RELIGIONS

VOLUME C

THE RUSSIAN-ORTHODOX TRADITION AND MODERNITY

BY

ANDREAS E. BUSS

BRILL
LEIDEN · BOSTON
2003

This book is printed on acid-free paper.

Cover photo: Church of the Nativity of the Virgin at the Far Caves in the
Kiev-Petchersk Lavra complex, Kiev, Ukraine. Photo by Ivo Romein.

Library of Congress Cataloging-in-Publication Data

Buss, Andreas E.
    The Russian–Orthodox tradition and modernity / by Andreas E. Buss.
    p. cm. — (Studies in the history of religions, ISSN 0169-8834 ; v. 100)
    Includes bibliographical references.
    ISBN: 9004133240 (alk.paper)
                    LC Control Number: 2003055870

ISSN   0169-8834
ISBN   90 04 13324 0

PRINTED IN THE NETHERLANDS

Uxori et filiae

TABLE OF CONTENTS

PREFACE

It might perhaps appear unnecessary to justify the publication of a book on the relationship between the Russian-Orthodox tradition and modernity at a time when, after the collapse of the Soviet Union, Russia is trying to adopt modern Western economic and political structures. But the need for this investigation seems even more urgent if one considers the lack of previous studies on the subject. Whereas there is an abundance of publications on the relationship between Catholic or Protestant religious traditions on the one hand and economic life and modernity on the other, there has hardly been any systematic attempt to study the significance and the possible impediments which the Russian-Orthodox tradition holds for the economic and political development of Russia, as well as the manner in which it affects Russia's acculturation to modernity. In this regard it may be hoped that this book will fill a gap and provide, at the same time, a necessary foundation for those who wish to formulate an opinion on Russia's future development and modernization.

But this is also a comparative study which finds its originality and justification in the fact that the Russian-Orthodox tradition and the Western religious tradition which led to modernity, have common roots in early Christianity. The intellectual journey to Russia can also teach us about the origins and the characteristics of the West, and can help to express modernity in more general sociological terms and, at the same time, from the point of view of traditional culture. By achieving this more general and comparative sociological understanding, the understanding of Russia and of its acculturation to the West will in turn be lifted to a higher level.

The book is mainly addressed to scholars of comparative sociology and socio-economic development, but it is hoped that others in the fields of religion (not only Eastern Orthodoxy), anthropology, Russian studies and historical sociology will also be attracted by it. It is the result of studies which, although interrupted from time to time, have continued for more than ten years. Some chapters constitute the revised and adapted forms of articles which are scattered in various scholarly journals, and new chapters of a more general perspective have been added. Financial support for research in the libraries of Heidelberg and Paris has come from the Social Sciences and Humanities Research Council of Canada.

ABBREVIATIONS

ASS   Archiv für Sozialwissenschaft und Sozialpolitik
EEWR Max Weber: 'The Economic Ethics of World Religions'
ES   Max Weber: *Economy and Society*
GAzRS Max Weber: *Gesammelte Aufsätze zur Religionssoziologie*
India   Max Weber: *The Religion of India*
PE   Max Weber: *The Protestant Ethic and the Spirit of Capitalism*
PE II   Max Weber: *Kritiken und Antikritiken: Die protestantische Ethik II*
PS   Max Weber: *Politische Schriften*
WG   Max Weber: *Wirtschaft und Gesellschaft*
WL   Max Weber: *Gesammelte Aufsätze zur Wissenschaftslehre*

INTRODUCTION

Traditional Societies and Modernity:
Two Approaches to the Understanding of Foreign Cultures

A century ago, scholars tended to believe that modern European development was unique in the history of mankind, that European culture in most respects represented the apogee of human achievements – and that the causes or origins of this uniqueness needed to be found and understood. One of the most well-known and nuanced formulations and explanations of the uniqueness of European culture may be found in the work of the German scholar Max Weber who tried to explain the rise of modern Western capitalism or, in a wider perspective, of the specific kind of Western rationalism – which is also visible, for instance, in modern bureaucracy, law, modern science and even music –, and who then inquired into the reasons why it failed to develop in the other major cultural areas of the world. Weber saw one of the main roots of modernity in the Protestant ethic and in its affinity to the spirit of capitalism, and he compared it with the spirit of the other world religions, in particular in China, India and in ancient Judaism. Nowhere else than in the Occident did he find the Protestant pursuit of ascetic ideals in mundane occupations, nowhere else the desire to prove one's faith in this specific type of methodical conduct. His studies led him to the conclusion that the kinds of rationalization, the ethos of the other world religions, differed considerably from those of the Protestants in the Occident and did not favour the development of the spirit of capitalism and that, moreover, the ethos or the spirit of these other religions was supported by very different institutional forms and organizations, equally unfavourable to the development of capitalism, and Western rationalism in general. It may be noted in passing that this distinction between the ethos and the institutions of a culture or, in his own terminology, between the spirit and the form, played an important role in Max Weber's approach – as a similar distinction between the institutions and the customs or habits had done in Tocqueville's study of the Old Regime and the Revolution in France. This distinction later led to the realization that the mere transfer of modern institutions to a traditional society may produce tensions between the traditional spirit and the new form.

The atmosphere in which the great cultural problems of the world were seen, has changed since the Second World War, and social scientists, also, have changed their standpoint, the questions they ask and, sometimes, their analytical apparatus and their methodology. Not only have they realized that in traditional societies there are internal dynamics and changes of various sorts which cannot be explained by the traditional approach, but an independent development of modernity is no longer considered to be out of reach for the cultures beyond the Occident. A search has been undertaken for the conditions which can further modernization, and many scholars, interested in questions of modernization in Asia or elsewhere, have tried to show that it is sometimes possible to find in other cultures functional equivalents of the Protestant ethic which can produce economic development.

While Max Weber used traditional cultures as sources of information for a sociology of the modern world, others have questioned the methodological approach which in the past had been applied to the study of traditional societies. According to this view, it may not be enough to remain within the occidental cultural configuration and to look at other cultures as strange entities which can be appropriately described by reference to occidental values and concepts. The French anthropologist Louis Dumont, for instance, insisted that each culture should be considered in its own right and as a whole, characterized by its ideology. The term ideology was not used by him negatively in a sense which would limit it to the view of social classes, deformed by interests or partial view-points; rather it refers to the configuration of ideas and values which are common to the global society and result from the necessity for its members to live in an understandable universe. Dumont also rejected the methodological view that grants real existence only to individuals and not to relations within a whole, and he believed that single cultural features or elements are deeply altered by their position within the social whole in which they are found, and that it would therefore be an epistemological mistake to compare a single cultural feature to a similar or corresponding feature in another society if this is done without any reference to the social whole. The concept of the individual itself is an example of the case in point: while modern culture is characterized by the ideology of the autonomous individual, the bearer of ultimate values, it is as such opposed to traditional culture in which the society as a whole is a paramount value and englobes the empirical individuals.

This approach does not ask any more why the Chinese or the Indian tradition did not develop modernity on its own, but rather why,
from a comparative point of view, occidental culture has had its
rather exceptional development. It is possible to say that it explains
the modern case in traditional terms. Modernity is here seen not as
being the end-point of the evolution of all societies, but simply a specific type of culture which is spreading all over the world and, while
other cultures may react, respond and adapt to it in different ways –
sometimes violently or in a state of shock –, is itself open to additions
and readjustments when it comes into contact with these cultures. In
this process of acculturation the great variability of symbolic and ideological responses to modernity is the result of the fact that traditional
cultures often seek to control modernization in the name of values
that are conceived as being independent of the process. Acculturation
does not generally create dual societies in which some aspects of traditional life simply become superfluous; rather, hybrids develop which
combine traditional holistic and modern features. Thus, the history of
Germany in the eighteenth and nineteenth century is that of a people
torn between traditional cultural identity and the individualistic ideology of the Enlightenment and the French Revolution. Dumont has
described how Johann Gottfried Herder in 1774 combined traditional German holistic features with the new features of modernity.
Against the Enlightenment which knew only the human individual
and the human species, Herder asserted the existence of cultures
whose interplay makes up the history of mankind. He had a holistic
perception of man, i.e. the view that man is a human being through
being a member of his culture. But he did not reject individualism out
of hand. Contrary to the naive ethnocentric devaluation of the out-
sider which is common to holistic societies, he granted all cultures
equal value. Cultures were seen by Herder as so many individuals of a
collective nature.

   The two approaches described here, represented by Max Weber
and Louis Dumont, are often thought of as being located at opposite
poles. It has become almost a commonplace to state that Max
Weber's approach to sociology was that of methodological individualism, i.e. that his approach implied that only individual human beings
are ontologically real. Methodological individualists argue that this
method, a form of heuristic eurocentrism, may and, in fact, must be
used in the study of all cultures, even traditional, non-individualistic
ones, and they tend to justify their position by the argument that

there is as little relationship between methodological individualism and individualism in general as there is between the dog as a barking animal and the dog as a celestial configuration. But it is necessary to be circumspect. With regard to Weber, such statements blind us to the fact that he managed, to some extent, to transcend the limitations of a sociology of the individual, for his interests were not directed towards individual men or events, but towards collective entities, even though they were conceived as ideal-types; he also realized that individual cultural elements or features in different societies, even if they may be identical on the factual level, may have a changing or different cultural significance within the conceptional whole or the "historical individual", which has been constructed by the social scientist (WL:183). Social wholes are everywhere in evidence in Weber's work, although they have become bloodless and shadowlike, as if night had fallen and the owl of Minerva were raising its wings. Max Weber's methodology – and perhaps the whole distinction, elaborated in Germany by the end of the nineteenth century, between *Naturwissenschaft* and *Geisteswissenschaft* – may itself be the result of a combination, resulting from acculturation to modernity, of holistic and individualistic factors.

Louis Dumont would probably have thought so, for he argued that methodology inevitably corresponds to ideology and that it is the society of the Individual which developed methodological individualism. He also reminded us of the irritation in a Hindu or a Japanese when he sees an individualistic Westerner claiming to express the fabric of traditional indigenous life in his own terms. In the end, the two approaches may not be poles apart and it may even be possible to interpret Weber's approach with the help of Dumont's categories or – *sit venia verbo* – to place Weber into Dumont. This will be attempted in the following study on the Russian-Orthodox tradition and its relation to modernity.

The motives for studying another culture, or aspects of it, can be manifold, but they can generally be divided into two categories. On the one hand, there are those who proclaim the desire to understand the other culture as such – out of pure curiosity perhaps or as a result of an attitude of escapism, the longing for a 'better' political or economic system or a 'truer' religion, or finally the intention to use the knowledge gained to better dominate this culture – and, on the other hand, there is the motive, pursued by some, who study a different culture to better understand their own. Men like Alexis de Tocqueville, Max Weber and Louis Dumont belong to this second category. In Tocqueville's *The Old Regime and the French Revolution* the centre of interest is France, although we learn a lot about England and Prussia. Max Weber wrote his essays on China and India mainly in order to test his hypothesis about the Protestant ethic and his more general ideas about a particular process of rationalization which he saw in the Occident; and Louis Dumont asked in his *Homo hierarchicus* what good there is in going to India if not in order to discover how Indian culture represents a form of the universal and how this contributes to the understanding of Western culture.

Similarly, the present study flows, on the one hand, from an interest in the possibility, the place and the characteristics of rational economic activity and modernity in Russia and, more generally, in the Eastern Orthodox tradition. It provides an interpretation of the Orthodox religious tradition with regard to its bearing on economic rationality, and makes the case that this tradition did not lead to the same sort of rationality which Max Weber associated with Protestantism. In examining another Christian tradition it rounds out Weberian scholarship.

Furthermore, the study also attempts a more general interpretation of Russian culture; it examines the underlying global ideology, the holistic set of ideas and ideals in Russia which was not conducive to modernity although, under the onslaught of the individualistic ideology of the West, hybrid new forms of thought were created.

On the whole, this study explores the deep cultural roots which nourish all human activity and thought in Russia and which strongly influence the direction which future development might take. Whereas there seems to exist the ineradicable belief, in the West as well as in Russia, that, once the structures of tsarism or of socialism have been eliminated and the legal conditions for capitalism and modernity have been put in place or rational choice can take its course, a development towards capitalism and modernity will automatically set in, the present approach implies that the radical Westernizers after the collapse of the Soviet Union ignored some of the age-old values and ideas that form the core of the mentality of the Russian people and that the mere transfer of modern institutions to a society which is grounded in a different tradition will necessarily produce tensions.

On the other hand, this study implicitly also attempts to provide a fresh understanding of aspects of Western culture and of modernity:

by pointing to the absence of a kind of ethic in the Orthodox tradition which might have an affinity to the capitalist spirit it underscores the significance of the Protestant ethic for the development of capitalism in the West; by contrasting the special path of development of the Occident with traditional (Russian) culture, it brings out its characteristic individualistic ideology; and by pointing to the hybrid forms of thought which developed in Russia under the impact of modernity it suggests that Russia in turn created and will continue to create new aspects of modernity which may be integrated in the modern configuration. Thus, as an example of large-scale comparative historical sociology, this essay attempts not only an interpretation of the Eastern Orthodox religious tradition and of Russian culture but also to shed new light on the development and the predicament of modernity in the West.

A brief overview may clarify these explanations and serve as a guide for the following chapters. In the introductory chapter Max Weber's reaction to modern science is analysed, his questioning of rationality, and his search in Russia for an alternative or solutions to problems which he saw in the Occident – although in the end the Russian alternative turned out to be unacceptable to him.

In the second part (chapters two to four), it will then be asked from a Weberian point of view and with the help of his analytical tools why the modern capitalist spirit did not develop within the tsarist structure and within the Russian-Orthodox religious tradition or even among the heterodox Old Believers and the sects, although some of them had much in common with the Protestants in the West. A short chapter on the related concept of pariah-ethics complements this part.

In the third part (chapters five to seven), finally, a different methodological approach is used, and the history of the Eastern Orthodox culture is now viewed from a different angle and in its own right, as a holistic tradition. It is shown that individualism as it is known today in the Occident does not have indigenous roots in this tradition. It thus goes behind the Weberian argument and points to the absence of the ideological preconditions of modernity in the Orthodox tradition without which neither modern science nor a rational economic ethic or a modern economic or political system would have a sufficient foundation. But, while the lineaments of the Orthodox tradition take shape, the corresponding Western features are also seen in a new light, for the mirror is then turned around and the comparative view permits a revised and perhaps more nuanced vision of how the development of modern inworldly individualism separated the Western world from the Eastern Orthodox tradition. Here, it will also become apparent that the ethos of a people, be it that of the ethical personality of the Protestants or of the Russian 'spirit', can best be understood when it is seen in relation to the dominant individualistic or holistic ideology: the economic ethic of the Protestants will be seen in its affinity to modern Western individualism and the Russian economic ethic in its affinity to traditional holism. These chapters thus provide the necessary context and foundation which the methodological approach of the study of the Russian economic ethics in the previous chapters has taken for granted. This is also what was meant by the earlier *boutade* that Max Weber would be placed into Louis Dumont.

The last chapter analyses some examples of acculturation in Russia, or of syntheses of traditional and modern ideas, which have taken place under the pressure of modernity in the social and political arena as well as in the arts and music – and which now have become part of modernity itself.

An epilogue comments on the conscious efforts of the last century either to reshape the ethos of the Russian people or to introduce new legal institutions. It concludes that any reconstruction needs to take account of the deep cultural meanings by which human beings live.

In the end, an appendix is concerned with a specific methodological tool, the concept of adequate causation (in contrast to the concept of elective affinity), as it is often used in the comparative study of cultures in general and particularly in the second part of this book.

PART ONE

BETWEEN TWO ALTERNATIVES

CHAPTER ONE

MAX WEBER AND LEO TOLSTOY ON SCIENCE AND CULTURE

Introduction

The title of an essay which purports to deal with the Russian Ortho-dox tradition as it relates to modernity might give rise to the suspicion that modernity is assumed to be the blindly accepted and favoured outcome of historical evolution. However, the scholars on whose shoulders the present study rests were not uncritical advocates of modernity and their scholarly excursions beyond the Occident were not intended to tell Russia or India what to do or how to become more modern; on the contrary, they wanted to learn from these cultures if this seemed at all possible.

In this chapter the German sociologist Max Weber's highly scepti-cal view of modern science will be summarized, and this will be fol-lowed by an examination of his brief forays into Russian culture and politics where he hoped to find solutions to the problems of his day as he saw them.

It is well known that Max Weber considered Western bureaucratic civilization to be trapped in a blind alley, on the way to becoming an 'iron-cage'[1] from which there was no escape and which would suffo-cate the individual. He worried about the rationalization and bureau-cratization of life, he perceived outlines of a petrified society similar to that of Antiquity or ancient Egypt in which concepts of freedom and personal responsibility of the individual would lose all meaning. The new 'House of Enslavement', he thought, stands everywhere ready for occupation. The system had been built with the help of the Protes-tant ethic, but its 'spirit' had left the 'shell', and now Weber asked how, in view of the overwhelming tendency towards bureaucratiza-

---

[1] The term 'iron-cage' is used with certain reservations and only because T. Par-son's translation of the German '*stahlhartes Gehäuse*' has been so widely accepted in the English-speaking world. The German term '*Gehäuse*' does not mean cage but rather housing, shell or cell (as in Dürer's engraving '*Hieronymus im Gehäuse*'). '*Stahlhart*' means 'hard as steel'.

tion, it might be at all possible to save anything of what is meant by individual freedom, how to preserve modern society from 'mechanical petrifaction'.

Even science, he thought, may be trapped in an 'iron-cage' of its own making, not only because of its institutionalization but also because of its very success in disenchanting the world. This is at least the implication which we can draw from Weber's writings, according to Friedrich Tenbruck (1974a). Following Tenbruck's lead (1974b) we shall analyse Weber's interpretation of the history of science. We shall then look at today's predicament of science and culture, as Weber perceived it, before we try to analyse how Weber tried to find solutions, alternatives and interpretations for today's historical situation in the politics, religion and thinking of Russia.

The History of Science as a Search for Meaning

Weber's lecture 'Science as a Vocation', originally delivered in 1917, may be understood as a question, according to Tenbruck: What meaning should we attach to the systematic pursuit of truth in which the social sciences and the humanities are as much involved as the natural sciences? The question, although it was new in Weber's time, and although science then seemed to have a fairly secure place in the life of society, stimulated rejoinders and lively discussions among German intellectuals (Troeltsch, Scheler, Spranger, Kahler). Since Weber's time, of course, the vocation of science has often been questioned.

On the surface, Weber's problem seems to be rather simple. He is concerned with the 'fact' that the truth which any kind of science (the German term '*Wissenschaft*', which includes the natural sciences, the humanities and even philosophy) pursues, does not prove its value.

We tend to believe that truth is an ultimate value. But evidently there are different kinds of truths which may be valued differently. Science presupposes in any case that "what is yielded by scientific work is important in the sense that it is worth being known". This sentence, obviously, contains problematic implications, for it cannot itself be proved by scientific means (1958c: 143). Weber shows this in detail. "Physics and astronomy presuppose as self-evident that it is worthwhile to know the ultimate laws of cosmic events...". The presupposition of medical science is that one ought to "maintain life and to diminish suffering... Yet this is problematical. Whether life is worth living and when – this question is not asked by medicine." "Aesthetics does not ask whether there should be works of art... nor does jurisprudence ask whether there should be law or whether one should establish just these particular laws."

Finally, the historical and social sciences: "They teach us how to understand and interpret artistic, literary and social phenomena... But they give us no answer to the question whether the existence of these phenomena has been or is worthwhile. Nor do they answer the further question whether it is worth the effort required to know them. That they presuppose this interest by no means proves that it goes without saying. In fact, it is not at all self-evident." On the whole, all science presupposes that it is worthwhile knowing, but we are unable to prove that this is so.

All this is the result of the fact that science, according to Weber, cannot give us an answer to Tolstoy's question, a question which is also most important to him: "What shall we do and how shall we live?" The positive sciences cannot provide us with a *Weltanschauung* and with a sense of the meaning of the world, and neither can philosophy. (Weber's philosophy is close to neokantianism).

Weber then goes on to state what science can contribute to practical and personal life. While he seems to play down the technology of controlling life and the methods of thinking which are a result of scientific work, he stresses that science can help us achieve consistency in our aims and clarity as to their meaning. "If we are competent in our pursuit... we can force the individual... to give himself an account of the ultimate meaning of his own conduct" (1958c:152). Weber believes that consistency in aims and clarity as to their meaning are important values, because they lead to integrity. Nevertheless, science is unable to establish ultimate values; all its pursuits must remain subject to what is called value-neutrality[2].

Clearly, what Weber says in his lecture about value-neutrality is largely a reiteration of what he has set forth in earlier essays, especially in his essay on objectivity in the social sciences. But the characterization of science is only one part of his subject. The other part is what

---

[2] In his writings on the theory of science (*Wissenschaftslehre*) Max Weber opposes value-neutrality and value-relatedness. Although this distinction cannot be discussed here, it should perhaps be mentioned that the research results of the social sciences are a moral force and that Weber failed to take account of this moral force when he insisted on the value-neutrality of science.

we may call the historical situation of science. Weber seems to be
looking at science, at its causes and its effects, in a rather new way. In
particular, the history of science is looked at in a way which explains
the development of science over the centuries as a continuous striving
for meaning.

Plato, he says, discovered the concept, one of the great tools of scientific knowledge, and it seemed to him that if one only found the
right concept of the beautiful, the good, one could also grasp the true
being and how to act rightly in life. And for these reasons one
engaged in science.

Weber then explains how the rational experiment, without which
today's empirical science would be impossible, originated during the
Renaissance period. Leonardo and the experimenters in music were
characteristic. "To these experimenters, science meant the path to
true art and that meant for them the path to true nature."

In what follows, Weber proceeds to the seventeenth century. He
recalls Swammerdam's statement: "Here I bring you the proof of
God's providence in the anatomy of a louse." The task of the scientist
of that time was, according to Weber, to show the path to God. God
was thought to be hidden. "In the exact sciences, however, where one
could physically grasp His works, one hoped to come upon the traces
of what He planned for the world."

Finally, quoting Nietzsche's criticism of "the last men" who
"invented happiness", Weber mentions with disdain the naive opti-
mism, still found in some circles, which celebrates science as a way to
happiness.

This account in a nutshell of the history of science could easily be
expanded, even from Weber's own writings. With regard to the attitude of Protestant asceticism, especially that of Spener, the decisive
point was that

> just as the Christian is known by the fruits of his belief, the knowledge
> of God and his designs can only be attained through a knowledge of his
> works... It was hoped from the empirical knowledge of the divine laws
> of nature to ascend to a grasp of the 'meaning'[3] of the world.
> (1958a:249, fn. 145)

In this context, one should perhaps also mention Bacon's belief that
man's dominion over nature was sacrificed at the Fall, but that

---

[3] Parsons has incorrectly translated the German word '*Sinn*' (meaning) (1920,
I:142, footnote 5) as essence. He also omitted the quotation marks.

through science man could achieve a restoration of his dominion over nature, a second Eden. For puritan millenarianists influenced by Bacon, science was to be pursued not as an end in itself, as Webster (1975) has shown, but for its value in confirming the power of providence, and as a means of bringing about a new paradise on earth. When millenarianism finally waned, it became transmuted into a general secular belief in progress.

This account of the history of science is completely at variance with ordinary assumptions regarding the nature of science. It is less concerned with the results of scientific efforts than with motivations which were, at least partially, religious. Science, Weber contends, was seen consecutively as a way to true art, a way to true nature, a way to the true God, and a way to true happiness, and he denies "that modern natural science can be understood as the product of material and technical interests alone" (1958a:249, fn. 145).

While it is frequently assumed today that the scientist is an uncommitted searcher after truth who collects, examines and interprets the bare and objective facts and whose allegiance is to such facts alone, Thomas Kuhn has tried to revise this conception of science. But whether we talk about facts or about paradigms is not the question here. Weber asserts that the scientist has traditionally a stake in his findings, and that the findings received their significance in the last analysis from their ulterior meanings.

The End of an Epoch

What has happened to this search for meaning and certainty today? Weber appeared to believe that, as scientific rationalization increases, the irrational also grows in intensity. Not only, as he argued, are all sciences based on presuppositions which cannot be proved by scientific means and which are, in this sense, non-rational, but also the progress of science or of the sciences itself leads to a more irrational and meaningless world. To grasp this more clearly, it must be understood that the terms 'rational' and 'rationalization' are used by Weber in at least three different ways. There is, first of all, the most widespread use of the term: scientific-technical rationalism which describes man's capacity and desire to dominate the world by calculation. Then there is metaphysical rationalism, which is the consequence of the need of man to comprehend the world as a meaningful cosmos, and which systemizes the structures of meaning[4]. And there is, finally, practical rationalism, which describes a methodical conduct of life (Schluchter, 1976:259).

Weber believed that there is a tension between the several aspects of the rational and that, as more rationality is produced in the scientific-technical sphere, rationality of the structures of meaning will disappear or at least become less obvious.

> The tension between religion and intellectual knowledge definitely comes to the fore wherever rational, empirical knowledge has consistently worked through to the disenchantment of the world and its transformation into a causal mechanism. For then science encounters the claims of the ethical postulate that the world is a God-ordained, and hence somehow meaningfully and ethically oriented, cosmos. In principle, the empirical as well as the mathematically oriented view of the world develops refutations of every intellectual approach which in any way asks for a 'meaning' of innerworldly occurrences. Every increase of rationalism in empirical science increasingly pushes religion from the rational into the irrational realm. (1958c:350/51).[5]

Science has disenchanted the world. But today – and this is, according to Weber, the historical situation of our civilization, perhaps its tragedy – science can no longer count on our belief in the ultimate meaningfulness of knowledge as it could during most of the former centuries. It has renounced the claim to know the meaning of things and pretends to have insight only into aspects of these things; it has admitted, thanks particularly to Weber himself, that it cannot provide us with norms; and thanks to Popper we know as well that all knowledge is provisional and temporary, and that it may soon be falsified. Science no longer creates a personality which can lay claim to universal knowledge and wisdom. This is the end of an epoch.

In the same way as capitalism, according to Weber's memorable

---

[4] Weber even distinguishes two types of physics (1958c:293) based on different rationalizations. This distinction is perhaps based on Pierre Duhem's book *La théorie physique: son object, sa structure*, Paris, 1906.

[5] Let us note in passing that today's much talked about 'split' or 'divorce' (Bell 1973; Berlin 1974) between the technical intelligentsia who are committed to scientific-technical rationalism and the literary intellectuals who are often critical of the technocratic modes of operation may be caused by the tension between the several aspects of rationalism which Max Weber described. Indeed, the modern world may be characterized by a paradox. On the one hand, there are many specialized viewpoints and disciplines which are pursued according to a means-end rationality. This rationality develops freely within the distinct disciplines, while the reason for their existence and their arrangement in a hierarchy of ends would need another rationality, but is at best left to a shifting consensus.

pages in *The Protestant Ethic and the Spirit of Capitalism*, as soon as it had become institutionalized, became self-sufficient and independent of the 'spirit' of capitalism and led to the 'iron-cage' (*stählernes Gehäuse*) which is the predicament of today's economic situation, so science may now be trapped in an 'iron-cage' of its own making from which there is no escape (Tenbruck, 1974a). The 'spirit' of past centuries, their belief in the meaningfulness of science, has departed, and within the dead and meaningless structure which remains we have to carry on.

Youth may sometimes look for redemption from this science in subjective 'experience' and countercultures, as Weber suggested, but more important is the fact that science, even when it is practised, may only be regarded as a fatalistically accepted necessity in today's world, or even sometimes as a relatively optimal means to achieve the relatively best goals; in either case it is not any more the expression of a style of life which is meaningful for the total personality.

Science, as part of a general process of rationalization, has destroyed the meaning for which it has been searching. It is now up to science, Weber believes, to explain its vocation. The disenchantment of the world has reached science itself.

In his *Sociology of Religion*, (part of *Economy and Society*), Weber described the quest of today's intellectual in a world without meaning.

> The intellectual seeks in various ways... to endow his life with a pervasive meaning, and thus to find unity with himself, with his fellow men, and with the cosmos. It is the intellectual who transforms the concept of the world into the problem of meaning. As intellectualism suppresses belief in magic, the world's processes become disenchanted... As a consequence, there is a growing demand that the world and the total pattern of life be subject to an order that is significant and meaningful. (1946b:125)

Weber then went on to describe the intellectual's characteristic flight from a world without meaning:

> This may be an escape into absolute loneliness, or in its modern form, e.g. in the case of Rousseau, to a nature unspoilt by human institutions. Again, it may be a world-fleeing romanticism like the flight to the people untouched by social conventions, characteristic of the Russian *narodnichestvo*. It may be more contemplative, or more actively ascetic; it may primarily seek individual salvation or collective revolutionary transformation.

Weber did not believe that new religions ever resulted from the needs of intellectuals for meaning[6]. But he realized that the general disenchantment could turn into an attack on science itself. He saw intellectual romanticism turn directly against science, doubting the meaningfulness of knowledge or demanding directions from science.

Two options for the intellectuals' flight were mentioned by Weber: the ideas and proposals of Rousseau and of the Russian *narodnichestvo*. To these ideas we shall now turn. Weber himself more than once turned to Russia, once because he thought that Russia might be able to provide an alternative to the Western bureaucratic 'iron-cage', and then again to look at the ideas of the Russian writer Leo Tolstoy as an alternative to the impasse of Western science and civilization. Rousseau[7], however, does not appear to have attracted Weber.

---

[6] Weber could be wrong here: Buddhism probably resulted from the needs of intellectual *ksatriyas* for meaning in a society intellectually dominated by *brahmins* (Buss, 1978:70).

[7] Like Weber, Rousseau in his *Discours sur les sciences et les arts* (1750), opposed the sciences on the one hand to religion and society on the other, and, like Weber, Rousseau believed that the progress of science does not add anything to man's happiness. But Rousseau also tended to think that the sciences (and arts) corrupt our morals. Our vices (ambition, avarice, curiosity) are, according to him, the causes of science, and in turn the sciences produce more vices and finally destroy the community of men.

Rousseau opposed a social philosophy which begins with fully formed individuals. He would ask: Where do individuals get all their capacities except from society? Within a society, there may be individuality, freedom, etc; outside it, there is nothing moral. Virtue meant the entire submission of man to his society or nation. Without this virtue, there is no society. And as science destroys virtue, it destroys society. Against our (perverted) society Rousseau set an idealized simple society without parties and factions. This 'true' society is in harmony and under the guidance of the General Will which 'moves and disposes each part as may be most advantageous to the whole' (*Social Contract* II, 4).

Weber's conception of society is very different. Indeed, in their conception of society lies the main difference between Weber and Rousseau, whereas many opinions or statements on science are remarkably similar in both authors. For Weber, society consists of autonomous individuals, the only 'real' beings. Churches, communities, states, etc cannot be considered as substances. The sciences have contributed to the dissolution of the substance of these institutions. Only individuals exist in the true sense of the word, and the war between individuals, factions and classes.

L. Strauss (p. 65) noted that "Weber puts peace in quotation marks whereas he did not take this precautionary measure when speaking of conflict. Conflict was for Weber an unambiguous thing, but peace was not: peace is phony, but war is real."

Weber's Turn to Russia

As has already been noted, Weber foresaw and feared the appearance of a bureaucratic apparatus which would deprive man of his freedom and which would produce some kind of 'Egyptian petrifaction'. He also anticipated the tendency of European culture to move in the direction of progressive irrationalism and meaninglessness and that science was contributing to this development. Both his attachment to the ideals of freedom and individualism and his interpretation of the predicament of science turned his attention to Russia.

For Weber, if there was any hope for the preservation of liberty and individualism, it lay outside Europe, in the United States and, above all, in Russia. Russia seemed to him to be a country where the culture was much less advanced than in the West and which might – at the beginning of the past century – provide the last opportunity for the construction of a free culture 'from the ground up' (1971:66). He hoped that Russia would perhaps follow a path which might avoid the pitfalls of Western scientific, economic and political development.

Russia, in Weber's time, was a country where capitalism and European science had only recently started to make an imprint, although they had already provoked strong reactions, for instance in the *narodnichestvo* movement which claimed that the village commune is the ideal embryo of the future society. Russia's main characteristics, according to Weber, were the primitive (in the sense of antique) Christianity of the Orthodox church and the peasants in their peasant community (*obshchina*).

Political Perspectives

This was Weber's understanding of some basic phenomena of Russian social life, when he became deeply intrigued by Russian politics. He learned enough Russian to read Russian newspapers and to publish two long articles[8] on the Russian political situation at the time of the revolution of 1905. He approached Russian political life from his already mentioned conviction that Western culture was moving

---

[8] Max Weber, 1906a&b. These articles, orginally published in the *Archiv für Sozialwissenschaft und Sozialpolitik*, have been partially reproduced in Weber's *Gesammelte Politische Schriften* (1971).

towards ever greater rationalization within the 'iron-cage' and towards a concomitant decrease of freedom.

> The edifice for the new bondage stands everywhere in readiness... All the economic weather signs point in the direction of diminishing freedom... Against the current of the material constellations are we individualists and party followers of democratic institutions. (1971, p. 63/64)

Freedom was not a national problem for Weber, but a human problem relating to the human destiny. He asked whether the Russian revolution of 1905 would provide more space for freedom, but he did not think that the emergence of Russian democracy could be based on peasant institutions, such as the *obshchina*. He was convinced that such 'romantic populism' would with time be undermined by capitalist forces and give way to Marxism (1971:62). Nor did he believe that the spread of the capitalist economy in Russia would automatically guarantee the acquisition of those liberties which had accompanied its emergence in European history.

Modern freedom, according to Weber, had been born under unique circumstances. One of its preconditions had been the conquest of life by science[9]. But, Weber added, the rational structuring of the exterior life has, after the destruction of countless 'values', destroyed freedom... – and science as such does not any more create a universal personality (*Universalität der Persönlichkeit*) (1971:64). Countries like Russia which began their industrialization late, missed out that epoch of social development which had provided the basis for free political institutions and a liberal tradition. Therefore, the spread of Western civilization and science in Russia or elsewhere would neither automatically guarantee the rise of freedom there, nor of "free" personalities or "altruistic" ideals. On the contrary, capitalism had forever destroyed the optimistic belief in the natural harmony of free individuals (1971:43).

Only *zemstvo* liberalism (a kind of local self-government) seemed for a moment to be able to oppose the bureaucracy of the Russian empire and to propagate the individualistic principle of human rights, but Weber realized that it could not succeed because it lacked the support of groups materially interested in the realization of its goals.

---

[9] The preconditions of liberty which Weber enumerates (1971:63/64) were 1) overseas expansion; 2) the economic and social structure of the precapitalistic epoch in Western Europe; 3) certain value concepts which originated in religious thought; 4) the conquest of life by science.

Weber's research convinced him, therefore, that it was in vain to look to Russia for new forms of liberal civilization.

Russian Christianity

At the same time, however, these studies on Russian politics may have led Weber to consider more closely the 'spirit' of the Russian people, grounded as it is in Orthodox Christianity. While still looking for the emergence of individualism and freedom in Russia he noted that one sometimes finds in this country the rejection of an ethic of success even in politics, and that a biblical sentence had deeply entered not only the spirit of L. Tolstoy but of the Russian people as a whole: Do not resist evil (1971:39). Russian Christianity, and particularly Leo Tolstoy's version of it, has played an important role in Weber's interpretation of the situation of Western science and culture.

As for Weber's understanding of Russian Christianity, we have a beautiful passage from a talk given by him at a sociological meeting in 1910, in response to a paper by E. Troeltsch:

> Russian Christianity was and is even today in its specific expressions to a high degree antique Christianity. If one looks at an authoritarian church, one tries to find out: which instance is invested with the last infallible power which can decide if a person belongs to the church or not... We know that in the Catholic Church it is today the Pope, we know that in the Lutheran Church it is the "Word", the Scripture, and those whose office it is to interpret it.

> If we now ask the Greek (Orthodox) Church who incorporates that instance, the official answer is...: The community of the Church, united in love... There is in the Orthodox Church a specifically mystic belief that brotherly love, love of one's neighbor, those peculiar human relationships which seem pale to us but which have transfigured the great salvation-religions, constitute a way not only to certain kinds of social effects..., but to the understanding of the meaning of the world, to a mystical relationship with God. It is known of Tolstoy that he was interested in this mystical belief, and great Russian literature generally has this kind of mysticism as a foundation.

> If one reads Russian fiction, Dostoevsky's *Brothers Karamazov* or Tolstoy's *War and Peace*, one first gets the impression of a complete meaninglessness of the events. This effect... is caused by the secret conviction of the actual meaninglessness of this politically, socially, ethically, literarily, artistically formed life as against the foundation which extends

underneath and which is personified in the most specific characters
which Russian literature possesses. These characters are difficult for us
to understand because they represent the antique Christian idea, that
what Baudelaire calls the 'Holy Prostitution of the Soul', the love of
our neighbor, i.e. of anyone, of the fellow creature – that this amorphous, unformed love relationship opens the doors of the Eternal,
Timeless, Divine... The artistic unity which appears to be lacking, the
forming principle of Russian art, is actually on the reverse side of what
we read.

On this acosmistic foundation of all Russian religiosity is founded a
specific natural law which one also finds developed in the Russian sects
and in Tolstoy's works, and which is sustained by the continuous existence of agrarian communism (Max Weber, 1924a : 466; my translation).[10]

Weber goes on to explain that many ideals in Russian life are based
on this foundation, and that these ideals are related to Tönnies' concept of *Gemeinschaft*, not *Gesellschaft*.

Russian Christianity, to summarize Weber's argument, was characterized by brotherly love which not only had social effects but also
gave meaning to the world.

Leo Tolstoy

In later years, Weber was much intrigued by L. Tolstoy's writings, so
much so that he had been planning a book about him (Marianne
Weber, 1975:446). Tolstoy expressed many of those aspects of the
Russian culture and particularly of Russian Christianity which Weber
considered relevant (Tolstoy was also mentioned in Weber's above-
quoted speech on Russian Christianity), and he was close to the *narodnichestvo* movement. Tolstoy was Weber's contemporary, and in many
ways, Weber's critique of science and his general *Kulturkritik*, his questioning and probing of the cultural situation of his day, was more than
equalled by Tolstoy's.

Tolstoy never ceased to denounce the notion that mankind can be
made eternally happy and virtuous by rational and scientific means.
Since his earlier works he had only contempt for the faith placed by

---

[10] Weber's characterization of the three branches of Christianity in the first part of
this quotation is almost identical to that provided by Soloviev (1968) in his *Short Story
about the Antichrist.*

modern man in science, and he had a very sceptical attitude towards all experts and all techniques and efforts at social improvement by these experts. He wanted to contrast the real texture of life with the unreal picture presented by historians and to destroy the illusion that individuals can understand and control scientifically the course of history.

Only the wise and good man, he thought, senses the truth. In *War and Peace*, Pierre gropes for it, Kutuzov feels it in his bones and attains to intermittent glimpses of it, while Napoleon and Western military experts are described as ignorant and bombastic.

Isaiah Berlin, in his study on Tolstoy's view of history (1953), has written that Tolstoy defended the 'deep currents', the *raisons du cœur* which he did not himself know by direct experience, but besides which, he was convinced, science was but a snare and a delusion. Tolstoy, in Berlin's words, built his case against liberal theories of progress, German military expertise and confident social engineering of all kinds, but was unable to attain the solid bed-rock of truth on which alone a secure interpretation of life and history can be built. This irritated awareness that no final solution was ever to be found by science caused Tolstoy to attack all bogus solutions of science all the more savagely with his intellectual mastery, for "what oppressed (him) most was his lack of positive convictions" (Berlin, 1953 : 36, quoting B. Eykhenbaum).

Later in life Tolstoy was less interested in the truth about the course of history than in the question of how we should live. Science, according to him, was unable to answer this question. In *What then must we do*, originally published in 1888, he wrote that science has lost its meaning and purpose and true science has come to be contemptuously called 'religion'. Science in the past, he said, has always dealt with the true welfare of each man and of mankind, but today the domain of human knowledge is so wide and the different fields so scattered that man loses himself unless he has a clue to enable him to decide what is most important for him. Whatever those learned men and artists call themselves who excogitate the theory of penal, civil and international law, who invent guns and explosives, who compose obscene operas and operettas, he added, we have no right to call such activity science and art; for that activity has not the welfare of society or of mankind in view, but is on the contrary directed to the injury of man.

To the question of how we should live, Tolstoy answered with the Sermon on the Mount: love all men, do not hurt anyone, do not resist evil. And he thought that this implies that one should abolish military organizations, police, prisons, judges. Moreover, it is not a sign of love, he continued, that in our 'civilization' the rich exploit the poor. We should leave behind us this civilization which does not conform to the Truth of the Sermon on the Mount, return to the villages and work for our own bread.

Tolstoy now favoured simple men and peasants because their observation of men and nature is less clouded by empty theories. The simple peasant became for him a repository of almost as many virtues as Rousseau's noble savage. He thought that simple people often know the truth better than learned men, he raged against Western sophistication, refinement and ethics, and sought escape from his scepticism in the uncorrupted human heart and in simple brotherly love.

Weber often seized the opportunity to use Tolstoy's ideas when he wished to underline the irrationality, the unbrotherliness, the meaninglessness of Western civilization.

A large part of his 'Intermediate Reflection' at the end of the first volume of his *Gesammelte Aufsätze zur Religionssoziologie* describes the tensions which develop with increasing rationalization between salvation religions and the various spheres of the "world", e.g. economics, politics, science, the erotic sphere. This tension between the various cultural spheres on the one hand and salvation religion on the other finally leads to the 'meaninglessness' of all cultural values, according to Weber. The late novels of Tolstoy helped Weber to formulate the discovery that today's general 'progress', of which science is part as well as motive force, is meaningless.

> All the broodings of Tolstoy revolved around the problem of whether or not death is a meaningful phenomenon. And his answer was: for civilized man death has no meaning. It has none because the individual life of civilized man, placed into an infinite 'progress', according to its own immanent meaning should never come to an end...
>
> Abraham, or some peasant of the past, died 'old and satiated with life' because he stood in the organic cycle of life... Whereas civilized man, placed in the midst of the continuous enrichment of culture by ideas, knowledge, and problems, may become 'tired of life' but not 'satiated with life'... And because death is meaningless, civilized life as such is meaningless; by its very 'progressiveness' it gives death the imprint of meaninglessness (1958c:139/140).

We can assume that the idea that a peasant dies 'satiated with life' while civilized man dies 'tired of life' was important to Weber, because he noted it also in another context, using almost the same words:

> The peasant like Abraham could die 'satiated with life'... for (he) fulfilled a cycle of existence beyond which he did not reach... But the 'cultivated' man who strives for self-perfection... cannot do this. For the perfectibility of the man of culture in principle progresses indefinitely, as do the cultural values... All 'culture' appears as man's emancipation from the organically prescribed cycle of natural life. (1958c:356)

Not only are the peasant and the 'cultivated' man distinguished here, but we are perhaps entitled to think that this was also the difference which Weber saw between man in Russia and man in the West. Russia had peasants[11], *Gemeinschaft*, brotherly love and meaning, while the West had 'culture', not in today's anthropological sense, but in the sense of the philosophical and literary tradition, namely refinement in the realms of science and art, and the pursuit of the ideal of the 'cultured person' who appreciates and perhaps contributes to the richness of the cultural tradition[12]. 'Culture', the ideal type of refinement in science and art, appeared to him far remote from the organically prescribed natural life. The advancement of cultural values... "seems to become a senseless hustle in the service of worthless, moreover self-contradictory, and mutually antagonistic ends" (1958c:357), whereas the life of a peasant, or indeed of an American Indian or of a Hottentot, is meaningful, because they have a greater knowledge of their tools and of the conditions of life under which they exist (1958c:139).

As mentioned earlier, Weber showed that tensions develop with increasing rationalization between salvation religions and the various spheres of the 'world'. He described, for instance, the tension between the unbrotherly euphoria of eroticism and all religiously oriented

---

[11] It may be noted in passing that Weber was very conscious of the fact that the honour and esteem in which peasants are sometimes held, is quite recent in Western civilization (and unheard of in most other great civilizations) and that it can be explained as a reaction of the Churches against the rationalism and scepticism of the bourgeoisie (Weber 1958b:84).

[12] Whenever the traditionalism of peasants comes to Weber's mind, he relates it to Tolstoy's writings. Even in his essay on China (1964a:96), in describing the relationships between the peasants and the patrimonial bureaucracy, Weber mentions the peasants in Tolstoy's *Resurrection* who never chanced upon the idea of 'disinterested' motives.

brotherliness, and thought that the psychologically most thorough portions of Tolstoy's *War and Peace* may be cited in this connection (1958c:349).

A little further on in the same text (p. 350) there is a passage which may be interpreted as an expression of a desire in Weber to look for an answer to this particular kind of unbrotherliness. Like Tolstoy, Weber had studied the Quaker ethic, and he found in this ethic (as displayed in William Penn's letters to his wife) a genuinely humane interpretation of the value of marriage: its linkage with the thought of ethical responsibility for one another 'up to the pianissimo of old age'[13]. The existence of this passage on the Quaker ethic and its concept of ethical responsibility for one another is particularly interesting, because it is not part of the original version of this text[14] (*Zwischenbetrachtung*) published in 1916, but has been inserted by Weber as a new insight in the edition of 1920. Only in the smallest circles, in marriage and friendship, does Weber seem to have found a sense of community which he could share.

In addition, bound by the charisma of mind and taste, culture values like the intellect or the pursuit of science presuppose modes of existence which generally run counter to the demand of brotherliness, Weber wrote, for the intellect is independent of all personal ethical qualities of man. The aristocracy of intellect is hence an unbrotherly aristocracy (1958c:355).

What then is the meaning of science, Weber asked finally, and again Tolstoy provided him with the answer:

> Tolstoy has given the simplest answer, with the words: Science is meaningless because it gives no answer to our question, the only question important to us: what shall we do and how shall we live? (1958c:143)

In the end, there remained two questions for Weber: Tolstoy's question 'how should we live?' and 'how can science help?'. By again comparing Tolstoy and Russia on the one hand and the West on the other, he arrived at two alternatives.

---

[13] 'Up to the pianissimo of old age' was also used by Weber as part of the dedication of Vol. 1 of his *Gesammelte Aufsätze zur Religionssoziologie* (1920) to his wife Marianne.

[14] *Archiv für Sozialwissenschaft und Sozialpolitik*, Vol. 41 (1916).

The Two Alternatives

Max Weber's wife Marianne once wrote that he saw two possible ideals diverge to form two opposite poles of tremendous tension.

> For one thing, cultural values may be maintained even if they come into an irreconcilable conflict with all ethics. And conversely, an ethic that rejects all cultural values is possible without inner contradiction – like that of Tolstoy. (1975:322)

In this quotation we notice the important Weberian distinction between cultural and ethical values. Ethical values address themselves, in Weber's thought, to the conscience of the autonomous individual and affect the conduct of life from the inside. They are often related to motivations of salvation in the great world religions and they imply the suppression of the "natural" needs.

Cultural (and political) values refer to collective ideals which the single human being may have as a member of a political or cultural community. Such values which one wants to further and ethical values which one ought to further are of a different dignity, according to Weber, who also thought that only those who accept ethical guilt can realize cultural values. Scientific truth is such a cultural value.[15]

This distinction played an important role when Weber started to develop the concepts of two kinds of ethics.

Again it was Russia which provided him with an example. In his study on the Russian revolution of 1905 – the time when in Russia there was an intense discussion about the question whether the Russian people should receive the right to vote in spite of a total lack of political experience and in spite of the fact that most of them could neither read nor write –, at this time Weber wrote:

> I know Russian democrats who defend the point of view: *fiat iustitia, pereat mundus* (justice must be done even if it leads the world to ruin). Even if the Russian people reject all cultural progress or are likely to destroy all cultural progress, we can only ask what is just and we have

---

[15] Both ethical values and cultural values imply duties. Opposed to duties are desires of happiness, based on interests (riches, health, long life, success, etc.). Actions related to them are not value-rational, but goal-related. Weber fought against the primitive idea that happiness is the highest goal of human actions. He said that social policy must not try to provide human happiness, but rather create the exterior conditions within which what we consider valuable in human beings can best develop. Otherwise, we become specialists without heart who only imagine to have climbed the summits of humanity.

done our duty if we give them their right to vote... It is preferable to
suffer cultural darkness for many generations to come rather than to
do a political wrong. (PS:39)

Fiat iustitia pereat mundus : this is an example of the belief that only an
ethical value may be recognized as a rule of conduct in all regards –
even if, as a consequence of it, the world goes to ruins, a belief which
consciously denies any responsibility for the probable consequences of
one's actions and which, from the perspective of the results, may even
be considered irrational. Weber called it an ethic of conviction. A
person who follows an ethic of conviction is not characterized by the
fact that he does not foresee the consequences of his actions, but by
the fact that he does not feel entitled to include those consequences in
the evaluation of his actions and that he does not recognize, besides
ethical values, the right of existence of political or cultural values.

   On the other hand, there is, according to Weber, the ethic of
responsibility. Those who follow this kind of ethic, do not only accept
ethical but also non-ethical values (which does not mean that they
replace the ethical by non-ethical values). Neither success nor adaptation to the "realities of life" (whatever that may mean) characterize
the ethic of responsibility, but the taking account of the consequences
of one's actions. This evaluation of the consequences, though, does
not lead to an art of the possible for, as Weber wrote, "that which is
possible sometimes was attained by grasping the impossible".

   The ethic of responsibility is the ethic of the modern scientific
world, for it is science which helps in the investigation of the consequences which the execution of given value-judgements would have
as they are tied to unavoidable means as well as because of possible
undesirable side effects. In a society which does not have a value-free
science about causal relationships, it is very difficult to act according
to an ethic of responsibility. A value-free science, although it may not
create meanings any more, is able to create the preconditions, the
foundations of an ethic of responsibility so that, as Schluchter writes,
decisions in modern society pass through science without being taken
by science.

   But the ethic of responsibility is also the ethic of the modern individualistic world, for the actor is here not only considered to be
responsible for the exterior results of his actions, but also for the
choice of his beliefs, his inner convictions: he is expected to make a
choice between different values or, in Weberian terms, between different gods by an act of will.

Whereas Weber considered the attitude expressed in the sentence *fiat iustitia pereat mundus* as an example of what he defined as the ethic of conviction, it is necessary to remain circumspect. Few Russians, and certainly not Tolstoy, may have agreed with its curtness and perhaps even unbrotherliness (in fact, it seems to have been, originally, the motto of the Holy Roman emperor Ferdinand I who signed the peace of Augsburg after the rise of Lutheranism). Max Weber later turned to Tolstoy's ideas as an example of the only possible alternative to this-worldly individualistic and scientific culture. In a short article, entitled "Between Two Ethics" (*Zwischen zwei Gesetzen*, included in PS), Weber ironically talked (during the first World War) about what American ladies "of both sexes" assert to be pacifism, while at the same time doing good business. If one opts for pacifism, he wrote, one has to take it seriously –

> and then Tolstoy's inner consequence is the only possible one: Whoever takes only one penny of interest which others – directly or indirectly – have to pay, whoever owns a commodity or eats any food produced with another person's sweat, lives off the machinery of that loveless and pitiless economic struggle for existence which bourgeois phraseology tends to call 'peaceful civilization', but which is in fact another form of the struggle of man against man in which millions or even hundreds of millions see their body and soul wither away every year...

> ... The position of the Gospels is clear, they do not just only oppose war – which they do not even mention –, but the laws of the social world, if this world wants to be a world of this-worldly culture and of the greatness of creaturely man. Those who do not opt for this alternative – Tolstoy did it when he was close to death – must know that they remain bound by the laws of this world. (1971:144, my translation)

In the same vein, Weber's wife Marianne (1975:412) mentioned that pacifists were unacceptable to Weber unless they not only enjoyed the conclusions which Leo Tolstoy reached as a literary dessert, but also put them into practice in every respect.

What Weber considered to be a valid alternative to the ethic of responsibility, appears in this text to be an outworldly ideal, to be lived outside of the constraints of what characterizes modern society; it is, in his opinion, "not of this world" (PS:557). But can Tolstoy's ethic of love properly be characterized as an ethic of conviction in Weber's sense, i.e., not concerned with the consequences of actions and "not of this world"?

Davydov (1995) has suggested that in a deeper sense, and in contrast to the ethic of responsibility, the ethic of conviction presupposes the faith in the existence of God or of the good, and that the human being in this case is not faced by a choice between different but equal gods (values), but between good and evil. Davydov's argument is convincing, particularly when he analyzes the ontological contexts in which the two ethics operate. Whereas Weber's conception of being is nominalistic, starting from the individual human being and, on the value-level, from the "battle of the gods" among whom the individual must choose, Tolstoy's is realistic in the mediaeval sense, starting from the living whole which he considers to be God and love and, on the social level, the *obshchina*. For him, therefore, acts of love, by which man participates in the essence of being, have a higher and more real level of being than the particularizing forces of evil. They are also effective and have consequences in this world in an empirical sense, for the self-change of human beings, resulting from love, furthers, in his view, the change of other human beings and this, in turn, promotes the change of unjust institutions. Within this conception of the world, physical force is not rejected because it is unethical, but because it appears to be ineffective. Clearly, Tolstoy did not overlook the consequences of his ethic: on the contrary, he thought to have a responsibility for the world.

Max Weber seems to have erred when he attributed to Tolstoy an ethic of conviction as defined by him, for Tolstoy's teachings were rooted in a holistic world-view in which the consequences of actions did matter. The ethic of conviction which Max Weber had in mind rather seems to be the ethic of those who place themselves outside of the modern world and particularly outside of the cultural tradition impregnated by modern science, but who retain an individualistic view of this world. It may also have an elective affinity with traditions which recognize the outworldly individual, e.g. the Indian renouncers (*samnyasin*), or with outworldly sects.

Conclusion

Weber wrote essays about China, India and Ancient Judaism. These essays were written for the purpose of understanding aspects of Western civilization. Weber's interest in Russia, however, was fed by his desire to find solutions and alternatives to the historical situation of his day (*die Welt, in die wir hineingestellt sind*), its political and its civilizational aspects. This situation is characterized, he thought, by the resignation of many within a petrified culture which does not provide meaning and liberty and which is without a messiah or prophet.

Weber did not find in Russia what perhaps he had hoped for. The Revolution of 1905 did not create a 'free' civilization which might have limited the growth of bureaucracy in the rest of Europe. And while he seems to have had a profound esteem for Tolstoy and to have thought that his ethic of brotherly love is a valid alternative for those who live in the 'iron-cage' of Western science and civilization, an ethic without inner contradiction, Tolstoy's ideas and ethic had no dominion over him.

This does not imply that Weber considered a *Gemeinschaft* of brotherly love and meaning as a 'realistic' alternative in our time, but rather as an (ethically) valid alternative. Nevertheless, Weber also knew that religious convictions and the religious charisma of saints and prophets are the principal driving force of history. "Not the matter-of-fact men who always find a way to adjust themselves to given conditions, but those who reach for the stars are the ones who influence the course of world history." (Mommsen 1965:33)

Weber was torn between his desire for meaning and what he felt to be his commitment to science, a sceptical renunciation of the possibility of understanding the meaning of the world. While Weber had an undeniable admiration for Tolstoy and accepted his interpretation of Western civilization and science as unbrotherly and meaningless, he did not accept his solution for himself. Weber was critical of the "unbrotherliness" of Western individualistic *Gesellschaft* and identified Tolstoy and peasant *Gemeinschaft* with mysticism and brotherliness (Mitzmann 1970:220); he may have dreamt of the times when science was not only a link in a chain without end, but fulfillment and accomplishment. But although he may have considered intellectualism or rationalism as the worst devil of our time, he suggested that "if one wishes to settle with this devil, one must not take to flight before him." In order to meet the demands of the day, "each of us should find and obey the demon[16] who holds the fibres of our very life" (Weber 1958c:156).

---

[16] Schluchter's (1976:282) evaluation of Weber's philosophy is most appropriate: "Weber has been called a *nihilist*, a relativist, a decisionist. He is all of these things if you believe in the existence and discernability of an objective meaning of the world. With Nietzsche, Weber believed that neither exists any more" (translated in Roth & Schluchter, 1979:59).

We live in an age of many gods, Weber thought. As the Greeks sacrificed in turn to Aphrodite, Apollo and the gods of the City, we attempt to serve peace, justice, truth, etc. If we select any of these values, even temporarily, we might offend and vex the rest. But this modern polytheism of values is really an expression of the primacy of one value: the value of the individual who chooses among these different gods; all values are masks of this unique value. The "battle of the gods" of which Max Weber spoke is the result of the era of individualism.

It is perhaps not surprising that only on the individual level, concepts like pneuma and demon, relics of an enchanted world, were still meaningful to Weber. He suggested that we meet the 'demands of the day', that we pursue, with practical rationalism, a methodical and consistent conduct of life. In this, at least, science can help. Not society as a whole, but only its smallest units, marriage and friendship, seemed to him to provide a sense of community in the modern world.

Isaiah Berlin (1953) distinguished between two kinds of writers and thinkers: the hedgehogs and the foxes. The hedgehogs relate everything to one organizing principle in terms of which alone all that they say and do has significance; the foxes pursue many ends, often unrelated, and their thought is scattered and diffused. Tolstoy as well as Weber were foxes; they both had an enormous skill in the art of describing or analysing life. But both also longed for an organizing principle or meaning. Tolstoy believed in being a hedgehog; he tried to find the natural law by which all history is determined and he finally chose a life according to his interpretation of the Sermon on the Mount and in accordance with his society's holistic conception of the world. Weber applied to the history of Western civilization the concept of rationalization – but this was a heuristic concept, an ideal-type – and he remained a fox within the 'iron-cage'.

PART II

THE ECONOMIC ETHICS OF RUSSIAN-ORTHODOX CHRISTIANITY

CHAPTER TWO

THE PATRIMONIAL STATE AND THE SPIRIT
OF ORTHODOXY

Introduction

Although Russia did not provide Max Weber with solutions to the historical situation of his day as he saw it, the study of the Russian-Orthodox tradition can serve – as he knew himself – to place his studies of modernity and particularly of the Protestant ethic in a much wider perspective. In his path-breaking essay on 'The Protestant Ethic and the "Spirit" of Capitalism', Max Weber had tried to show that the teachings of the early Calvinists, Methodists and Baptists had contributed to the formation of an ethically coloured maxim or ethos for the conduct of life as an aspect of modern vocational culture: the spirit of capitalism. They had done so, according to him, because the Calvinist doctrine of predestination had created the feeling of unprecedented inner loneliness of the single individual and, as the individual was expected to consider himself elected by God and looked for signs of his election, this in turn had led to the idea (unforeseen by the reformers) of the necessity of proving one's faith (*Bewährung*) in worldly activity, and particularly in the systematic control of one's state of grace by rational ascetic work in one's calling. The outcome was, in contrast to the traditional disapproval (*deo placere vix potest*), a pharisaically good conscience in the acquisition of wealth, combined with an ascetic compulsion to save, an inner-worldly asceticism of great intensity[1] combined with an attitude of rational world-mastery which led to a historical development of great internal consistency, for this inner-directed ethos had an elective affinity to the capitalist system.

Weber's essay did not remain unnoticed in other countries and cultures. If religion had such a profound influence in the West, which were the religious points of view which guided the rationalization of life elsewhere and in which direction?

---

[1] That practical rationality, related to values, is more intense and stable than simple technical or means-end rationality is an important point in Max Weber's PE-thesis. For a detailed analysis *vide* Kalberg 1994: 62 sqq.

The Russian economist and theologian S. Bulgakov, after reading
Max Weber's essay a few years after its first publication in the early
twentieth century (1904-5), expressed his regret about the lack of similar studies on Russia's economic ethics. Although he saw fundamental differences between Russian-Orthodox Christianity and Protestantism, he nevertheless thought that Orthodox religion is just as able
as Protestantism to influence the personality in a powerful way, that it
can awaken sentiments of responsibility and duty, and can provide
religious foundations for a work-ethic. True, the influence of Orthodox discipline on economic activity may have been less obvious in
recent times, he added, less in any case than that of the Russian schismatics, but this must simply be interpreted as the sign of a temporary
disease, and not as a definitive decline (Bulgakov I:197 sqq).

Whereas Bulgakov's initial assessment of the possible relationship
between Orthodoxy and economic ethics may have to be reexam-
ined, the need for such a study is certainly as pressing today as it was
in Bulgakov's time.

Max Weber himself, a few years after the publication of his essay
on the Protestant Ethic, turned to the study of the economic ethics of
some of the other major religious traditions of the world, in particular
the religions of China, India and ancient Judaism. The goal of these
new essays, published originally in *Archiv für Sozialwissenschaft und
Sozialpolitik*, and later, in a partially revised and amplified form as part
of the *Gesammelte Aufsätze zur Religionssoziologie* (GAzRS), is still under
debate. Were the essays on India and China mainly intended as control tests of the so-called Weber thesis on the relationship between
Protestantism and capitalism or was the major purpose the elabora-
tion of a sociology and typology of rationalism? Scholars agree only
that these essays, by means of a tour of the major cultures of the
world, somehow characterise Western humanity and culture.

It is generally assumed that Max Weber up to the end of his life
planned to supplement his essays on the economic ethics of world
religions (EEWR) with further studies on Islam and Christianity –
early Christianity, oriental Christianity and Western Christianity.
Our knowledge of this plan is mainly based on a letter which Max
Weber wrote in 1919 to his publisher Siebeck and Marianne Weber's
preface to Vol. III of GAzRS (Schluchter 1981:148). It is true that F.
Tenbruck (1980:349, Fn. 40) questions this generally accepted view,
suggesting that Weber abandoned his plan for chapters on Islam and
Christianity after having drawn the result of his comparative investi-

gation in the 'Introduction' and in the 'Intermediate Reflection' of EEWR. Tenbruck bases this opinion on a supposedly clear statement of Weber's in the 'Introduction' of EEWR,[2] but Weber's abandonment of his design is far from obvious if one compares the original and later version of the 'Introduction'. Only temporarily during the First World War might Weber have believed that he would not be able to return to his former intellectual preoccupations.

In any case, the project which Weber did not conduct to the end still waits to be done. In this and the following chapter we shall try to get a grasp of a part of oriental Christianity, namely Russian-Orthodox Christianity, from a Weberian viewpoint and with Weber's analytical method. The question about the economic ethics will be pursued in such a manner that, as Weber did himself in his studies, at the outset the socio-political structure will be described and then the 'spirit' which lived in it, followed by an analysis of the heterodox movements and sects. The scattered remarks which can be found in Weber's own writings about Russian phenomena, particularly but not exclusively in *Economy and Society* (ES), will serve as navigational supports and will be incorporated into the context.

In any discussion about economic ethics, the term economic ethics itself needs some clarification. In Weber's *Protestant Ethic*, although not in his studies on the *Economic Ethics of World Religions*, it referred not only and not even mainly to the ethical theories and doctrines of theological textbooks (ethics in the narrow sense of the term), because such doctrines do not necessarily create in the people the psychological motives which will produce the required type of conduct. Rather, in the centre of Weber's analysis was that type of ethics on which the religious context as a whole (for instance, the content and the means of salvation) places psychological sanctions, and only in so far as these sanctions work and in the direction in which they work, which is

---

[2] In the original version of the 'Introduction' (ASS 41; 1916:1), Weber says that he sent the essays on the economic ethics of world religions to print in unfinished form because his conscription made further work on them impossible for the moment, and also because after the war (of 1914-1918) further work on them would be impossible. For the break produced by the war would be so radical that it would be out of the question then to return to the former train of thought. Other work would then be more important.

In the second version of the 'Introduction' (GAzRS I:237), Weber says, however, that the essays were printed earlier only because it *seemed* (my italics) at that time that it would be impossible after the war to return to the former train of thought. Weber implies here that he did return to his former projects after the war.

sometimes very different from the doctrines of the theologians. Only ethics understood in this way have an independent influence on the conduct of life, according to Weber. Furthermore, Weber was also interested in the psychological motives created by religious organisations such as churches or sects.

Having defined ethics in this way, we shall ask in which direction the ethics of Russian-Orthodox Christianity directed human attitudes towards the world and influenced economic conduct; at the same time we shall ask why the Western kind of economic ethics did not evolve in Russia on its own – with the exception of certain similarities in some sectarian movements. The formulation of these questions does not imply a normative ethnocentrism, for what Weber called the 'iron-cage' of Western culture with all the consequences for those who have to live in it, remains undisputed. But it should be admitted that the content as well as the means of knowledge in comparative research, if it is undertaken in the Weberian tradition, necessarily have their conceptual and terminological origin in the occidental scientific culture of the person who undertakes it.

The Patrimonial State

Russia has always been essentially an inland area of a strongly agricultural character. The quality of the soil in the mixed forest area where the cradle of the Russian state was located was poor; in the taiga, around Novgorod and Leningrad, the agricultural season hardly exceeds four months and the rainfall is unreliable. The agricultural yield until the nineteenth century was not higher than it was in the rest of Europe in the Middle Ages when one sown grain produced three or four new grains, while the more advanced agriculture of other European countries in the nineteenth century showed a yield ratio of 1:10 (Pipes 1974:7). Until the sixteenth century slash-and-burn techniques were used, subsequently the three-field system and, well into the nineteenth century, a primitive plough called *sokha*. As cities have never played a significant role in Russia, there were few markets for agricultural products and therefore no encouragement for yield improvements.

The great difficulties in agriculture were counterbalanced by a very good network of navigable waterways which facilitated trade. Since the time of the Normans who invaded Russia from Scandinavia and made Kiev the headquarters of their settlements in their trade with Constantinople, traders have sailed on the Russian rivers.

The state of the Kievan Normans disintegrated in the twelfth century and was divided into virtually independent principalities and regions (the appanage period). Among them was Novgorod in the North-West, in close contact with the Hanseatic League and with a system of government which resembled that of the city-states of Western Europe. Most political functions were concentrated in the so-called *veche* which was in the hands of a patriciate composed of forty leading families.

The South-Western region was occupied by Lithuania and Poland which entered into a dynastic union, although the Orthodox population opposed the Catholic church to which the Polish nobility largely belonged. Finally, there was the relatively backward Volga-Oka region in the North-East of the country which, however, was to become the cradle of the Muscovite state.

Although the environmental conditions were relatively unfavourable and the population small (no more than ten million in the sixteenth century), and although precious metals and money were available only in minimal amounts, nevertheless the existence of a good system of navigable waterways, Novgorod's system of government and trade, and generally the competition for power and ideas between the different principalities might have been able to bring about a capitalistic formation of the economy. We shall ask why this happened neither then nor later. The answer will be found, on the one hand, in the existence of the patrimonial and then patrimonial-bureaucratic state and, on the other hand, in the 'Russian spirit' (Weber 1906a:322), which was mainly rooted in the Russian-Orthodox religion.

The Muscovite princes considered their country with the eyes of landlords as their property (*votchina*, the equivalent of the Latin *patrimonium*), as goods and powers inherited from their fathers. The administration of the state evolved out of the patriarchal administration of the prince's private domain. Now it is when patriarchal domination, based on a definite rule of inheritance and legitimated by tradition, expands from the familial group to political subjects and new territories with the help of a personal administrative staff – but remains organised as in the exercise of patriarchal power – that Weber speaks of a patrimonial state (ES:1013).

Weber also appears to talk of a feudal system in mediaeval Russia

(*Rus'*) and the Muscovite state, but his concept of feudalism is more extensive than in the definition of French scholars, such as Marc Bloch. If, however, one wishes to study the reasons for the development of Western institutions from a comparative perspective, it may be useful to distinguish the Western feudal system from all others. Characteristic for Western feudalism was vassalage, along with political decentralisation and the service-related fief. Vassalage was based on a bilateral contract which was entered into by personal consent and not through inherited obligations and which was binding not only for the vassal but also for the lord (Bloch 1968:617). The tradition of contractual obligations created by vassalage, which in the Occident has contributed to the separation of the administrative and the legal system, was lacking in Russia. While in a dispute with his lord the Western vassal was entitled to public legal proceedings (and while this contributed to the creation of an independent legal system), Russia did not have an independent legal system before the reforms of 1864, and partially not even afterwards. In the Russian patrimonial state a rationally calculable law and administrative system was lacking.

The qualities characteristic of the Muscovite patrimonial state were intensified by the Mongol conquest of 1237-41. As long as a tribute had to be paid to the Golden Horde, the functions of the state were reduced to the levy of tributes and the maintenance of order, and a sense of responsibility for the well-being of the people was entirely lacking. The patrimonial mentality began to change slightly after the dissolution of the Golden Horde at the end of the fourteenth and during the fifteen century and after the collapse of the Byzantine Empire in 1453. The Muscovite princes increasingly thought of themselves as *defensores fidei* of all Orthodox Christians and began to adopt the title of Tsar; at the same time they continued to consider themselves as the owners (*gosundar'*) of the state and political administration as their private affair, to be handled with despotism and arbitrariness. The *oprichnina* under Ivan IV was only an extreme example. The slowly growing patrimonial bureaucracy operated in purely personal submission to the ruler, so that it served only him and not impersonal purposes (ES:1031), in spite of the gradually developing division of functions and rationalisation (official channels, written records).

The Russian population was easily divided into four groups: the nobility, the monastic and clerical estate, the peasantry and the urban population. Each of these four groups was treated differently by the administration in regard to taxes, legal matters and military service; it has even been suggested that these groups existed in the interest of the throne and not for themselves because of their own tradition, for the Tsar had the power to shift his subjects from one group or category to another. What the nobility and the monastic and clerical estate had in common was that they were exempted from military service and from corporal punishment, but between the nobility and the clergy there was no solidarity on the basis of family ties or education. Even within each of the four groups or categories there were no common interests or feelings.

The Nobility

The old land-owning nobility of the appanage period, mainly the boyars, had been of the opinion that they owned *votchiny* (alodial property) and that they were free to enrol in the service of the prince of their choice. But the more the Muscovite rule expanded, the more the rulers tried to reduce the freedom of the boyars and to tie their *votchina* property to services to the Muscovite prince and later the Tsar (particularly from the time of Ivan III). In addition, a service nobility (*dvorianstvo*) was created and received service fiefs (*pomest'e*) which could not be sold or bequeathed. Differences within the nobility were apparent, and from the beginning of the fifteenth century until 1682 the system of the *mestnichestvo* determined social ranking in the sense that the service fief and the rank assigned to the first acquirer became hereditary for all his descendants, as Weber says (ES: 1066), and hence that the rank order of the noble families became relatively stable so that nobody was obliged to serve under a person whose ancestors had had a lower position than their own. According to the highest official rank in the office hierarchy achieved by an ancestor, and according to the number of generations elapsed since that time, the young noble began his career. The system of the *mestnichestvo* forced the nobility, the more so the higher the hereditary rank of a person was, to enter the patrimonial bureaucracy for the sake of preserving social status and career chances. Privately owned land (*votchina*) as basis for social rank declined more and more in favour of the service fief (*pomest'e*). It was this situation which Peter the Great encountered. By burning the lists of family rank which contained the claims of the noble families and by treating the *votchina* and the *pomest'e* as legally equal in the *ukaz* of 1714, he abolished the customary social ranks and legal rights of the Russian nobility in favour of two simple principles (in the argument of Max Weber, ES:1065):

1. Social rank (*chin*) was obtained only through service in a patrimonial-bureaucratic (civilian or military) position, and depended upon a person's standing in an office hierarchy of fourteen ranks. In theory there was no monopoly of the existing nobility and no landed property qualification but rather educational qualifications were required.

2. Any aristocratic privileges lapsed after two generations if their holders did not take on an office.

All this appears to be similar to the practice of the Chinese patrimonial bureaucracy, but the privileges of the Russian service nobility included the right of owning land settled with serfs, and this kind of seigneurial bureaucracy was unknown in China. It is true, though, that in Russia, in order to ward off the appropriation of offices and to avoid the formation of local monopolies of honoratiores (notables) on offices, the Tsarist patrimonial government never sent provincial administrators (*voevody*) into the areas where they possessed landed property. The loss of title to landed property, because of failure of a nobleman to take office, was abolished in the reigns of Peter III and Catherine II, but the *chin* within the patrimonial bureaucracy continued to be the official basis of social prestige, and all opportunities for economic advancement depended upon office holding and court connections and no more solely upon inherited titles (ES:1065).

In this way the *mestnichestvo*, an office hierarchy based on the positions which a family and its ancestors had occupied, was followed by a new hierarchy which was almost completely based on the actual holding of office (the so-called *tabel' o rangakh*). The title of boyar was abolished. Wrangling for positions and a certain bureaucratic spirit were the natural consequence, and because the officials, according to their respective rank, were often moved between the various branches of the administration (military, judiciary, diplomacy), modern specialised knowledge was generally lacking and the career rather resembled the *cursus honorum* of the Roman nobility.

The power of the Tsar was based on the firm solidarity of interests with him of the *chin*-holders and on the complete lack of a status-based solidarity of interest among the nobility. Max Weber as well as Leroy-Beaulieu before him (Leroy-Beaulieu 1897 I:356-72; ES:1067) have underlined the fact that the nobility remained deeply divided through ruthless competition in so far as it strove for the social rank of the *chin*, and through animosity and hatred towards the officials (*chinovnik*) as it remained owner of a *votchina* or a *pomest'e*, for not every owner of landed property remained in the service of the state and not every official immediately received his *pomest'e*. The monopoly of serf ownership did not create status solidarity. For this reason, Weber believed (ES:1068), one fundamental feature of mediaeval Western nobility could not develop in Russia: a central orientation of an internalised conduct of life, the common social honour as it had been created by the occidental knighthood. The split basis of social rank merely provided an external impetus for economic interests and did not produce an inner standard of self-assertion and honour or an *esprit de corps*. One might say that Russia had noblemen but no nobility. Manors or castles, similar to those in which the French nobility resided, did not exist in Russia. The public service attracted the nobles from the country to the metropolis. Compelled to acquire a *chin*, they left their estates in the hands of incapable administrators. Moreover, a large part of the service nobility was of foreign origin – in Leroy-Beaulieu's opinion approximately half of them – and therefore had few roots in the country.

The Merchants

Cities, in the occidental sense with institutions and freedoms, have not existed in Russia. Novgorod and Pskov were exceptions, but the Muscovite patrimonial state which captured them put a quick end to their liberties. In the first place the climate and later also serfdom may have been responsible for the lack of developed cities. The long winters with their long nights make it necessary for the Russian peasant to find activities beside agriculture during a large part of the year. Small cottage industries existed everywhere and for this reason there was no special need for the output produced in cities during long periods of Russian history. This was no fertile ground for specialisation and division of labour. There is also the fact that landlords often established commercial enterprises, cottage industries and even factories with the help of serf labour and this was, according to Weber (ES:1101), one of the reasons why the development of modern capitalism as a system was impeded in Russia; for capitalism depends on the development of mass purchasing power for industrial products.

However, the frequently heavy tributes of the peasants to the landlords confiscated much of their purchasing power. Moreover, the
landlords' purchasing power, which was created by the peasants' tributes, did not promote mass-produced articles on which modern capitalism depends, but rather luxury products and the maintenance of
personal servants. Weber also notes that the manorial industrial
enterprises operated with the forced labour of serfs, who received no
wages, and that in this way labour was withheld from the market.
Moreover, the owners of these serf enterprises tried to impede capitalist development in the cities through political repression.

The Russian city was mainly an administrative centre, military
base and market place, not to be compared with the West European
city, a commune with an autonomous status. There were originally
no corporations nor guilds in Russia,[3] but they were created by the
government in the eighteenth century. The rich merchants (*kuptsy*)
belonged to the two upper guilds, among the others were the poorer
shopkeepers and traders (*meshchane*), who were subject to the capitation tax. Distinctions between the guilds were made merely according to income. Together with the small group of *gosti*, who were entitled to participate in international trade, the rich merchants were
part of the privileged classes and enjoyed almost all the privileges of
the nobility except to own land inhabited by serfs. And yet a bad
deal, a serious financial loss could, because of the classification
according to income criteria, result in descent into a guild of
meshchane. It is, therefore, not surprising that precisely the richest
merchants made every effort to be raised into the nobility and into
the public service, for it alone provided relative security from such a
fall. This, and not an expansion of business or new investment, was
their highest goal; and as soon as they belonged to the nobility, their
capital was usually not reinvested in business or trade. The division
into guilds with different privileges and different fiscal and administrative duties to the state, which was imposed upon the merchants
and, furthermore, the endeavours of the more affluent merchants to
become accepted into the nobility did not create moral solidarity and
thus did not add to an *esprit de corps* and a common social honour
among the bourgeoisie.

The absence in Russia of independently developed corporations
and guilds, which in Western Europe were able to control and to

---

[3] Exceptions existed mainly in Novgorod (Kaufmann-Rochard 1969:250).

increase the trustworthiness of their members and the quality of production, was of no little significance for the poor development of an economic ethic in the narrow sense of the term (Gerschenkron 1966:48; 1970:59-60). This could at least partially explain the fact that the Russian merchant was notorious for his dishonesty as a seventeenth century proverb indicates (*kto torguet tot voruet*; those who trade are thieves).

Very strong status differences stratified the town dwellers of Russia even after the abolition of serfdom. Max Weber notes in this context that the city dweller from the countryside continued to be legally bound to his village of origin and could be forced to return when his travel permit was revoked. Under such circumstances no legal status of urban citizenship arose, but only an association for sharing the burdens and privileges of those who happened to inhabit the city at any given time (ES:1245). Before the abolition of serfdom the town-dwelling serfs paid a money tribute (*obrok*) to their lord, but otherwise were in fact economically independent burghers. The possibility of purchasing their freedom probably intensified the economic effort of these unfree city dwellers. In Weber's opinion (ES:1238) it was no accident that a large part of the first fortunes acquired through continuous rational operation in trade or industry was found in the hands of freedmen.[4]

If, however, one takes into account the extreme scarcity of money in circulation (paper money has existed in Russia only since 1768), furthermore, the fact that well into the middle of the nineteenth century there was virtually no commercial credit or banking, and finally also the general ignorance of book-keeping even among the affluent merchants (Pipes 1974:207), some of the obstacles to modern capitalism become clear. Add to this the fact that a differentiated law of sodalities like that of the mediaeval Occident or the rational concept of the corporation, as it was produced in the confluence of Roman and mediaeval law, remained unknown in Russia (ES:726). Finally, Russia lacked the Roman legal tradition with its rational mode of proof which excluded the (irrational) ordeal – a tradition which had been rediscovered by the great mediaeval universities of Western

---

[4] It is interesting to note that in Rome the freedmen also found themselves barred from the typically ancient, politically oriented type of capitalism, and therefore found themselves pushed onto the path of relatively modern ways of gaining a livelihood (ES:1359).

Europe. The churchmen of mediaeval Russia were conversant not so much with classical Roman law as with the Byzantine law of the Ecloga (Kaiser 1980:173).

On the whole, the legal situation of the Russian merchants was not uniform and, therefore, did not produce status solidarity, and it was precarious. In the state of Muscovy they had to fear the nobles who sometimes seized hold of their commodities or even the Tsar who might confiscate them. Fairs were allowed only in designated towns and trade beyond the borders of the state was generally forbidden. In the sixteenth and seventeenth centuries the Tsars claimed a monopoly of wholesale trade, mining and parts of manufacture production, if it appeared to be profitable. The surest way of becoming rich in Muscovite Russia was to obtain a concession for a business on which the Tsar claimed a monopoly; later, under Peter the Great and in the eighteenth century, the political capitalism of the purveyors of the state flourished. 'Entrepreneurs' who had been hired by the Tsar (especially under Peter the Great) obtained tax advantages, government contracts, cheap labour from state peasants and they were protected by tariffs. Their success depended at least as much on political favours as on entrepreneurial know-how.

When towards the end of the nineteenth century industrialisation intensified, this happened mainly because of government initiatives with foreign capital and foreign technology and know-how.

The Peasants

During the Middle Ages the Russian peasants were free and, as tenants, could choose their lord and location. In the sixteenth century, however, when elsewhere in Europe the bonds of serfdom started to break, Moscow began to tighten them. The terror of the *oprichnina* under Ivan IV had depopulated the central areas of Muscovy and the conquest of Kazan and Astrakhan had opened up to Russian colonisation much of the attractive black-earth belt. The complaints of the service nobility whose peasant-workers were moving away as well as military and fiscal considerations persuaded the government to gradually deprive the peasants of their freedom of movement, to tie them to the land in a process extending over a century or more and to submit them to the administration and jurisdiction of the *dvorianstvo*. The expression of *muzhik* for the Russian peasant is really the diminutive form of *muzh* (man); the *muzhik* was the little man who had the duty to serve his lord.

To be sure, the peasants of the border regions (White Sea, Siberia, Cossacks), and certain ethnic groups like the German colonists who settled in Russia under Catherine II, were able to maintain their liberty, and almost half the peasants who were state peasants were tied to the land but were not serfs of a *dvorianin*; but those who carried the burden of serfdom never quite came to terms with it, as the peasant uprisings initiated by Stenka Razin and later by Pugachev demonstrated.

As in the northern parts of Russia agriculture was not very profitable, serfs were often allowed merely to pay a money tribute (*obrok*) to their lord. Such peasants were often successful traders and their conscientiousness and honesty was recognised by many foreigners; in the nineteenth century some peasants even became owners of large cottage industries and factories, especially in the production of cotton. But all these activities were limited by the fact that these peasants were practically without rights with regard to their lords and that they were dependent not only on their protection and their goodwill but also on their greed (Kulischer 1931:330).

When finally in 1861, after Russia's humiliating defeat in the Crimean War, the emancipation of the peasants eventually arrived, the authority of the landlord over his serfs was abolished but not the bonds which tied the peasant to the *mir*, the village community, to which the land belonged in common and which redistributed it periodically. It may be true that the *mir* in the sense of an organisation responsible for the village community's tax payments was known since the late Middle Ages, but it gained importance as the administrative agency of communal land and as a land-distribution organisation during the time of serfdom, because, from the point of view of the state and the *dvorianstvo*, it rendered the agricultural organisation of the village more rational, especially after the introduction of the capitation tax (Goehrke 1964:184). However, in spite of the periodical redistribution of land to the families of the village community, the peasants remained owners of the product of their work. Where the *mir* did not exist at the time of emancipation, it was often brought in for reasons of financial control, for the village community as a whole was now responsible for the taxes of all its members.

Russian law, as Max Weber has noted (ES:725), recognised liturgical collective liability and the corresponding collective rights of the compulsory organisations, e.g. of village communities. The Russian population which did not belong to the service nobility or the monastic and clerical estate, in particular the peasants, manual workers and merchants, owed the state a variety of obligations in money and labour, called *tiaglo*. All *tiaglo*-bearers formed communities whose members were jointly accountable for the monies and labour services imposed on their group. The system of liturgies,[5] as Weber called this system of satisfaction of state needs (ES:1097), was applied comprehensively by many patrimonial-bureaucratic empires of Antiquity, for instance, Egypt. The various classes of the population were stratified along occupational lines and the burden of state requirements was imposed on these occupational groups on the principle of joint liability, so that the members could not withdraw unilaterally. In this sense the compulsory guilds of ancient Egypt and the hereditary attachment of the Russian peasants to the village are comparable (ES:350). It is obvious, according to Weber, that everywhere, where it was introduced, the system of liturgies considerably reduced private capital formation and the realm of capitalist acquisition. In the late Roman state this meant the throttling of ancient political capitalism and for the same reasons Russian political capitalism (trade concessions, 'entrepreneurs' who were financed by the Tsar) was never very successful.

In any case, the retention of the *mir* after the emancipation of the serfs inhibited the emergence of a more vigorous farming class because the hard-working and enterprising members of the *mir* had to share financial responsibility with the incapable and unwilling ones. Moreover, important sums had to be paid as compensation to their former landlords by the affluent serfs who had become successful in trade or industry (in fact, all peasants were obliged to make redemption payments to their former landlords). These sums were therefore not reinvested as capital (Kulischer 1931:354).

The emancipation of the serfs was progress, particularly if it is seen in connection with the revolution of 1905, the year in which 'redemption payments' were finally abolished and the peasants were allowed to leave the *mir* even without its consent; it was an economic advance because of the greater freedom of work and competition, and a moral

---

[5] The notion of liturgy is derived from a Greek verb (*leiturgeo*), which means that someone administers a public office and defrays the costs connected with it out of his own pocket.

advance since it increased the feeling of responsibility. The old patriarchal customs were weakened and replaced by greater individualism. It was precisely the success of the reforms, however, which created new millenarian hopes and an increase in the desire for more profound changes which would eliminate the disappointments of the
past.

In spite of the fact that it eliminated important obstacles, the emancipation of serfs was hardly an independent driving force towards the
development of modern capitalism, just as little as the increase of
population in the nineteenth century (the population increased from
35 million in 1750 to 125 million around 1900) or as the discovery of
important gold deposits in the Urals in the time of Nicholas I. For
deposits of precious metals, although they can be highly significant for
the speed of capitalistic development, are by themselves unable to
create it; the enormous deposits of precious metals in Ptolemaic
Egypt, for instance, did not produce capitalism to any significant
extent.

The Patrimonial State and Capitalism

The patrimonial state no doubt blocked the development of commercial capitalism (but not of political capitalism) because of the lack of a
rationally calculable functioning of administration and jurisdiction
and because of the lack of a clear separation between them. This did
not even change in the eighteenth century when – according to Pipes'
thesis which is basically also Leroy-Beaulieu's thesis – a partial dis-
mantling of the patrimonial structure could be detected. It resulted
from the fact that the *dvorianstvo* and the patrimonial bureaucracy
achieved a certain independence with regard to the patrimonial ruler
(the *dvorianstvo*, because it was exempted from state service in 1762,
and the bureaucracy, because in 1767 civil servants achieved auto-
matic promotion on the basis of seniority). On the one hand, the
reforms did not produce more rationalisation and objective norms in
the administration and, on the other hand, according to Weber, history shows that the strengthening of patrimonial bureaucracies has
always and everywhere smothered capital formation and hence private capitalism.

This is perhaps the place to discuss the thesis of Samuel Baron
(1970) who claims that the liturgical patrimonial state as a whole was

the main cause of the poor development of capitalism in Russia
before the middle of the nineteenth century, because the diverse trade
monopolies of the Tsar and the general lack of legal security set
unavoidable barriers in the path of private economic activities.

Baron has *expressis verbis* formulated his thesis in contrast to Weber
who, in his opinion, would have attached more importance to the
religious element. It should be asked, however, what Baron under-
stands by capitalism, and it will then be noticed that he seems to identify capitalism, at least the cause of capitalism, with the passion for
trade and gain. That, however, has nothing to do with modern capitalism as Weber described it, for he saw in it a restriction of the passion for gain and an incorporation of economic striving within an ethical system of rational inner-worldly conduct (GAzRS II:372;
India:337). For the rest, it cannot be assumed that capitalism is, as it
were, the 'natural' organisational system of humankind which immediately evolves as soon as all obstacles have been removed. Weber has
particularly shown that in the absence of the Protestant ethic modern
capitalism did not develop on its own (although, naturally, it could be
imported as a system), even if there were few institutional or other
obstacles to its development; but that modern capitalism did develop,
even when the obstacles were considerable, if the Protestant ethic was
also present. There seems to be sufficient cause, therefore, to turn to
the question of whether somewhere in the ethos of the Russian people
it is possible to find motives which may have contributed to the formation of a rational conduct of life and a capitalistic spirit, or whether
such motives were absent. In Russia itself, the relationship between
religion and a certain cultural superiority of the West was already
alluded to by Chaadaev who believed that no extolment of work and
no principles and rules (common interests, the building of a socialist
state) will suffice if there is no deeply rooted inner ethos with regard to
life and work. In his opinion such an ethos which must be acquired in
the course of a long education, was provided in the West by Catholicism (he did not consider the Protestant churches and sects), but was
lacking in Russia (v. Schelting 1948:36 & 139). In the following, the
Russian-Orthodox religion and, further on, the *raskol* and the main
sects will have to be examined in the context of this question. Preceding this examination is a brief analysis of the development of the situation of the Orthodox Church within the Russian patrimonial state.

The Orthodox Church and Monasticism

In 988 Prince Vladimir of Kiev was converted to the Christian faith, although the mass of the population continued to adhere to pre-Christian customs for a long time to come. It has had far-reaching consequences for Russia that Vladimir was influenced by missionaries from Byzantium and not from Rome, for the classical conception of the emperor as *rex-sacerdos* continued to survive in Byzantium. The emperor exerted an influence on the synods, played a part in the appointments of bishops and patriarchs and called together the church councils (like that of Nicaea) which made legally enforceable decisions on dogmas, while the patriarch of Constantinople had no political or legal authority whatsoever.

Because of a political vacuum in the Western part of the Empire, the Roman Church had begun to develop in a different direction. One contributory factor was an imperial law of 451 which made the Bishop of Rome the supreme judge of all bishops of the Western part of the Roman Empire; another factor was the lack of control which Constantinople could exert over Rome. The creation of the Papal States and the crowning of Charlemagne in Rome accentuated this development. While in Contantinople a strong state and an old civilisation englobed and dominated the Church, in the West a new state was created with the help of an independent church which gained increasing influence over worldly matters. The investiture controversy, for instance, was not about the separation of the *sacerdotium* and the *regnum*, but rather about the claim of the Church (which was sometimes even realised in practice) to be the state, as Figgis said (1956:4), for the existence of society as separate from the Church was not conceived. The state was the political part of the Church. The bull *Unam Sanctam* (1302) and the doctrine of the two swords were the final stages of this development which only afterwards turned into the gradual separation of Church and State as two different societies, a separation which is known from early Christianity and again in modern times.

The Orthodox Church has never known an Archimedean point, in the form of a Pope, outside or even above the sphere of the state. It was divided into national branches which had to adapt to the respective states. Under Mongol domination, which was a heavy burden for the rest of the population, the Orthodox Church was granted protection and exemption from tributes and taxes in return for its favour and for the pledge to pray for the *khan*. The number, prosperity and

landed property of the monasteries grew considerably during this
period because of colonisation as well as donations from the princes
of Moscow whose claim to monocratic power was backed by the
Church. The monks were no longer able to till their land and had to
resort to tenant labour. They were also among the first to petition the
Crown for charters binding peasants to the soil. Around 1600 the
Troitse Sergeev Monastery owned approximately 2,500 villages, and
at the same time the Solovetskii Monastery employed 700 workers in
its salt works and in its own fishing and merchant fleet on the White
Sea. By the end of the sixteenth century, approximately one third of
all arable land in Russia was in the hands of the Church and the
monasteries, although it could not be called their property in the legal
sense of the term, no more than the land of the *boyars* and the *dvorianstvo*.

Besides their worldly activities (the administration of their lands) a
certain lack of education could often be detected among monks and
priests and, as a consequence, religion retained magical and ritualistic
aspects. Reactions against these conditions developed in those parts of
the country where contacts with abroad were possible, for instance, in
the fourteenth century among the Strigol'niki sect in Novgorod and
in the fifteenth century when Novgorod fought for its independence,
in the anti-trinitarian and anti-monastic Judaising movement, and
finally in the mystical Hesychast movement with connections to the
monks of Mount Athos.

A deadly conflict developed which involved the two kinds of
monasticism of that time in Russia: on the one hand, the hermitage or
skete (from *skity*) monasticism, which turned away from politics and the
church hierarchy, preached gentleness and love even towards heretics
and schismatics and pursued missionary activities in Northern Russia
and in Siberia; on the other hand, the cenobitic founders' monasteries, which were friendly towards the state and where the princely
founders appointed the abbots and were in charge of the land-hold-
ings. The *skete* movement was annihilated and a whole spiritual trend
of old Russia, represented by charismatic monks, was forced under-
ground, while the prevailing submissive monasticism of the state
church only contributed to the petrifaction of religious life. These so-
called Josephite monks also developed the idea of Moscow as the
Third Rome (after the fall of Constantinople) and the thesis that the
rulers of Russia were universal Christian sovereigns and had the right
to rule all Orthodox people as well as the Orthodox Church. It was in

conformity with the idea of the Third Rome that the rulers of Moscow assumed the title of Tsar (Caesar) and that a patriarchate was established in Moscow in 1589. When the Josephite monks, and with them the Russian-Orthodox Church, placed themselves voluntarily under the tutelage of the Tsar, they were able to uproot certain heresies and to retain the church lands but, in the long run, this led to their total dependence on the state. It soon became customary for the Tsars to make their own appointments of bishops and metropolitans and to interfere with church justice.

But neither the late Byzantine nor the Russian caesaro-papist rulers, Weber notes (ES:831), have ever claimed to be able to create new sacred laws (in the absence of both an infallible agency for the exposition of doctrine and of conciliar legislation). As a result, Eastern canon law, confined to its original sphere, remained entirely stable but also without any influence on economic life. For the rest, the caesaro-papist rulers of Russia could not normally afford to intervene in questions of dogma and even less in questions of sacred rights. For every change in the ritual was assumed to endanger its magic efficacy and thus would have mobilised the interests of the subjects against the ruler. From this perspective, the great schism (*raskol*) of the Russian church in the second half of the seventeenth century – over whether one should cross oneself with two or three fingers and similar issues – appears readily understandable (ES:1174). The reaction to the reforms, which were initiated by the Patriarch Nikon and supported by the Tsar, and which drove the more religiously interested parts of the population to separate as so-called Old Believers (really *staroobriadtsy*, Old Ritualists) from the official church (and who therefore were called *Raskol'niki* or 'splitters' by the official church), nevertheless hardly touched the relationship between the official church and the state. More important for this relationship was the fact that a few decades later Peter the Great abolished the patriarchate, transformed its administrative, jurisdictional and fiscal offices into branches of the patrimonial bureaucracy and confiscated its revenues in return for fixed government salaries to the clergy. About the same time the secularisation of church properties, which was completed under Catherine II, had begun. The office of the Patriarch was replaced by the Holy Synod, a purely bureaucratic organisation of state-appointed clerical dignitaries, and headed by a lay procurator. At this point of the development, the Russian-Orthodox Church completely lacked a hierocratic apparatus with a monocratic head (ES:1192).

If one considers in this context the obligation imposed on the clergy by the state to denounce political dissenters (consequently no con-
fessional secret), it becomes obvious that the organisational form of
the Orthodox Church excluded any possibility that it could set itself
up as an advocate of civil rights and liberties against the power of the
patrimonial state (Weber 1906a:274). Support in the population was
also lacking, particularly since many peasants switched to the Old
Believers and the sects, while the intellectuals were uninterested and
religious thinkers, like L. Tolstoy and V. Soloviev, were expelled from
the Church.

The experience of the West has demonstrated, as Müller-Armack
(1959:350) has already noticed, that the dualism of emperorship and
papacy, developed during the Middle Ages as the basic form of status
plurality, also strengthened other status positions (nobility, cities).
Because in Russia the tension between state and church was lacking,
the sociological phenomena connected with it, i.e. an autonomous
nobility and the essentials of the occidental city based on an independent bourgeoisie, could not develop either.

In a special way the already mentioned monasticism was connected with the official church, a monasticism which had preserved, to
some extent, the early Christian ideal of the monk (*monachos*, unique,
perfect). The monastic rule of Pachomius (fourth century) took a still
relatively anachoretic (although to a certain extent already cenobitic)
position and forbade monks to become clerics, so as not to aspire to
glory and control over others, but the rule of Basil the Great, which is
authoritative for all Orthodox monasticism, introduced a middle
position, for not only did it introduce the cenobitic monasteries (*koinobion*), but it also accepted the compromise that in every monastery a
few monks became ordained priests (*hieromonachoi*). They were allowed
to perform the sacraments, although the institutional order of the
Orthodox monastery is intended to create the conditions which facili-
tate the complete separation of the monk from the 'world' and his
complete abandonment to prayer and contemplation. Therefore,
when the Trullan Council (*Quinisextum*) in 691 brought about a certain rapprochement of the monks and the Church by its decision that
only monks can become bishops (while the ordinary priests of the
Orthodox Church had to be married), this led to a certain tension in
the monks' conduct of life, a tension which led to the fact that monks
who followed the strictest monastic rule (*skhima*) evaded the office of
bishop.

Here, then, lies one of the great problems of every hierocracy, according to Weber (ES:1166): How is the 'official apparatus' to cope with the emergence of a charismatic following of God, the monks, who strive for individual salvation through finding a personal and direct path to God, while the hierocratic church as an institution of salvation seeks to monopolise the way to God (*extra ecclesiam nulla salus*) by means of the sacraments. Nevertheless, each of the great churches was forced to compromise with monasticism. One possible solution, adopted by the Roman Catholic Church, was the reinterpretation of monasticism as a specific vocation within the ranks of the church: on the one hand, the adherence to the *consilia evangelica*, which is too demanding for the ordinary believer, was considered an extraordinary achievement, to be utilised by the Church as a repository of blessings for the benefit of the less charismatically gifted; on the other hand, Western monasticism subdivided into functionally different orders which, according to their objectives, were active as auxiliary troops of the Church, as it were, in missionary work, hospital work and education, and whose social range included mendicant orders and orders of knights. From the rules of St. Benedict to the Jesuits, the emancipation of Western monasticism from planless otherworldliness increased, the monks left the monastic cell, as Weber said (ES:1167), and tried to dominate the world; through their competition they imposed their own way of life upon the office-holding priesthood and partook in the administration of the charisma of office vis-à-vis the laymen. The integration of the monks into a bureaucratic organisation as the troops of the monocratic head of the church and subject to a specific discipline was, according to Weber (ES:1168), a consistent solution of the tension between the official church and monasticism. However, the solution of the Eastern churches, which increasingly reserved all higher-ranking offices for the monks was, in Weber's opinion, inconsistent (because of the mechanical combination of personal charisma and office charisma) and could be explained only because the development of the hierocracy itself had been deflected by caesaro-papism.

Within the Orthodox religion one does not find the Western fragmentation into different monastic orders which actively try to intervene in the 'world'; and as Orthodox monasticism tends to see the means of salvation in liturgy, mysticism and contemplation, the Orthodox monasteries were no breeding grounds of science, while Western monasticism was the originator of the most diverse scientific stimuli. Indeed, the distinctiveness of the scientific thought of the Occident can be ascribed in large measure (i.e. in its rational-theoretical aspects) to Benedictine, Franciscan and Dominican monasticism (ES:1169), in the same way, incidentally, as the development of the specific rationality of harmonic music in the Occident can be ascribed to its monasticism. (It was not only because of the absence of the stave notation that a rational polyphonic and harmonic music did not originally exist in Russia; the chant in unison according to neumatic notation is still practised to this day among the Old Believers.)

Incidentally, it should also be noted that other contributory factors to Western scientific development have been absent in Russia. In addition to its theoretical aspects, which can largely be attributed to Western monasticism, Western science has one of its roots in the technical experiment which was born in Renaissance art (GAzRS I:439). Experimentation in art, however, which originated in the desire to raise art to the level of science, could not develop within Orthodox religion because the painting of an icon was a liturgical act, the creation of a heavenly archetype, which it would have been blasphemy to change in the process of experimentation.

Finally, a normal condition for the development of scientific theological speculation in Russia would have been the existence of an independent official church.

Besides the monks, who were popularly called the black clergy, there existed the mass of married priests, the white clergy (*popy* in popular language). They were exempted from the capitation tax, from corporal punishment and, in earlier times, also from military service. As a serf hardly ever received permission from his landlord to become a priest, and as a noble who took up priesthood would have lost his privileges, membership of the priesthood had practically become hereditary: the priests had their own educational institutions; in order to obtain a position, they married the daughter of another priest, and their sons also became priests. Their income, however, was in most cases very inadequate, and they tried to increase it by requesting payments from peasants for various religious services. For this very reason many peasants had very little respect for the *popy*, in spite of their respect for the Orthodox religion, and some of the peasants may have had financial reasons for becoming members of the heterodox and sectarian movements which will be discussed later. With regard to the relationship between the mass of the population and the priests, it would be accurate to say, according to Weber (1906a:274, fn.), that the magical powers, which were at the disposal of the priests and were believed to be needed for salvation, were highly valued but that this had no influence at all on the opinion generally held about priests. With regard to the relationship between the white clergy and the black clergy, a certain antagonism was apparent because of the different interests and because of efforts on both sides to increase their influence. Max Weber therefore thought that the problems of the regeneration of the Russian Orthodox Church (in 1905) could be attributed not only to the caesaro-papist government, but also to the social differences between the peasant-like and proletarian white clergy, on the one hand, and the celibate black clergy for whom all the higher positions in the hierarchy were canonically reserved, on the other (ibid.). It should be noted though that, although monasticism was formally in control, since all high-ranking religious positions were occupied by monks, the caesaro-papist subjection of the Church broke the influence of monasticism (ES:1173), so that its influence on the governing structure of the Church and on the conduct of life of the lower clergy can in no way be compared with the influence of Western monasticism.

The 'Spirit' of Orthodoxy

But in the system described so far, what kind of 'spirit' lived in it and influenced the conduct of life of Russian-Orthodox humanity? It was a spirit composed of magical-traditional, ritual and mystical aspects. Pre-Christian polytheism survived in many places in the belief in *domovoi*, *vodianoi* and *rusalka*, and even in the Christian veneration of saints magical ideas often survived: many peasants used to cover their icons, which in every house were positioned in a place of honour, with a piece of cloth when it was assumed that what they intended to do would not be approved of by one of the saints (Leroy-Beaulieu 1896 III:37). If by this means one could successfully conceal one's sins and avoid punishment in this or the other world, the motivation for a rational conduct of life was considerably reduced – in the same way as the scarab on the heart of the Egyptian, who tried to deceive the judge of the dead and thus get into paradise, made all ethics futile. Weber also mentioned, in connection with magical ideas,[6] that the fear of giving serious affront to two dozen saints by omitting in one year the days sacred to them has hindered the reception of the Gregorian calendar in Russia until the beginning of the twentieth century (ES:405).

In the eyes of many peasants the rites of the church were nothing more, but also nothing less, than particularly effective magical performances; without knowledge of the Bible, any dogmas, or even the Lord's Prayer, they were accustomed to the rites and saw the essence of Christianity in them. To change them, as the reforms of Nikon did, not only was an act against the holy tradition, but also made the rites, for instance, the three-fingered instead of the two-fingered sign of the cross, magically ineffective.

In this context, it should be stressed that peasants, as they are more dependent on organic processes and natural events than town populations, are little oriented to rational systematisation. While urban artisans who work for clients tend to develop ideas of duties and rewards, and then also of religious rewards, namely of salvation, peasants usually are much more remote from this notion of compensation and try to coerce their gods by magical means. Theodicies and ethical speculation are uncommon among them. The more agrarian a culture is, Max Weber said (ES:469), the more likely it is that the agrarian element of the population will fall into a pattern of traditionalism and that the religion of the masses will lack ethical rationalisation. At any rate, caesaro-papism was most successful when the type of ethical and salvation religion was not yet dominant in the respective culture; in Russia the caesaro-papist formula gained control in a religious context with a considerable magical-ritual orientation (ES:1161).

But Eastern Christianity, in Weber's opinion, cannot be classified only according to its magical-ritual aspects because they are mainly a

---

[6] Magic is a much debated issue in the social sciences (cf. Wilson 1979). Here it will be assumed that magical ideas and practices predominate in those cultural contexts where cult and beliefs have not been systematised and where the relationship between the human being and the supernatural seems to be reduced to ad-hoc relations and interests and where these interests are then pursued by stereotyped means which 'compel' or 'pacify' or 'bind' the irrational powers or spirits. In Weber's sociology practically all religions, even monotheism, contain magical elements somewhere. The decisive consideration is then: who is deemed to exert the stronger influence on the interests of the individual in everyday life, the theoretically supreme God or the lower spirits and demons? In the Catholic religion the sacraments are considered by Weber to contain magical elements to the extent that they reduce or do not further an ethically rational conduct of life (ES:561). In *The Protestant Ethic* (PE:117) Weber calls the Catholic priest a magician who performed the miracle of transubstantiation.

matter of the orientation of the religious masses. In addition, and especially among the religious elites, there has always existed a mystical aspect, a kind of antique mysticism (Weber 1924a:466). On this level, the rites of the Church, and especially the liturgy of the Eucharist, are not magic but guidance and direction to mystical experience in a complicated mystery play, the structure of which was essentially shaped by Hellenistic mystery religions and which originally offered the creed as a secret formula (Benz 1971:32).

Furthermore, Orthodox mysticism reveals itself in the fact that the highest authority, which decides who belongs to the church and which religious teachings are dogmatically correct, is the church as a communal group united in love, the *consensus ecclesiae* (Weber 1924a:466) – and not the Pope, as in the Catholic Church, nor the Scriptures, as in the Lutheran Church (Russian translations of the Bible from the Church Slavonic were published only in the second half of the nineteenth century). For one finds in Russia the firm conviction, related to mysticism, that Christian brotherly love will lead to unity in all things,[7] or that people who mystically love each other will think and feel in the same way and act in solidarity with each other (ES:551). This view is basic to the Eastern conception of church community (*sobornost'*). It is symbolised in the brotherly kiss during the night of Easter which the believer shares with everybody who happens to come along the way, because this acosmism, this 'sacred prostitution of the soul ', is the way to a mystical vision of God (ES:589).

A particularly clear picture of orthodox mysticism can be obtained from Hesychasm which tried to achieve the vision of divine light as the result of methodical contemplation. Under the influence of Symeon, the New Theologian, hesychasm had been cultivated among the monks of Athos in the fourteenth century and then had permeated the spirit of the Orthodox Church with its world-renouncing attitude.

The goal of salvation in Hesychasm was the personal deification in the mystical *theoria* and the means of salvation was the 'spiritual

---

[7] Weber's interpretation of Orthodoxy, in particular his comparison of the Orthodox, Catholic and Protestant concepts of truth, has great affinity with the thought of A. Khomyakov. Khomyakov taught that the whole truth is not accessible to individual thinkers, but only to an aggregate of thinkers, bound together by love. Khomyakov's indictment against 'Latinism' was that the Western Church accepted a new dogma (*filioque*) in the eleventh century without the consent of the Eastern Church, and thus undermined the moral conditions of knowledge, isolated itself from the truth and fell under the dominion of rationalism (Zenkovsky 1953 I:191-3).

prayer'. Ascetic practices (e.g. manual work, little food and sleep) were a precondition. All acting towards the 'world' was devalued so that it could be said: the bodily action resembles the leaf and the inner spiritual action resembles the fruit (Smolitsch 1953:110).

In this context the *startsy* also need to be mentioned. Certain monks, who lived in the vicinity of their monasteries and concentrated on 'spiritual prayer' (although they also sang the monastic offices), attained a reputation and influence among the surrounding population who came for advice and help, like the *starets* Zosima in Dostoevsky's *Brothers Karamasov*. Numerous alleged miracle healings indicate, however, that the influence of the *startsy* often was not only of a mystical but also of a magical character. For the rest, in the phenomenon of 'staretsism' a tendency towards a form of hagiolatry, a hagiolatry of living saviours with a personal charisma, becomes apparent. This development, which has been even more pronounced in the India of the gurus, has been prevented in Western Europe by the rational office-character of the office-church which took the monastic orders under rigid official discipline.

On the whole, therefore, Weber saw the Orthodox Church as permeated by mysticism, and this mysticism did not only, like the mysticism of Tauler in the West, represent a heterodox movement. It was, on the contrary, central.

Mysticism, in Weber's terminology, is set in opposition to asceticism. He connected asceticism with salvation by works and with activity proving one's religious merit; in mysticism, however, he saw passive contemplation and quiet repose in God. Neither asceticism nor mysticism affirms, according to Weber, the world as such. The ascetic rejects the world's ethically irrational empirical character, while at the same time affirming rational activity within the world as a personal means to become God's instrument for securing certification of a state of grace. On the other hand, the innerworldly mystic regards action within the world as a temptation, against which he or she must maintain the state of grace as God's vessel. Therefore activities are minimised by resignation to the routines of the world, and activity within the world is characterised by a distinctive 'brokenness' (*Gebrochenheit*) because for the mystic no success which may crown innerworldly activities can have any significance with respect to salvation (ES:549), and because of an inner conviction of the senselessness of this politically, socially, ethically and artistically formed life. Early and oriental Christianity are mentioned particularly by Weber in connection with this mystical attitude to life, and he also argues that when an innerworldly salvation religion is characterised by mysticism, the normal consequence is a relative indifference towards the world and a humble acceptance of the given social order.

The acceptance of the social order out of an attitude of world indifference could also be the reason for the apparent apathy of the Russian Orthodox Church and of the upper strata of society towards the surrounding social misery, particularly in the nineteenth century; this apathy cannot be explained only, as Müller-Armack once did (1959:353), by the relative absence of a sectarian movement whose critical attitude once woke the social conscience of Western Europe.

Harnack (1913:162-3) has emphasised the mystical character of Orthodox religion with analytical means which are related to those of Weber. In all salvation religions, he writes, the question arises, from what, to which end and by which means the human being wants to be saved – the motivation, the goal and the means of salvation. While in the Occident the wish to be saved from one's sins appears to be more prominent, in Orthodox religion man is more preoccupied with death and transitoriness (while thoughts about sin are certainly not absent). In the Occident, therefore, Christians strive for means which atone for their sins or prove their salvation from sins – and these are usually ascetic means. In Orthodox contexts, however, means are sought after, which make people forget the transitoriness of this world and life, and which promise a foretaste of happiness in the hereafter, the mystical enjoyment of heavenly goods. The ethical impulses are here of the more mystical and world-fleeing kind.

Mysticism and asceticism as methods of salvation have also been linked by Weber to the concept of the divine, be it the concept of a transcendental and absolutely omnipotent God, which is predominant within the Western religious traditions, or be it that of an impersonal immanent order as it is found in the traditions of the great religions of Asia. The concept of a transcendental God implies a tremendous distance between God and humanity, and as a consequence human beings often see themselves as instruments of God and seek salvation in actions pleasing in the sight of God, while the followers of the great Asiatic religions see themselves as passive vessels of immanent divinity. Therefore, Weber says, the decisive difference between the predominantly oriental and Asiatic types of salvation religion, and those found primarily in the Occident, is that the former usually culminate in contemplation and mysticism and the latter in asceticism

(ES:551).[8] That this is not a necessary correlation, but rather one of elective affinity[9], can be seen in the Russian Orthodox tradition which, in spite of its mystical tendencies, conceives of God as a transcendental being and which is in this respect internally 'broken'. Some implications of this 'brokenness' will now be mentioned.

First of all, the concept of predestination, which has contributed to the increase of a methodical conduct of life in ascetic Protestantism, is lacking; the Eastern Church did not develop the idea, which it considers absurd, that the transitory actions of people can lead to eternal damnation, nor has it adopted the Western idea of a law-based relationship between God and the human being (for instance, the doctrine of justification by faith of Protestant theology which considers the human being corrupted by original sin and in need of God's grace, or the casuistry of sins and satisfactory deeds and the legal competence of the Catholic priests to grant absolution). Orthodox Christians are convinced that sinful actions imply only a diminution of their goodness, a loss of substance (but not a total elimination of their relationship with God); they are also convinced that they them-

---

[8] Of course, also in Weber's opinion, mystical heterodoxies have existed here and there within the occidental tradition with its transcendental God, but even for Meister Eckhart the pantheistic experience of God was, according to Weber, impossible without the abandonment of crucial elements of the occidental concept of God (GAzRS I:258).

Following the footsteps of Weber, Peter Berger (1980:172) has contrasted the mysticism of personality with the mysticism of infinity. According to Berger, the mysticism of personality is a form of inward experience where there is no dissolution of human personality nor a forgetting of the personal and transcendental character of God; the mysticism of infinity is a form where the individual self believes in a complete loss of his or her own personal qualities and in merging into union with the divine. Mysticism of infinity is at home in India since the Upanishads (*tat tvam asi*), but not in the monotheistic religions of the West whose religious authorities have often reacted vehemently against mystics of this type (there was the fate of the Muslim mystic al-Hallaj who was executed in 922 because of his saying 'I am truth'; and Meister Eckhart's teachings about the mystical experience of the soul which attains unity with the Godhead beyond all intercourse with God were condemned by the Catholic Church).

The theoretical matrix of the Indian philosopher Shankara also easily accepted the mysticism of infinity, while for him an encounter with a personal God (the Indian *bhakti* experience) is but an inferior step and in the last analysis an illusion (*maya*) on the way to the impersonal *brahman*.

On the whole, then, in the Occident mystical experiences could not, because of the concept of a transcendental God, attain the mysticism of infinity but had to stop at the mysticism of personality. In India, on the other hand, the fully flowering mysticism of infinity accepted personal Gods only at lower levels of experience.

[9] For the concept of elective affinity, please see the introductory pages of the Appendix.

selves are able to become similar to God, to attain *theosis*. But the consequences of these ideas have not been drawn in full clarity, because the doctrine developed by Origen, that at the end of many aeons all people will have turned to the divine *logos*, has been rejected as heretical (Benz 1971:47).

Additionally, a considerable reduction in preaching, which is so central in the Protestant churches, in favour of the dominating liturgy, can be noticed. The importance of preaching generally stands in inverse proportion to the magical components of a religion, and in the context of mysticism it is often, especially in Asia, related to exemplary rather than ethical prophecy. It is not surprising, therefore, that preaching was confined within strict conventional limits and then practically eliminated. And when in the nineteenth century preaching regained some importance, the main reason was the government's request to the priests to preach against 'nihilism' and for the Tsar — with the condition that the prepared sermons must be submitted for censorship.

Furthermore, the rather summary method of confession in the Orthodox Church, which lacked any kind of examination of conscience, must be mentioned. On the one hand, ascetic Protestantism provided no relief by confession and no institutional dispensation of grace by a minister and for this reason it compelled believers to obtain the *certitudo salutis* by their own efforts, i.e. by the development of an ethically systematised conduct of life. On the other hand, Catholicism supported the relatively effective control of each action by a father confessor, although a regular remission of sins and dispensation of grace by a priest generally weakened the demands of morality upon the individual because it spared him or her the necessity of developing an individual pattern of life based on ethical foundations. It should then be clear that, according to Weber (ES:561), the poorly developed and rather general method of confession, which was particularly characteristic of the Russian Church, frequently taking the form of a collective admission of guilt, was certainly no way to effect any permanent influence over people's conduct. The particularly lax practice of Orthodox confessions, which reduced the influence of the priests, has been connected by Weber (1906a:279; cf. also Leroy-Beaulieu 1896 III:159) with the lack of celibacy among the white clergy.

Finally, the above mentioned tension between the concept of a transcendental God and a basically contemplative-mystical attitude

could also explain the specific political ethic of Orthodoxy. Weber
mentioned in this context the resolute rejection of any success-orient-
ed ethics, because only the unconditional ethical rule is accepted as a
possible guiding star of positive actions. As soon as duty is done, however, and because all non-ethical values have been eliminated, the
biblical sentence comes unconsciously into force which deeply
marked the soul of Tolstoy and the whole Russian people: Do not
resist evil! (Matthew 5, 39; cf. Weber 1906a:255). Here is the reason
for the abrupt changes between furious storms of activity and surren-
der to the situation which, according to legend, induced the early
saints of the Russian church, Boris and Gleb, to let themselves be
slaughtered without offering resistance. The spirit of the Orthodox
religion does not appear to have an elective affinity with any type of
political regime but to be indifferent towards all.

An economic ethic in the narrow sense of the term, which might
have settled the questions of the 'just price' (*iustum pretium*) and of the
justification of interest, was not developed because of Orthodox
indifference towards the world. Therefore few ethical barriers were
set up against widespread usury. Work itself appeared as a plain fact
which had to be accepted, and even the doctrine of the fruit of work
and honesty in business, combined with the rejection of fun and
play, was not lacking, as can be seen from the *Domostroi*, a manual of
the sixteenth century on how to lead a patriarchal household. For
the rest, the accounts of Western travellers (e.g. Olearius) have suffi-
ciently borne out the existence of a healthy acquisitive drive in Russia (if this widely used but inadequately precise concept must be
retained here).

But what is the use of such doctrines and stimuli if the economic
ethic in the wider sense of the word, which is not the result of theological teaching and doctrines but of psychological motivations produced
by rationally structured ideas about salvation, points in a different
direction? What is the use of singing praises to work if the highest psychological premia are not placed on vocational activity within the
world, but on the monastic life-style which is considered to be the perfection of human conduct; and if the religion of the masses is interwo-
ven with magical ideas so that no rational innerworldly ethic of conduct is developed and advice and help are sought from *startsy* who
themselves have turned away from the world; and if, finally, a very
general confession provides an inner release from all sins? In the highest ethical ideals of Orthodoxy, for which innerworldly political or

economic success was irrelevant in terms of salvation, there was no motivation for a rational and methodical reorganisation of the world or for capitalistic gain as the practical outcome and objective of the pursuit of a vocation. No inner motivation led out of the spiritual conditions of the Orthodox Church to a reorganisation of political and economic life. The dualism between mystical ideals and the world was such that, on the one hand, worldly actions were ethically downgraded and, on the other, the religious means of salvation appeared irrational from the point of view of the 'world'. The works of A. Ostrovsky, for example, make it clear how little respect was accorded to merchants, and to the entrepreneur Stolz in Goncharov's *Oblomov* the deeper sense of life remains hidden. The proof of one's own value (*religiöse Bewährung*) was produced against the 'world' and worldly activities, not in and by them. The ethical transfiguration of gainful activity, which as vocational ethics contributed to the formation of the spirit of modern capitalism, was lacking.

Incidentally, the unbrotherly reality of the economic world produced within the mystical context the postulate of love for one's fellow human being and of unselective generosity which did not enquire into the reason and outcome of self-surrender nor into the worth of the person soliciting help. It asked no questions and gave even the shirt when only the cloak had been asked for (ES:589). A famous example of this attitude was the philosopher V. Soloviev who, during a single walk in St. Petersburg, gave to beggars all his money and even his shoes and handkerchief (Soloviev 1947:150).

No Renaissance, no Humanism, no Protestantism with a Luther or Calvin (the Raskol, to be analysed in the following chapter, cannot be compared with it) have opposed the spirit of Orthodoxy. Eventually also the development of science out of its own roots did not take place, partly because the rational form of a systematic theology (e.g. the *summae* of Thomas Aquinas; rational theology became one of the foundations of the natural and human sciences of the Occident) did not emerge in the more mystically oriented Orthodox environment (Müller-Armack 1959:351).

All in all, the specific roots of Russian Orthodox culture must be sought in the peculiarly mechanical combination of office charisma and monasticism and, furthermore, in the integration of the official church in the caesaro-papist patrimonial state. These roots produced until the last third of the nineteenth century a largely unified culture (ES:1193) in the sense that there were no strong and independent institutional or spiritual powers: no bourgeoisie, no independent nobility or hierarchy, no science and no legal profession and, finally, no ethical prophecy (with the exception of the founders of sects still to be discussed), which could break open the strong cage of the patrimonial state.

CHAPTER THREE

RUSSIAN OLD BELIEVERS AND SECTS

The Origins of the Schism

In the sixties of the seventeenth century, when Patriarch Nikon, in line with the Byzantine Church and supported by Tsar Alexis, had introduced several liturgical reforms, a schism (*raskol*) split the Russian Church in two. The schism appeared to be about seemingly trivial questions as to whether to make the traditional two-fingered or the three-fingered sign of the cross, of how to spell the name of Jesus and how to perform a religious procession, for, in the opinion of many, a religious ceremony, incorrectly performed, had no effect and no value before God. In this insistence on ritual there was a fundamental difference between the Old Believers or Old Ritualists, called *Raskol'niki* (splitters) by the official church, and Protestantism, which had little interest in what it considered to be mere exterior forms.

About the same time, though, there was in Russia an eschatological mood whose significance for the *raskol* should not be underestimated. The Antichrist was expected anytime after 1660, and any other relatively accidental event which could be interpreted as an attack on Orthodoxy would probably have produced a reaction similar to that of the *raskol*. Therefore, it is also possible to say that the real core of the doctrine of the Old Believers was not the reaction against the liturgical reforms, but the expectation of the rule of the Antichrist.

Russian populist and Marxist authors have thought that the socio-political conditions were mainly responsible for the emergence of the *raskol*. They mentioned in this context that the economic situation of the peasants had worsened during the preceding century and that their right to depart from their landlord had been abolished in fact since the end of the sixteenth century and legally since 1649; furthermore, that the growing centralisation and bureaucratisation of the Russian patrimonial state and the growing foreign influence caused the resistance of large sections of the patriarchal society, threatened in their independence, towards the impersonal ways of thinking and forms of organisation of Western Europe. But, while it is true that all these circumstances had prepared the ground, the *raskol* would not have developed without the seed of Nikon's reforms and the expectation of the Antichrist.

Those who decided on a break with the official church, the Old Believers, then faced many further decisions concerning not only ritual but also conduct of life. When a church council in 1667 had excommunicated all those who continued to perform the old rituals, when their leader, the Archpriest Avvakum, had been burnt at the stake and when an *ukaz* of the Tsarevna Sophia in 1685 threatened all those, who continued to cling to the old belief, with death by fire, and those only suspected to be schismatics with torture, the reaction of many Old Believers was the total break with the former conditions of life and the flight to the uninhabited woods, either as hermits or in self-sufficient communities. Some, the so-called *stranniki*, cut all ties with family, state and society, others chose death by self-immolation when the troops of the Tsar, the instruments of Antichrist, approached (waves of mass suicide swept the country at times, particularly in the area of Olonets among the Filippovtsy, but also in Siberia and elsewhere). The *ukaz* of 1685 was not generally enforced, but the Old Believers were prohibited from testifying in courts against those belonging to the established church; for a long time they were also excluded from elective offices in the villages and towns and could not register their births and marriages, as this was the responsibility of the priests of the official church. Even though under Peter the Great the attitude of the government became more tolerant towards the Old Believers, because Peter distinguished between political and religious opposition, they nevertheless were obliged to pay double the regular capitation tax. All the same, the repressive attitude of the government produced the advantage that the communities of Old Believers were (until 1738) exempted from military recruitment and that their merchants were freed from liturgical services as collectors of state revenue, because the government regarded them as subjects of suspect loyalty. Further relief was granted under Catherine II, especially since those who had fled abroad or to inaccessible border regions were given the opportunity to return. But in the nineteenth century under Nicholas I the persecutions of the Old Believers increased again, and only in 1905 did they obtain full legal equality.

If one takes into account that in the long run the government policy towards the Old Believers, despite all its fluctuations, must be described not as extremely but persistently intolerant, and if one further takes into account the inhospitable geographical location where many of them had to live, it may be surprising to find that not only the number of Old Believers increased significantly during the eighteenth and nineteenth centuries (although precise estimates are very difficult to obtain because of the persecutions to which they were exposed),[1] but that on the whole they were also more prosperous than the members of the official church. In the nineteenth century, owners and managers of factories had a preference for hiring Old Believers as industrial labourers, primarily because of their honesty and their temperance (Gerschenkron 1970:44; Leroy-Beaulieu III:386), and disproportionately many rich entrepreneurs – e.g. the Grachev in Ivanovo and the Guchkov and Morosov in Moscow – especially entrepreneurs in the textile industry who either themselves or whose fathers had been serfs and had been able to buy their freedom, were Old Believers (Portal 1961:45). They enjoyed the reputation of being the most honest businessmen in Russia (Pipes 1974:238), even if the novels of Melnikov do not bear out this reputation (Pleyer 1961:113). Prosperous communities of Old Believers grew not only in the far-away Urals, along the Volga river or near the White Sea, but soon even in Moscow.

Old Believers and the Weber Thesis

Some authors (e.g. Gitermann 1965 I:315) have gone on to assume that the connection, which Max Weber tried to establish between ascetic Calvinism and the development of modern capitalism in Western Europe, might also be true in the case of the Old Believers. Billington (1966:193) finds the parallel between the Calvinists of Western Europe and the Russian Old Believers striking, because both movements were, according to him, not only puritanical, replacing a sacramental church with inner-worldly asceticism, but both saw hard work as the only means of demonstrating one's selection by God.

On the other hand, there are authors like Gerschenkron (1970:34, 45) who have arrived at the conclusion that the Old Believers consti-

---

[1] Some estimates are given in Note 17, p. 88.

tute a rather uniquely suitable case for testing Weber's hypothesis (or
what they take for Weber's hypothesis) and for proving it wrong. As
the Old Believers did not leave the established church for any doctrinal differences, their case appears to show, according to Gerschenkron, that the social condition of a penalised or persecuted
group affords sufficient impulse for such a group to engage in profitable economic activities and to produce the features of honesty, fru-
gality, industry and thrift, that were generally observed to characterise the Old Believers. In a similar vein, Crummey has pointed out
that because Old Belief did not differ from official Orthodoxy in doctrine (although it differed in details of ecclesiastical practice), the
'Weber thesis' (in the sense of a parallel between the Calvinists and
the Old Believers) does not apply, because otherwise Old Believers
and Orthodox should have conducted their affairs with roughly the
same degree of success (Crummey 1970:136). Instead, Crummey suggests that the economic success of the Old Believers should be related
to their pariah position which was similar to the pariah position of the
Jews, analysed by Weber.

With regard to the identity of doctrine in Old Belief and in official
Orthodoxy, assumed by Gerschenkron and Crummey, it should at
least be pointed out that there were differences in the teaching about
Antichrist and also, as will be seen later, in the teaching about the
sacraments. And with regard to Crummey's thesis about the influence
of the pariah position, it must be stressed that the pariah position of
the Jews was precisely one of the reasons which prevented the development of the modern capitalistic spirit among Jews because it
required them to hold out in the given situation. While it is true that
the Jews could treat those who did not belong to their people in an
objective and impersonal way, as Crummey points out, it must also
be pointed out that this was only permitted action, an ethical *adiaphoron*, not duty and vocation to dominate the world by impersonal
action. To the extent that the Jewish conduct of life was auto-methodical and systematic, it was not motivated by their pariah position
(ES:611-23), just as little as the economic ethics of the Old Believers
can be explained by their pariah position alone.

Moreover, the reference to doctrine by Gerschenkron and Crummey is also erroneous because Weber did not derive economic ethics
from theological dogmas, but rather, as mentioned earlier, on the one
hand, from psychological motivations which often grow out of the
concepts of God and salvation, and on the other hand, as the result of

church organisation and ecclesiastic institutions.[2] This will be exemplified later.

Finally, Weber was, of course, conscious of the fact that national or religious minorities are likely, through their voluntary or involuntary exclusion from positions of political influence, to be driven to a particularly large extent into economic activity and that their ablest members seek to satisfy the desire for recognition of their abilities, which cannot be satisfied in the service of the state, in the economic arena. The Huguenots in France under Louis XIV and the Jews for two thousand years are well-known examples (PE:39). Weber equally knew that the exile or a change of residence with a breakdown of traditional relationships can be among the most effective means of intensifying labour (PE:43). But, although the external conditions often had important consequences for the economic development of minorities, Weber did not leave it at that, because Catholic repressed minorities, as he noted, were never driven into particularly remarkable economic activity and never showed a particularly prominent economic development (PE:39). In this context it is possible to mention the Dutch and English Catholics who were persecuted or only tolerated in the past, or also the French-speaking Catholic Acadians of Canada who were resettled in peripheral areas whose political rights were curtailed by the English and who have never distinguished themselves in the economic field (Deveau 1987). Thus, the reasons for the different economic conduct of incompletely tolerated religious minorities should not be sought mono-causally in the external historico-political conditions of these minorities, but also in their religious organisation and in their ethos and intrinsic character. Let us look at the Old Believers from this point of view.

---

[2] 'Where, in spite of different doctrinal basis, similar ascetic features have appeared, this has generally been the result of Church organisation. Of this we shall come to speak in another connection' (PE:128). Weber refers here to his article on the Protestant sects in GAzRS I: 207-36. The quoted passage is, by the way, an insertion which cannot be found in the original Protestant Ethic essay of 1904-5. Similar references to the importance of church organisation in the context of Weber's thesis can also be found in PE II: 307-12.

The Economic Ethics of Old Believers

As the expected end of the world did not occur, it appeared more and more necessary to somehow manage in this world ruled by the Antichrist. The Old Believers were now faced with psychological as well as practical difficulties. On the psychological level they had to somehow come to terms with the cognitive dissonance which resulted from the fact that the end of the world did not occur, although, in the anticipation that it would come, far-reaching religious and material steps had been taken. Festinger et al. (1956) have shown that precisely in the case of a delay of the Second Coming (*parousia*) missionary activity often sets in and this can indeed be noticed with regard to the Old Believers. Cognitive dissonance can sometimes also be reduced if one considers oneself or one's own group as different from the mass of the population and if then, as a result of this view, an ethically higher conduct of life is developed. The Old Believers tried to do this too.

The practical difficulties resulted from the fact that no bishop had joined the Schism and that therefore no new priests could be ordained. The shortage of priests grew worse, to the extent that the priests who had been ordained before the reforms of Patriarch Nikon and had joined the Old Believers, died out. One part of the Old Believers, the so-called priestists (*popovtsy*), decided to accept priests ordained by the official church; the others, however, the so-called priestless (*bezpopovtsy*), arrived at the view that those sacraments which can only be performed by ordained priests – the Eucharist and the sacrament of marriage – were not accessible to them any more. While some of them now got married without priests, by simply vowing within the family circle to remain true one to the other, and while others insisted that they now had to remain celibate, the contradictory situation developed that the most faithful followers of the old ritual completely gave up the orthodox ritual. Here is an example of the fact that religious positions can also have other sources than the social conditions of the strata which support them, namely the inner consistency of logic, which unexpectedly and against the requirements of interests, tradition and feeling, leads to certain conclusions and consequences. The great problem of marriage among the *bezpopovtsy*, which arose as a result of the lack of priests, was solved by some of them (Alekseiev; Liubopytnyi) by saying that the ritual of marriage is only a formality and that marriage existed in the 'natural law' (*estestvennyi zakon*) long before the written law of the Church (Miliukov 1899

II:80-1). The idea of natural law, whose origin and possible connection with individualistic ideas in Russia needs further clarification,[3] thus served as a justification for some *bezpopovtsy* to enter into marriage-like unions – sometimes even without any ritual (as in the case of the *bezbrachniki*). For the rest, the Old Believers nevertheless made many, and for a long time unsuccessful, attempts to attract an orthodox bishop from across the borders and thus to establish a new church hierarchy.

To the extent that the influence of priests diminished, the Old Believerdom developed the character of a congregational religion,[4] i.e. a religion which was influenced to a large extent by the laity. This can be said not only about the *bezpopovtsy* but also about the *popovtsy* for they subjected the priests who deserted from the official church and came to them, often motivated by greed, to a humiliating procedure (the so-called *isprava*) and treated them more as employees, who can also be dismissed, than as their religious shepherds (Leroy-Beaulieu III:401; cf. S.A. Zenkovsky 1970:435). Authority and leadership lay in the hands of the laity and this led to the idea that any mediation between God and man (the ecclesiastical provision of grace) is necessary only to a very limited extent. There was therefore more self-responsibility and the conduct of life of the Old Believers became more auto-methodical and systematic.

The greater self-responsibility in the conduct of life did not, however, lead the Old Believers out of their traditionalism. The patriarchal life-style and the family discipline, as described in the Domostroi, were held by the Old Believers in particularly high regard. They also valued the book of Jesus, the son of Sirach (Ecclesiasticus – not regarded as apocryphal by the Russian Church), which conveyed to them the traditional idea that one should remain in one's calling, and consequently a certain indifference to advancement on the social lad-

---

[3] The idea of natural law began to develop markedly in Russia during the second half of the eighteenth century (V.V. Zenkovsky 1953 I:39) and has played an important role in the Russian Revolution of 1905-6 because of irresolvable inner contradictions (formal versus material natural law – ES:872).

[4] Weber talks of congregational religion when the laity has been organised permanently for common activity in such a manner that they can actively participate and make their influence felt – as opposed to a parish which is a mere administrative unit and merely delimits the jurisdiction of priests (WG:277; ES:455). Rational ethical congregational religions have combined frequently in the past and in a striking manner, according to Weber, with capital continuously and rationally employed in a productive enterprise for the acquisition of profit (ES:479).

der (Gerschenkron 1970:37). In Ecclesiasticus 12, 1-4, they read, too, that one should help the righteous but not the sinner, and in this sentence may well be seen the theoretical foundation for the solidarity and the mutual confidence and readiness to help which have so often been attributed to the Old Believers (but not, as must be mentioned again, in Melnikov's novels). In contrast to ascetic Protestantism, the Old Believers also kept the magical and ritual aspects of their religion (the traditional worship of icons and relics) and thus the world remained for them a magic garden.

Furthermore, Old Believerdom was different from Protestantism because, to some extent, it upheld the division of ethics into monastic ethics and lay ethics. While the ecclesiastical provision of grace lost some of its importance, the monastic ethics practised in the *skity* of the Old Believers continued to have exemplary significance. It is true that there were usually more nuns than monks in the *skity*, but many women, who as girls had lived and been educated in the *skity*, brought the more rigorous religious and ethical ideas of those who had renounced the world, back into the family.

During the first hundred years after the Schism a monastery in the valley of the Vyg River near the White Sea played an important and influential role among Old Believers. Not far from the Solovetskii Monastery, which after its revolt against the liturgical reforms had been destroyed by government troops, a group of *bezpopovtsy* had founded the Vygovskaia Pustyn' (Vyg Monastery), whose members, men as well as women (the women lived in a convent twelve miles away), were bound by monastic vows of chastity, poverty and obedience to the chosen elders. The severe northern climate often destroyed an entire crop of grain and therefore the Vyg community was able to survive the first years only because of the solidarity shown to them by the Old Believers of the Volga region. Thereafter they diversified their economic production under the leadership of A. Denisov (1674-1730): traditional agriculture was supplemented by fishing and even speculative trading ventures. Now it is certainly true that ascetic celibates can easily underbid the indispensable minimum wage or revenue required by married workers or entrepreneurs, but to this external reason for the relative success of Vyg and of other communities of celibate Old Believers must be added internal reasons.

In the first part of the eighteenth century Vyg was the religious and cultural centre not only of the *bezpopovtsy* but of all Old Believers, particularly since it succeeded in being considered as the successor of the

Solovetskii Monastery which was still renowned among them. The inhabitants of Vyg followed strict norms of congregational discipline. It was recognised that all members of the community, the general assembly, would decide on questions of dogma, ritual and political principle (Crummey 1970:110). Newcomers were tested during a period of fasting and then rebaptised and severe cases of disobedience were punished by banishment from the community. Every day there was a three-hour morning service, although it was canonically impossible for the Old Believers to celebrate the Eucharist and other sacraments in the usual manner. But in the *Pomorskie Otvety*, an apologia of Old Belief written by the leader (*nastoiatel'*) of Vyg, A. Denisov, the thesis of the division of the sacraments into two categories had been put forward: on the one hand, the sacraments which are absolutely indispensable (*muzhno potrebnye*) for the attainment of salvation, namely baptism and penance, which can be performed by laymen; on the other hand, such sacraments which, although required (*potrebnye*) in principle and to be performed only by priests can be dispensed with in case of necessity (Chrysostomus 1957: 119-20). This theory provided the theoretical and dogmatic foundation of the congregational lay religion[5] of the priestless Old Believers. Confessions, made to experienced older monks,[6] were longer and more specific (as was the practice of all Old Believers) than in the official church (Leroy-Beaulieu III:158), and thus had a greater influence on the conduct of life.

For the rest, the rule of the Vygovskaia Pustyn', for the most part written by A. Denisov, put an emphasis on the benefits of hard work and on the importance of guarding the community's material resources (Crummey 1970:123). Although there is a resemblance here with the rule of Joseph of Volokolamsk which also required manual work or work in the administration of the Monastery's enterprises[7]

---

[5] The use of the term laymen or lay is often confusing in texts on Orthodox religion, because lay people may be either opposed to priests or they may be opposed to monks who have no priestly function. This second use of the term can be found in Crummey (1970:151-2).

[6] Traditionally in the Orthodox Church the confession was addressed to monks. This changed from the time of the Council of Lyons (1274) when the Eastern Church accepted the doctrine of the seven sacraments and the hearing of confession became the duty of priests.

[7] It is true that already the Benedictine rule insisted on manual work in a more detailed way (the precise times for work are indicated, the reading of books is advised at other times) than the rather general passages in Joseph's rule. Only in the Occident did the Christian asceticism become an asceticism of work, as Weber says.

(with the biblical reason that if any would not work, neither should they eat, cf. Zimin 1959:311), it certainly makes a difference whether the individual is subjected to the external control of an abbot or whether the congregational discipline of formal equals is motivating one's actions.

All economic activities were undertaken by the community as a whole, in contrast to other branches of Old Believers, which were often combinations of small monasteries and peasant villages or, in the case of Moscow, congregations of merchants and artisans who never gave up control of at least part of their wealth and of their business ventures.

In the Vygovskaia Pustyn' apologetic (the Pomorskie Otvety) and devotional literature was written for the growing population of Old Believers, and schools were organised in which children from the surrounding area were taught reading and writing, because it was realised that it was indispensable to read the Scriptures if one wanted to defend oneself against the attacks of the official church. Thus a great percentage of Old Believers (more than in the official church) received a basic education.

The initial survival and development of Vyg no doubt resulted from the fact that A. Denisov achieved a *modus vivendi* with Peter the Great by accepting that the inhabitants of Vyg would prospect for and send iron ore, which was much in demand during the Great Nordic War, to the metallurgical factories in Olonets. Sectarian groups rarely ever enter into an alliance with a political power because of their anti-political or at least apolitical tendencies and also the *modus vivendi* with Peter the Great, whom many Old Believers considered to be the Antichrist, did not imply a recognition of the legitimacy of his power, for the Vyg monks continued to avoid praying for him. And when they finally, in 1739 under massive governmental threats, declared themselves willing to pray for the Tsar, their more radical members left them in protest.

The more or less passive resistance of the Vyg inhabitants towards the state can be characterised, on the whole, as pariah-ethical, as a pacifism in the sense of the Sermon on the Mount ('Do not resist evil'), combined with inconspicuous but stubborn opposition. This attitude must be seen in contrast to the eruptions of violence during the peasant uprisings when the return of the 'true Tsar' and of better times was expected, even though Old Believers may also have participated in the peasant uprisings of the seventeenth and eighteenth centuries. But, in contrast to the English Puritans, the Old Believers did not bequeath a political ideal to the Russian people. Their attitude towards the world was not world-domination, nor was it world-indifference, as in the case of the members of the official Russian church, but rather an attitude of world-endurance combined with passive resistance.

The situation of the Old Believers was significantly relieved under Catherine II who repealed several discriminating laws (by the end of her reign, the Old Believers were free from all special taxes, could give evidence at trials and hold certain elective offices) and provided the opportunity for return from the border regions. The Old Believers received areas in the north of Saratov and along the Irgiz River and they soon took charge of almost all the economic activities in the areas of the middle and lower Volga: wholesale trade, fisheries and various industries. At about the same time the state-owned iron foundries in the Urals were under the direction of the Demidov brothers who were Old Believers, hired almost only Old Believers as workers and were responsible for the administration of their region.

From 1767 on Catherine II also passed laws allowing the establishment of textile manufactures without registration, and this was to the advantage of a disproportionately large number of entrepreneurs who belonged to the Old Believers. Moscow now became the centre of the Old Believers who flocked back from the border regions. During this time of official toleration, Thedosian merchants (the Theodosians were a particularly ascetic branch of the priestless Old Believers) founded, at the height of a plague epidemic in 1771, the so-called *Preobrazhenskoe Kladbishche*, a cemetery combined with a hospital and a home for the aged (almost at the same time the priestists founded a very similar institution, the *Rogozhskoe Kladbishche*). Soon some chapels, shops and more residential buildings were added and, since the beginning of the nineteenth century, the activities of the institution, which continued to be called *kladbishche* (cemetery), were extended to the commercial field.

Since the Councils of Novgorod 1692-94 the priestless Theodosians had established the principle of equality of all members, but they were not allowed to associate with the members of other religious groups. They were also against the consumption of alcohol and the shaving of beards, and hostile to private property, sex and marriage. Their congregational discipline was severe, for any violation of these rules was punished by temporary expulsion; in the case of the

violation of the rule of chastity, if repeated three times, even by complete expulsion (S. A. Zenkovsky 1970:441). For the rest, they taught
that idleness breeds evil (*prazdnost' uchilishche zlykh* – Zenkovsky
1970:448).

In view of their discipline and of their belief to be special or chosen,
the Theodosians have sometimes been compared to the Puritan *electi*,
but the doctrine of predestination was not part of their belief system,[8]
their teaching with regard to ownership and property was very different and, in contrast to Calvin who considered the state to be necessary, the Theodosians kept away from everything connected with the
state as belonging to Antichrist. While Max Weber was able to say of
the Puritans that they left the monastic cell and tried to dominate the
world, it was the tendency of the Theodosians to strengthen the personality ideal of the world-renouncing monk who lives in chastity and
poverty. If nevertheless the life-style of the Theodosians led to an
accumulation of wealth of the community (and later also of the individual Theodosian), this is a phenomenon which the history of
monastic orders has revealed again and again.

In the forties of the nineteenth century there lived within the walls
of the *Preobrazhenskoe Kladbishche* a central community of monks and
nuns (approximately 500 men and 1100 women; cf. Ryndziunskii
1950:210), and outside lived the lay followers who were religiously,
and often also financially, committed to the *kladbishche*. The *kladbishche*
soon obtained a monopolistic position in the manufacture of icons of
the old style and of candles and sacred books. Moreover, large
reserves of capital were obtained through gifts and inheritances, for to
join the community and to enjoy the use of its shelter entailed the
signing over of one's entire estate to the community, although members were allowed to continue to manage their business affairs during
their own life-time, often borrowing funds from the commune's trea-
sury.

As Russia had virtually no commercial credit or banking system
until the sixties of the nineteenth century, the community banks,
which were established by the Old Believers because of their obligation to solidary help, were of particular importance. Serfs were able to
obtain credit here to cover their redemption, on the condition of con-
verting to the Theodosian creed and discipline and of taking up

---

[8] Another priestless group, however, the Netovtsy, came close to the doctrine of
predestination, according to Zenkovsky (1970:475).

employment in a factory of the *kladbishche* to work off their debt. The economic and financial activities of the *kladbishche* were controlled by a council of 26 members, mostly leading merchants (Ryndziunskii 1950:202-3), who were also able to receive credit from the community and to invest it in their enterprises. In fact, one of the most important economic functions of the *kladbishche* was to offer investment capital.

In the nineteenth century, there were Old Believers among the richest merchants of Moscow. They used their money to defend themselves in case of persecutions, for mutual solidary help and to come to an arrangement with the corrupt administration. The private life-style of the old-believing entrepreneurs and merchants, however, at least in the initial stages, was kept at a very modest level (Kulischer 1931:348-9). Even rich entrepreneurs who owned millions lived in seclusion with their families in a little gloomy hut, did not smoke or drink and grew long beards. This ascetic life-style naturally added to the increase of property. Those who belonged to the Theodosians refused to eat or drink together with members of the official church (according to the rules of the 'Council of Vetka', 1751) and even with other Old Believers (Leroy-Beaulieu III:431; Kovalevsky 1957:51). This ritualism, with a certain resemblance to Indian caste rules, certainly obstructed a rational conduct of life.

In the course of the nineteenth century the Theodosians became more reluctant to sign over their private estates to the *kladbishche* and many of them wished to enter a formal conjugal union. Some withdrew to join other groups of Old Believers, such as the Pomortsy who had begun to recognise marriage. When in 1847 new persecutions set in and the *kladbishche* came under state administration, the reaction of many was compromise or indifference and some of them just joined the Edinoverie movement, a kind of officially recognised and institutionalised form of Old Believerdom. If the Edinoverie movement, in which the Old Believer priests were ordained by the official church, was nevertheless of limited success, one explanation may be that the liturgical reforms were not any more the only reason for the continuing existence of the *raskol*, for the Old Believers had now become accustomed to refuse any interference of the state in religious matters.

Max Weber's opinion about the Old Believers was quite rightly full of nuances: they were, at the beginning of the twentieth century, a culturally and economically very differentiated group, Weber said, in whose lower strata one could still find the old belief that Antichrist

rules the world, and consequently a completely apolitical attitude; but
there were also vigorously individualistic elements, and finally, in line
with the capitalistic abilities which the Old Believers share with most
sects, a continuously increasing opportunistic upper stratum (Weber
1906b:192). Weber also notes that the affinity of the economic and
political ethics of the Russian rationalistic sects[9] (although not of all
Russian sects) with the Protestant ethic did not escape Leroy-
Beaulieu's notice (Weber 1978:153-4 and 321; cf. Leroy-Beaulieu
III:389), but that this affinity was obstructed in the most numerous
sects, the *raskol* proper, by the pecularity of their 'innerworldly asceticism' (Weber 1906a:280, fn 42).

Indeed, the inner-worldly asceticism which can be noticed in the
life-style of most Old Believers, was 'broken' (*gebrochen*) by traditionalism and ritualism, taboos and magical influences in the search for salvation. And what is said in the Domostroi, much esteemed by the Old
Believers, about thriftiness in a patriarchal household, or in the rules
of the Vyg Monastery about the necessity of hard work, amounts to
worldly wisdom or literary theory, not to be compared with the religious motives of the ascetic Protestants which led them to seek the
proof of their own value (*Heilsbewährung*) in their inner-worldly calling
and to dominate the world by rational inner-worldly action. The
Protestant ethic and the capitalist spirit, that individualistic attitude
which objectifies the relations between people, could not be detected
in the life-style of the Old Believers, and while some aspects of their
teachings must even be interpreted as implying a preference for
poverty (Beliaev: passim) and as resisting technical innovations as
works of the devil (Kulischer 1931:349), so that the Old Believers contributed only to a small extent to the later industrialisation of Russia
at the end of nineteenth century. But it must also be taken into
account that the ascetic renunciation of consumption and the vow of
poverty paradoxically have often produced economic rationalism and
have contributed to the prosperity of many Occidental monasteries,
and that a similar ethical attitude could also further the economic
well-being of the Old Believers. In spite of its 'anti-mammonistic' doctrines, the 'spirit'[10] of Old Believerdom has produced economic ratio-

---

[9] Weber did not make a clear distinction, as is customary today, between Russian
Old Believers and Russian sects.

[10] The difference between the doctrines and the 'spirit' of a religion is stressed in
PE: 259. This Weberian distinction is also underlined in the Russian language by
Neusykhin (1974:432).

nalism, even if it was partially 'broken' by traditionalism and ritualism. One simply has to distinguish clearly between the ideals and the
doctrines of a religion and its practical influence on the followers.

Even if the unifying bond of the Protestant self-fulfillment
(*Bewährung*) in an inner-worldly calling was missing, several separate
motivations, for instance, the increase of personal responsibility and
of a systematic life-style, produced by the development of congregational religion, furthermore the solidary mutual help, the community
banks and concepts of ownership which partially were a result of the
form of religious organisation, have contributed to the economic success of the Old Believers. It goes without saying that the persecutions
by the government and the official church and the exclusion from
public life were likely to further individualism and commercial abilities, in the same way as happened to other minorities (Jews, Parsis,
Armenians, Copts).

The Khlysty

The Old Believers can be distinguished from the Russian sects, to be
discussed now, by the fact that they clung to the old rituals of the
Orthodox Church, while the sects produced completely new belief
systems and rejected all rituals as means of salvation. The Khlysty are
usually considered to be the root of all Russian sectarianism, in particular of the Skoptsy, the Dukhobors and the Molokans. The name
Khlysty seems to be derived from the name of Christ (although it has
been perverted by a pun to Khlysty or flagellants), for the Khlysty
believed in the repeated reincarnation of Christ in living human
beings and even in the possibility of the existence of several Christs at
the same time. They called their belief system Christovoverie or
Christovshchina and are known to have existed at least since the middle of the seventeenth century. They have been mainly attractive to
peasants and monks (Klibanov 1982:58). They rejected the sacred
books of the Orthodox and of the Old Believers, and had received
from their founder, a certain Danila Filippov, twelve commandments,
among which were the prohibition of stealing, the drinking of alcoholic beverages and sexual relations even within marriage, and the
commandment to keep these rules a secret (Grass 1966 vol. I:15).

The incarnation of God in Jesus of Nazareth was, according to the
Khlysty, a filling of Jesus with the Spirit of God, and was only one of a

series of such fillings which we witness in many human beings at all
times (Conybeare 1921:342), for according to them the possession of
the Holy Spirit in combination with suffering and asceticism turns
men into Christs. All Khlysty believed themselves to be filled to some
degree by the Holy Spirit, and they therefore used to bow to each
other as more or less perfect Christs. All congregations, or 'ships' as
they called them, had their own Christ or prophet who was appointed
by Danila Filippov or his successors.

Salvation for the Khlysty consisted in the liberation of the soul
from the body; the perfection of the human being in the fact that the
soul, liberated from the flesh, comes to God. Therefore they thought
nothing of the resurrection of the flesh. Their dualistic idea of a good
soul and a sinful body and world also made the idea of the closeness
of the end of the world, to which the Old Believers clung, impossible
(Fedorenko 1965:49). Thus the goal and content of salvation for the
Khlysty was the receiving or the ecstatic contemplation of the Spirit
of God, the so-called *radenie*; the method of salvation (in the sense of
systematised means of salvation) consisted in calling down the Spirit
of God during a religious-ecstatic dance after ascetic preparations.
These ecstatic dances, performed in secret with the simultaneous
singing of spiritual songs (in contrast to the Orthodox Church where
congregational singing does not exist) and with rhythmic movements,
led at their height to ecstatic visions, often of Christ, and in some cases to glossolalia.

As the ecstatic effects of the *radenie* were for the Khlysty the only
source of revelation, it was only natural that they had a mixed attitude towards the Bible and towards tradition. It appears, however,
that they read the Bible and that they did not reject all education, but
the knowledge of reading (in which they surpassed the Orthodox people) and of the Bible (which they interpreted allegorically) mainly
served to convert the members of the Orthodox Church to the Christovoverie.

The *radenie*, the temporary ecstatic possession of the Holy Spirit,
required as a preparation a weakening of the flesh, the vessel of the
Holy Spirit, by ascetic means. Therefore the Khlysty practised flagel-
lation, and hence their whole life-style consisted in the systematic-
rational suppression of all physical urges and desires. Sexual relations
with a woman, even one's own wife, was a great sin. Married Khlysty
did not have to separate from their wives and unmarried Khlysty
were often allowed, perhaps for economic reasons, to take a 'spiritual

sister', because the help of a wife was indispensable for a peasant, but all these relations were supposed to be purely spiritual and to prove the domination of the Spirit over the flesh.[11] Furthermore, the Khlysty suppressed their physical desires by fasting. The Christs prepared themselves for the receiving of the Holy Spirit by fasts, lasting several weeks, and even the ordinary Khlysty did not eat for several days of the week, and particularly on the days before their congregational meetings, leading to the *radeniya* (Grass I:311).

K.K. Grass has noted that the Christovoverie must be considered as an attempt to turn monastic asceticism into the required life-style of everyone, as an attempt to abolish the difference which the Church has established between monks and lay people (Grass I:320). If Grass is right, there seems to be a parallel with Western Protestantism which also abolished the distinction between the religion of the *virtuosi* and the religion of the masses. But, while Protestant asceticism is inner-worldly and resulted in world-domination, the world-fleeing asceticism of the Khlysty was only directed towards the domination of the creaturely aspects of the human being and therefore was world-indifferent.

On the whole, the Christovoverie may be characterised as a combination of a methodical world-fleeing asceticism with the ecstatic *radenie* which, as ecstasy generally, is only temporary, does not result in a permanent conduct of life and therefore leaves few marks on daily life and on economic ethics. Here, then, a certain tension or paradox revealed itself which led, as will be seen, to more consistent forms of life-style.

As a further means of salvation the *disciplina arcani* (*Arkandisziplin*) must be mentioned. In the same way as the liturgy of the Eucharist in the Orthodox Church originally offered the creed as a secret formula, the Khlysty asked their followers to keep their beliefs a secret. The *disciplina arcani* was not, or at least not mainly, a result of the persecutions under which the Khlysty suffered, but followed from the conviction that one loses the Spirit if one talks about Him to those who are not initiated. The *disciplina arcani* was expressed in the tenth commandment of the Khlysty: Keep these rules in secret, reveal them not

---

[11] One is reminded of the encratitistic tendencies of the early phases of Christianity, the cult of male and female virginity. These tendencies survived in different ways also in the Occident, e.g. in the chivalry of the Middle Ages with its idealised mistresses and in Dante's dream of Beatrice.

even to father and mother, and even if men scourge thee with whip or burn thee with fire, bear it (Grass I:15). Publicly the Khlysty belonged to the Orthodox Church, went to the Orthodox church service and were baptised there, but they disdained this baptism as a baptism by water, a religious *adiaphoron*, not to be compared with the baptism by the Holy Spirit during the *radenie*.

Although the congregational organisation fluctuated – besides the Christs and prophets there were also leaders (*nastavnik*) and elders (*starshina*) – the congregational discipline was relatively strong. During initiation the neophytes promised to keep everything that they heard or saw a secret and to obey the commandments; in case of disobedience expulsion was likely (Grass I:318). Moreover, the Christs and prophets promoted the congregational discipline by the fact that in their ecstatic condition during the *radenie* they beat and mistreated the sinners until they asked the congregation for forgiveness (Grass I:289). The commandments of the Khlysty – to those already mentioned can be added the ban on going to any festivities or drinking sessions – in connection with their congregational discipline, can help to explain the often mentioned honesty, industriousness and solidarity of the Khlysty which contributed to their relatively well-ordered economic situation (Klibanov 1982:52; Grass I:505). To lend money at interest, and indeed commerce in general, are said to have been considered reprehensible by them, and they refused to sell their agricultural products above market value (Grass I:504). It has been said of the Khlysty (in the same way as of the Old Believers) that they represented the ethical ideals of the Russian people more consistently than others (Grass I : 507; Leroy-Beaulieu III:387).

There are various hypotheses about the origin of the Khlystic sect (Western sectarians, e.g. Jacob Boehme; Finnish popular religion; Bogomils; Domostroi and *Bezpopovtsy*). In the present context, the hypothesis of Leroy-Beaulieu (III:456) and of Grass (I:648) that the old Christian gnosis, transmitted in the Euchitic monasticism, has contributed to the development of the Christovoverie is of particular interest. For the gnostic interpretation of cosmic dualism with its irrational consequences of world-fleeing asceticism and ecstatic dances as means of salvation and the temporary *radenie* as goal of salvation did not give rise to a rational conduct of life in the world. It cannot be denied, however, that the thrifty life-style and the congregational discipline have produced relatively well-ordered economic conditions.

A special branch of the Khlysty since the beginning of the nineteenth century were the Postniki who emphasised certain ascetic practices (fasting) and reduced the ecstatic dances. They had a particularly rigid congregational discipline: every lapse (e.g. the consumption of wine or tobacco) was punished by a long fasting period and those who broke the vow of celibacy were expelled for two years. The reduction of irrational ecstasy, the permanent habit of asceticism, enforced by the rigid congregational discipline, where it can lead to financial savings, and the system of mutual help, make it plausible that the Postniki in the Government of Tambov, in comparison with the poor Orthodox masses, distinguished themselves by a high level of material well-being (Klibanov 1982:97).

While the Postniki sometimes still used the means of salvation of the Orthodox Church (icons, ritual), the movement 'New Israel', one of their branches, rejected them. Before the First World War parts of them emigrated to Uruguay where they hoped to build the utopia of Belovodie, an island of plenty.

The Skoptsy

It may have happened occasionally as an unwanted outcome that some Khlysty had sexual relations after the ecstatic dances which led to the *radenie* or also with their 'spiritual sister'. (Especially outsiders accused the Khlysty of such moral laxity.) The foundation of the Skoptsy sect reflected the desire to eliminate such possibilities (GAzRS I:557 fn; ES:602). Skopets is the Russian word for eunuch.

The Khlyst Kondrati Selivanov (who died in 1832) emasculated himself with a hot iron (destroyed his testicals) and later, as this kind of castration does not eliminate the possibility of sexual relations, completely cut off his sexual organ. A very determined man who was not intimidated by the knout and a long deportation to Siberia, Selivanov was intent on persuading as many people as possible to accept castration and to spread his new sect, for in Selivanov's mind, and then for the Skoptsy, castration was the only means of salvation. They based this doctrine on Matthew 19.12, equating the Jewish circumcision with castration (aided by the similarity of the Russian words *iskuplenie* and *oskoplenie*) and claimed that all prophets, and even Jesus and his Apostles, were castrated. In contrast to the doctrine of the Khlysty, according to which there have been many Christs at all times, the Skoptsy thought that there have existed only two: Jesus and Selivanov. Selivanov was also worshipped as the Tsar Peter III, and after his death the Skoptsy developed the messianic idea of Selivanov's return and of his inauguration of the Millennium as soon as 144,000 persons had been castrated (Revelation 7.4 as interpreted by the Skoptsy).

While the Khlysty interpreted their ascetic life-style as a preparation for the ecstatic *radenie* which alone facilitated the *certitudo salutis*, the Skoptsy maintained that only castration is the basis of the *certitudo salutis*. Everything else is secondary. In contrast to the Khlysty they were an essentially ascetic sect, while the ecstatic dances which they also practised initially, had no connection with their central means of salvation, castration and other ascetic practices (no consumption of meat and alcoholic beverages, no gaiety, no aimless strolls). Marriage was not allowed, already married Skoptsy were sometimes allowed (because of the danger of being recognised by the authorities as a Skopets) to remain officially married, naturally on condition that they lived 'in chastity'. Sexual continence was the subject of admonitions at most meetings and, while the Skoptsy were also asked not to be attached to vain riches, the absence of lust and sexual desire which can be attained by complete castration was always considered as the main means of salvation.

The Skoptsy followed the *disciplina arcani* in the belief, like the Khlysty, that religious achievements lose their value if they are made known to other people. Therefore, it was not only permitted to them but they were required to tell untruths to outsiders about the castration and about the veneration of Selivanov.[12] The literature about the Skoptsy raises the possibility that not even all members of the sect knew about the castrations, because, on the one hand, the initiation ritual (*privod*) was not identical with the castration, and, on the other hand, it was said, that only the person who castrates and the person who is being castrated, should ever know about it (Grass II:775). In any case, in the Skoptsy sect there was, besides those initiated by the ceremony of *privod*, the esoteric group of the castrated (ES:540), and among them the differentiation into those who were only emasculated and those who were completely mutilated. The castrations, which

---

[12] Western writers often tend to criticise a certain lack of truthfulness or even the 'hypocrisy' of certain Russian schismatics and sectarians in religious matters and even generally. These criticisms may be contrasted with the often praised honesty and trustworthiness of old-believing and sectarian merchants and may be a cause for the realisation that, even though the *disciplina arcani* prevents truthfulness in the religious field, this does not prevent a high level of openness and truthfulness in other areas.

were the centre of the religion, did not take place during the religious meetings but were very private events, quite in line with the separation from society and the total individualisation of the castrated Skopets (Grass II:785).

The slow drying up of the ecstatic means of salvation (because of the discrepancy of castration as the sole means of salvation and the traditional ecstatic dances) and the icy individualism, which followed from the separation of the castrated from all societal life, produced an impersonal and more rational conduct of life, similar to ascetic Protestantism, not only in the religious but also in the political and economic field. The Skoptsy did not worship icons and they had only contempt for the sacraments of the Church – which did not prevent them from participating in them if political reasoning or the *disciplina arcani* demanded it.

Because of the government persecutions the meeting places of the Skoptsy were located in hidden places. Here, in the presence of teachers and prophets, ecstatic dances took place during which the prophets, like the Christs of the Khlysty, accused single members of their sins and thus enforced the congregational discipline. In the case of simple transgressions (e.g. the consumption of meat) temporary exclusion was imposed; members who had been accepted formally by the *privod* ceremony but were not castrated yet, could be confronted with the choice of emasculation or expulsion; already emasculated Skoptsy could repair a severe offence only by complete mutilation (Grass II:875).

In view of the often noted great economic and financial successes which the Skoptsy achieved in spite of their very small number[13], and in spite of the persecutions, it may be asked whether the character of their religion had a motivating influence on their economic behaviour. Much more than the Khlysty, the Skoptsy lived in towns and cities, where they were active as goldsmiths as well as in commerce, industry and banking. It is often assumed that they chose occupations in towns because their physical condition made them incapable of heavy agricultural work, but it is also known that in the Siberian exile they were excellent farmers and craftsmen who distinguished themselves from their generally poor neighbours.

---

[13] The estimates of the total number of castrated and non-castrated Skoptsy in the middle of the nineteenth century vary between 10,000 and 100,000; the number of castrated male Skoptsy at the same time may have been between 2,000 and 10,000 (Grass II:891; Leroy-Beaulieu III:494).

Normally 'ships' (the term for local congregations) of merchants and industrialists were founded in places like St. Petersburg, Kostroma, Saratov and Tula, and castrated peasants came from villages to these centres in order to work for the Skopets entrepreneur, among them also women who preferred to work in common workshops organised on the basis of the popular *artel*'[14] (on the bodies of the women some-times the removal of the clitoris and cuts over the nipples were noticed). Nikol'skii has tried to explain the wealth of the Skoptsy entre-preneurs by the exploitation of this 'obedient herd' of workers (Nikol'skii 1983:355), but much more central for the understanding of their economic behaviour seems to be what Nikol'skii has said about their social position in society: the persons who had entered the sect and had been castrated, had become completely isolated from the rest of the world; they separated from their family or from the possibility of having a traditional family life; if they also separated from their peas-ant milieu and came to a city, they now met people who just like them-selves, had turned their backs on their former world. In this peculiar milieu all former ideas and aspirations changed and a new societal form with a new ideology developed (Nikol'skii 1983:354). The address 'dear orphan' (Grass II:833), which the prophets used when they talked to an individual Skopets, indicates the separation of the individual from traditional society from the point of view of the Skopt-sy, a separation from social ties which led to an individualism without illusions, excluded all traditionalism and opened the door to purely rational and impersonal action. It is, therefore, not surprising that, on the one hand, the sobriety and industriousness of the Skoptsy was often praised, but that, on the other hand, their conduct was often interpreted as crafty, mischievous and even cruel as soon as it did not conform to traditional expectations (Grass II:887).

As they emphasised asceticism in contrast to the mysticism of the Orthodox Church, and as they reduced the pneumatic christology of the Khlysty, which in principle conceded to all the dignity of Christ, the Skoptsy were less inclined to consider themselves as vessels of the divine Spirit but rather as tools in the plan of the world in which Christ and Selivanov had a central position. Their attitude was world-rejecting but nevertheless turned towards the world – and this not only in economic but also in political respects, for they considered it to be their task to

---

[14] In the Russian tradition, *artels* were associations of workers who joined together on the basis of equal rights and joint liability.

increase and complete the number of Skoptsy so that the Millennium of the Skoptsy be created. But as the Millennium appeared to be still far away, the question arose whether it might not be possible to reform the present Russian empire according to such principles that Skoptsy would effectively rule it. In 1804 a project was submitted to the Tsar Alexander I which proposed the restructuring of the Russian state according to Skoptsy instructions in the sense that Skoptsy should be the secret advisors or directors of all branches of the administration (Nikol'skii 1983:363) – a project similar to that which the English Puritans of the seventeenth century had realised in their own way.

Although this political project of the Skoptsy remained without success, economic and financial success did not fail to materialise, because without passion and youth, as Leroy-Beaulieu writes, the Skopets dedicated his whole life to the acquisition of wealth with the consistency and obsession which are normally the sign of maturity and old age (Leroy-Beaulieu III:491). This striving for wealth was certainly, on the one hand, motivated by the circumstances, for the financial possibility to bribe the officials in order to deflect the sometimes intensive persecutions was essential, and generous donations to the Orthodox Church and the monasteries appeared useful to the Skoptsy for propagandistic and political reasons, although they had only contempt for them in their heart; it was also advantageous for the commercial activities that the Skoptsy had given up all resistance to reading and education and that, without wife and family, they often led a more economical life (their property was willed to young adopted Skoptsy).

But, on the other hand, there were important inner motives too: first of all that cold individualism which leads to objectivity and to an unbrotherly calculating attitude in human relations; then the rejection of all sacramental means of salvation and the ascetic life-style connected with it; the ban on all joyful worldly activities and the necessity of economising and saving which followed out of it – and all these factors reinforced and controlled by the strict congregational discipline and duty to contribute to the coming of the Millennium of the Skoptsy.[15] Quite rightly, therefore, Max Weber says that the

---

[15] Whether the castration itself can lead to an activation of inner-worldly action or of the passion for gain or power, is a question which can only be speculated about in the present state of knowledge. Some information could perhaps be collected by a comparison with the castrates of other cultural areas (Chinese, Byzantine and Turkish eunuchs).

rational-ascetic Russian sects (not all sects) had economic features similar to those of ascetic Protestantism, and that the Skoptsy produced the most extreme combination of business qualification with ethical world-rejection (Weber 1978b:154, 321).

The Dukhobors

In Southern Russia in the eighteenth century, serfdom was much less developed than in the central regions. Most peasants still lived in their own farms (*odnodvortsy*) but they saw that the government policy threatened their independence. Here in the Ukraine, in the government (province) of Tambov, appeared in the second half of the eighteenth century the so-called 'Spiritual Christianity', mainly composed of the sects of the Dukhobors and the Molokans. Their followers rejected the traditional forms of Orthodox ritual as well as fasting, bowing to icons and priesthood. We are all priests, they said, and: the church is not in the boards but in the ribs. For this reason, they had no special buildings for religious services and they accepted the sacraments at best only in an allegorical sense.

The so-called 'Sons of God' who appeared initially among the Dukhobors, surrounded by twelve 'Archangels', seem to indicate Khlysty influence. A similar influence may be seen in the fact that the Bible was of little importance to the Dukhobors ('Wrestlers by the Spirit') and was not binding; decisive was the inner revelation by the Spirit and the gnostic opposition, also made by the Khlysty, between spirit and matter, but without the *radenie*. The mystic and philosopher Skovoroda, although he probably was not a member of the sect, had developed views almost identical with those of the Dukhobors: Our earthly existence is but a pilgrimage, he said, only the inner spirit really exists, everything else is but a passing shadow, an ever changing torrent of water and therefore we must not strive for worldly progress, but for inner greatness. Skovoroda probably had a major indirect influence on the so-called Ekaterinoslav Confession (1791) in which the original doctrines of the Dukhobors were detailed in the following way:

Human souls were created after God's image and the body is but a temporary prison. Every sin or weakness sends the soul deeper into the material substance, but it is the goal of salvation to restore God's image in man and to break the material bonds. The first people on earth, the tribe of Abel, had no need for any rituals or institutions, but the descendants of Cain oppressed the tribe of Abel which was dispersed throughout the world among creeds of various denominations. When people became more and more corrupted and when the craving for the pleasures of life produced discord among people, a need for external forms which would regulate social life was felt, a need for laws which would not destroy the sins but could prevent a small part. With no laws the people would have fought each other like dogs. Also in religious life, what should have been pure spirit, now materialised into outward formulae, ritual and biblical morality. Finally, spiritual wisdom, which formerly permeated the world, was incarnated in Jesus Christ, and then also in everyone of God's People. As they now have the Spirit, they have no need for authorities, human laws, Bible or sacrements (Miliukov 1948:96-7).

A consequence of this doctrine of the Dukhobors was the rejection of all government authority and the refusal of military service. Human beings, they said, should be equal and autonomous, they should be like brothers who live on the basis of common property and mutual help and they should work with their own hands. A 'Spiritual Christian' would also reveal the self in a virtuous conduct of life, they said, but it remained unclear whether the virtuous conduct of life was for them a means of salvation or perhaps a symptom of salvation (*Erkenntnismittel*).

At the beginning of the nineteenth century the Dukhobors were resettled by the government in an area north of the Sea of Azov. Here they tried to live separately from the neighbouring population, to develop their own customs and to avoid the *connubium* with members of the Orthodox Church or other sects. At the same time, though, they built within a few decades a thriving agricultural community.

But the doctrine of the equality of the human beings now fell into oblivion, for 'Dukhoboriya' fell under the rule of a dynasty of 'Christs', Kapustin and his successors (according to Kapustin's doctrine that Christ incarnates himself only in one person in every generation). These 'Christs' had considerable influence and any serious disobedience brought with it a boycott of the disobedient person and ruin. At the same time, individual economic initiatives and considerable private property developed in connection with a rejection of common property and communal life among parts of the Dukhobors.

In the eighteen-forties, when repressive measures by the government towards the Old Believers and sects were intensified, the Dukhobors were shifted to the Transcaucasus. In this new environment too, 'Dukhoboriya' soon achieved considerable prosperity (Klibanov 1982:112). Klibanov notes that Dukhobor agriculture was marked by a high level of technical equipment and that they founded a so-called 'Orphans Home', a kind of aid fund which often functioned as a bank (whose capital consisted of deposits by the entire population) and financed even entrepreneurial activities. In productivity, technology and prosperity the Dukhobors exceeded the local population (Kurds, Georgians, Armenians) considerably[16] (Klibanov 1982:115).

Conybeare (1921:285) believed that the comfortable circumstances of the Dukhobors were due to the aid they rendered to each other in misfortune, but among the reasons for the increase of their capital and prosperity their religion must also be mentioned. They rejected icons and ritual as means of salvation. Only a virtuous life to which manual work also belonged was thought to lead to the *certitudo salutis* or was at least a symptom for it. Besides, the mutual control of the conduct of life, produced by the congregational discipline of a community which tried to have few ties with others, had some influence.

When the dynasty of 'Christs' had died out and the old ideals of equality and communal property were revived by many Dukhobors, several thousand of them emigrated to Canada in 1898-9.

The Molokans

The Molokans who developed under the leadership of Simon Uklein out of a group which had split off from the Dukhobors, was the most numerous sect of the nineteenth century and had spread not only in the Ukraine but also in the Transcaucasus and in many parts of Siberia. Their name is derived from *moloko* (milk), perhaps because the members drank milk on fast days of the Orthodox Church, perhaps also because they called their doctrine 'spiritual milk'. Much less than the Dukhobors they revealed the desire to construct a utopian community away from the state and the official church with the con-

---

[16] It is symptomatic but nevertheless surprising that Klibanov, whenever he produced detailed information about the economic superiority of sectarians over the neighbouring population, avoids an explanation of this superiority (unless one accepts short remarks about exploitation as such). But the question is, why sectarians, in spite of persecutions and frequent resettlements, were able to succeed, while the rest of the population and particularly the Orthodox population, was not.

sequence of ghettoisation, and calls for equality and community of property were heard only to a limited extent. Rather, the Molokans wished, as much as possible to come to an arrangement with the authorities and the Tsar.

The accession to the throne of Nicholas I (1825-1855) brought a considerable deterioration in the conditions of all sectarians who so far had been tolerated. The Dukhobors and Molokans, who were classified by the government as particularly harmful, were ordered to resettle in Transcaucasia and in Siberia. This led to a far-reaching spread of Molokan ideas and their conduct of life in many parts of the Empire, partly also because the Molokans were not only peasants but also often merchants and *meshchane* who travelled from place to place.

In contrast to the more pantheistic and immanent concepts of God and Christ among the Dukhobors, the Molokans upheld the idea of a transcendental God which, as already noted in Part I, has more affinity with ascetic than with mystic tendencies. Moreover, much more than in the case of the Dukhobors, the Bible was the basis of the Molokan religion, even if it was not interpreted literally but 'in spirit and truth'. Wherever they settled, the Molokans founded primary schools for the learning of reading and writing in order to be able to read the Bible. Religious services, as far as we know, consisted of reading of Bible passages and the singing of psalms according to popular melodies.

While the Molokans rejected the Orthodox ritual and priesthood, they were not averse to all religious institutions; they had their own presbyters and their own religious norms (the ten commandments in Molokan interpretation) and they interpreted the sacraments 'spiritually'. They taught, for instance, that the sacrament of baptism is performed wherever someone leads a Christian life without sins (*tainstvo kreshcheniya polagayut v pokayanii i ostavlenii grechov* – Diedrich 1985:223, fn 575). Thus baptism, instead of being a single ritual act, had become a continuous conduct of life which, according to Molokan concepts, expressed itself in sobriety, honesty and industriousness and also in the fact that one gains one's daily bread with one's own hands (Diedrich 1985:232). Monasticism was rejected because of its 'idleness'.

These Protestant-like aspects – the general validity of the Bible, the kind of religious service, the reduction of the significance of the sacraments or their 'spiritual' interpretation as a permanent and in this sense rational conduct of life – must be contrasted with aspects which were more removed from Western Protestant ideas and which may have obstructed any tendencies towards an attitude of world-domination.

An elaborated doctrine of justification like the Lutheran *sola fide* or the Calvinistic doctrine of justification was lacking. In fact, large sections of the teachings, not only of the Molokans but of almost all Russian sects, were quite amorphous because of the general absence of a country-wide organisational structure and of institutions for theological training.

To this must be added a certain 'brokenness' (*Gebrochenheit*) or undecidedness in their attitude towards the world. While they certainly rejected the world, the question as to whether this attitude should lead to inner-worldly action or to resignation and world-renunciation remained unresolved. For, in spite of an active conduct of life, which was turned towards the world, and in spite of the fact that they never refused to pray for the Tsar and tried to adapt to the conditions of the Empire, the Molokans also thought that worldly authority and human laws are only meant for 'the children of the world' but not for 'Spiritual Christians'; they therefore rejected serfdom, military service and the taking of oaths and thought that they should hide from the state like the first Christians (Klibanov 1982:161).

Also the Obshchie, a separate Molokan group which anticipated in chiliastic expectation the approaching heavenly Jerusalem, had a mixed attitude towards the world. On the basis of the community of property (new members transferred their property to the community) and the respect of the collective will, they wished to lead a form of life which resembled that of the Apostles. Exceptional significance was attributed to confession and the system guaranteed a strict mutual control of the conduct of life. But after finishing the daily public work, members were allowed to undertake private activities for which they were even able to receive loans from the so-called 'Table Fund', a kind of community bank and a replica of the Dukhobor 'Orphans Home', on condition the believer receiving this aid submitted to a fast (Klibanov 1982:170).

In spite of a certain 'brokenness' or mixed attitude towards the world, the stress placed on the congregational and certain 'Protestant' aspects of religion contributed to the economic success of the Molokans. Compared with the Orthodox population, Klibanov writes, the Molokans of Amur Oblast were the richest group. They were at the head of all branches of economic and public life of the region and directed steamship companies, the lumber trade and the financial institutions. In a similar way their economic success in Transcaucasia, where they lived from agriculture, must be evaluated, for there the Russian Orthodox village lagged behind the Dukhobor one, just as the latter lagged behind the Molokan village in terms of economics (Klibanov 1982:198).

If the differences between Molokans and Dukhobors, which led to the greater economic success of the Molokans, were to be evaluated, the universal school education and the attempt not to be pushed into a ghetto in spite of difficulties with the state, must be mentioned. Furthermore, as an inner reason the interpretation of baptism as an inner-worldly conduct of life, combined with the concept of a transcendental God, must be added. On the whole, Molokans had a rational ethical congregational religion which, according to Weber, has frequently combined with capital continuously and rationally employed in a productive enterprise for the acquisition of profit (ES:479).

Stundism

Stundism, which will only be touched upon, developed in the years immediately after the emancipation of serfs, when the judicial reform gave rise to hopes for more religious liberties. Although the name (derived from the German word *Stunde* and referring to the hours of Bible study of the German colonists) seems to indicate German origin, Stundism was not a unified movement but was composed of Protestant-pietistic, Molokan and Khlysty sources which were welded together by exterior influences, e.g. the similar treatment by the government.

The Stundists developed strong anti-ritualistic tendencies; they rejected the Orthodox ceremonies and sacraments, fasting, icons and priesthood. Their rejection of the worship of icons was particularly intense, and it has sometimes been suggested that the birth of Stundism can be connected to the dates when they returned their icons to the Orthodox Churches because they did not need them any longer (Diedrich 1985:355).

The first public Russian translations of the New Testament appeared in the eighteen-sixties. It is therefore perhaps not surprising that the Stundists considered the Bible as the highest authority (instead of the community united in love, as was the case in the Orthodox Church).

Outsiders and government officials considered the Stundists as industrious, abstinent and thrifty and as the best elements of the rural population (Diedrich 1985 : 426). They abstained from all entertain-

ment and the consumption of alcohol, sometimes even from commerce and the use of money which they considered bad for morality.
Instead, work was obligatory. Everybody was supposed to work on as
much land as was necessary for their needs. Loan banks were created,
private property was held sacred, and contrary to other sects, state
and society were not rejected (Nikol'skii 1983:393). In the twentieth
century Stundism became part of the Baptist movement.

Concluding Remarks on the Old Believers and Sects

The Orthodox religion offered several different forms of salvation for
which the demand varied according to the different social strata. The
peasant masses with their magical world-view contrasted with the
personality ideal of the monk oriented towards a mystical world-view.
In contrast to the Western Church, which cultivated the world-dominating ascetic virtues and in which the inner-worldly and world-
ordering priest was more esteemed than the monk (Harnack
1913:170), in the Eastern Church the monk with a world-fleeing, or
at least world-indifferent, attitude and who aspired to a mystical content of salvation, was more esteemed than the priest. The active
world-dominating personality, this specific Western ideal of personality which also contributed to the shaping of the Western economic
ethics, has no affinity with the Orthodox religion.

The Old Believers and the sects laid partially new emphases. The
sects attracted the most intelligent and the most energetic elements of
the Russian population, as Tsakni said; they also continuously
increased in numbers, particularly since the emancipation of the serfs
and the judicial reforms.[17] In two respects, however, they had to

---

[17] Miliukov (1948: 116), at the end of the nineteenth century, gave the following
numbers:

In 1863			In 1880		
	Priestists	5,000,000		Priestists	3,640,000
	Priestless	3,000,000		Priestless	7,150,000
	Molokans and			Khlysty	65,000
	Dukhobors	110,000		Spiritual	
	Khlysty and			Christians	1,000,000
	Skoptsy	110,000		Others	1,145,000
		8,220,000			13,000,000

Bonch-Bruevich (1959:175) has the following numbers for the beginning of the twentieth century: at least 20 million Old Believers and 6 million sectarians.

adapt to the spirit and the circumstances of Russian-Orthodox Christianity. On the one hand, their demand for independence from the patrimonial state could hardly be achieved and this generally led to passive apolitism and pariah ethics; in some cases, however, when military service was demanded from the individuals concerned, it led to acute conflicts with the political authorities (ES:595). On the other hand, the Old Believers generally and many sectarians developed the acosmic (as Weber says) and mystic character of Russian-Orthodox religion and the specific natural law which is based on the concept of community and not of society (Weber 1924a:467) and which expressed itself, for example, in demands for the common property of production or of the means of production.

The religion of both Old Believers and sectarians was congregational religion. While in mediaeval Christianity, post-Reformation Lutheranism and in Orthodox Christianity the lay people were essentially members of a parish, a passive ecclesiastical tax unit and the jurisdictional district of a priest (ES:455), sectarians and Old Believers congregated in apolitical religious communities in which lay people played often important roles as prophets, intellectuals or administrators of tradition. Such rational ethical congregational religions have combined frequently and not only in the Occident, with rational economic development (ES:479), even if, as in the case of Old Believers, traditionalism and ritualism have partially hampered this development. The rejection of religious rites and icons and of sacraments, performed by priests, as a means of salvation by many Russian sects, i.e. the rejection of magical positions, led to the necessity for human beings to attain the *certitudo salutis* by their own efforts without a mediator. This led to the rationalisation of the conduct of life, and then possibly also of the economic conduct, only if salvation was not sought any more in the temporary ecstasy of the *radenie* but in a permanent ethos. This was not yet the case among the Khlysty, but in a certain sense among the Skoptsy and then more clearly among the Molokans. In contrast to the Old Believers, the Russian sectarians, at least since the development of 'Spiritual Christianity' also abolished the difference between monastic ethics and lay ethics, but without the consequence of a Protestant ethic in the Western sense.

It is rather rare in the history of religions that peasants became connected to non-magical, rational-ethical movements, particularly since in early Christianity the heathen and the peasant (*paganus*) were equated and since the official doctrine of the mediaeval church treat-

ed the peasant as a Christian of lower rank (ES:471). Max Weber noted that the Russian peasant sectarians, threatened by proletarisation,
turned against the official church as the recipient of tithes and as the
bulwark of the financial and landed magnates (ES:469), but Weber
also talked of the pariah intellectualism of the Russian peasants who,
at the bottom of the social hierarchy, and therefore not impeded by
material considerations, were capable of an original attitude and of
intense ethical emotion (ES:507).

The Russian sectarians have been transfigured by the *narodnichestvo*,
the agrarian-communist protest movement against modern rationalism in the eighteen-seventies; and even under the socialist regime of
the Soviet Union the scholar and government minister Bonch-Bruevich had a very high opinion of their economic abilities and proposed
the unusual policy that until the end of the nineteen-twenties religious
collective estates were to be financially supported by the state (Kolarz
1963:287). This policy seemed to be based on the insight, which has
also been the outcome of the present study, that not only the political
and economic system but also the economic ethics in the sense used
here (not only the economic ethics of the sects but also of the Old
Believers and of the members of the official church) have contributed
to an important degree to the economic development of Russia in the
past and perhaps even today.

CHAPTER FOUR

PARIAH-ETHICS AND THE RUSSIAN-ORTHODOX TRADITION

The analysis of the economic ethics of Russian-Orthodox Christianity can be complemented by the introduction of the concept of pariah-ethics which was also formulated by Max Weber.

The term pariah can be derived from an old South-Indian weaver-caste, the Parayan. The Abbé Raynal, in his *Histoire philosophique et politique des établissements et du commerce européen* (1770) used it for the "savages" in the colonies and for the serfs and poor artisans of Europe. Later, the term was employed more precisely for those who lived in a legally inferior and precarious situation and at a social and ritual distance from a dominant ethnic community, for example the metics in ancient Greece. When Max Weber (1920) introduced the concept in his essay on the economic ethics of ancient Judaism, he referred to a distinctive hereditary social group, lacking autonomous political organization, socially disprivileged, and characterized by internal prohibitions against commensality and connubium. More-over, he stressed the importance in ancient Judaism of the teaching of Isaiah (40-55) that suffering, particularly if it is unmerited, as well as the situation of a pariah in exile are to be accepted and even are signs of honour and dignity before God – while everywhere else the well-to-do and healthy were thought to be the favourites of the gods. The Jewish pariah-situation resulted, according to Weber, in a dualism of in-group and out-group morality which prohibited within the group what was permitted or an *adiaphoron* in relation to the outside – and Weber used this dualism in his explanation regarding the question why the Jewish religious ethic did not contribute to the development of the 'spirit' of capitalism.

Whereas certain pejorative connotations of the term pariah and particularly Weber's use of it in the interpretation of ancient Judaism have been criticized, the concept can also be widened and there is no need to limit it to one culture, as particularly Mühlmann (1961) has shown.

1) For instance, passive resistance or even non-resistance to evil can be connected to pariah ethics. The historian Flavius Josephus

recounts in *Bellum Judaicum* that a Roman governor had the image of the emperor brought into the temple at Jerusalem. The Jews were shocked, went to the governor's palace and, for five days and nights, stayed there on their knees. When the governor threatened to have them killed by his soldiers, they just bared their necks and answered that they were willing to die rather than to act against their religious laws. Amazed by this attitude, the governor removed the image of the emperor from the temple.

If we turn to another culture, it will appear that Mahatma Gandhi's strategy of non-violent resistance must be related to a pariah-ethic. Gandhi also identified himself with the "Untouchables", glorified by him as harijans (people of God), and, on the international level, the role of India in its struggle for independance was conceived by him as a typical pariah-role: he accepted the West's political and economic superiority while he thought India to be morally superior.

The belief in non-resistance to evil was of course not only expressed among Jews and in India, but the Sermon on the Mount has made it a part of the Christian heritage. In modern times it has been revived in Russia by L. Tolstoy in his book *The Kingdom of God is within you* and in the subsequent *tolstovstvo* movement.

2) Another aspect of the pariah-ethic, meekness and the willingness to serve, is particularly prevalent in Russia, as can be observed in the novels of N. Leskov who, perhaps more than any other Russian writer, knew the common people and the serfs, and who did not only describe the negative aspects of serfdom. In "A Fallen Family" he tells us about a former serf, now a freedman who, in a kind of thoughtless rapture, 'forgot' to register the papers which would have shown his new status as a freedman because he was a fanatic in his servility. To serve was his vocation and his honour, according to Leskov; he preferred to serve even when he had become free, and he feared to be ridiculed for allowing his former master to sink into poverty. In another story, "The Sealed Angel", we read about Father Pamwa: 'When you insult him, he blesses you; when you beat him, he bows down before you. A man of such humility is invincible!'

3) Russia can also serve as an example of the idea of the pariah as a future elite. In exile and oppression there grew among the Jews the identification of the despised and rejected with the elected people, the future elite. This millenarian idea can also be found among

the early Christians: "Those who are meek and weak in the eyes of the world, those God has elected", says Paul. The cultivated Greeks and Romans disdained those uneducated artisans and slaves who pretended to be elected by God. The Platonic philosopher Celsus described these Christian beliefs as not founded in reason, as illogical and unproven (ἀλογως πιστευουσιν – Nestle 1941:72). Russian philosophers of history, particularly those of the nineteenth century, often compared the situation of the Russian people with that of the Jews. Like the Jews in Egypt or Babylon, the Russian people had been oppressed by the Mongols and, later, by their own rulers, but now, steeped in the Orthodox Christian tradition and patiently waiting, Russia would become the bearer of salvation for the world. Prince Myshkin in Dostoevsky's *Idiot* proclaimed that the Russians were the elected people and that the Russian idea would be at the basis of the resurrection and the renewal of all mankind.

4) The higher castes of the Orient, for instance the brahmins in India, generally were intellectual workers and left all physical work to the lower castes. Equally, classical Antiquity lived according to values opposed to physical work (which was done by slaves and metics). But it was among slaves and small artisans that Christianity had its early successes, and Christian monks were the first to include physical work among their monastic rules; they valued physical work, even methodical physical work, although everywhere else it was the lot of pariahs.

Wherever afterwards the ethos of Christian monasticism was adopted, physical work was valued and not rejected. This was so in the Occident at least since the Reformation; within the Orthodox tradition some Old Believers who, as has been shown, adopted quasi-monastic rules and enforced them by congregational discipline, as well as some of the sects were known for their hard physical work, especially in the harsh climatic conditions of the Russian north; Tolstoy insisted on the necessity of physical work, and even Mahatma Gandhi, who as a student in England had imbibed Western ideas and combined them with traditional Indian ideas when he identified India with a people of pariahs, rejected the traditional disdain of the higher castes for physical work and insisted that everyone should produce his own garments at the spinning wheel.

On the whole, pariah-ethics can be characterized by passive perseverance and prudent adaptation, and by secret and non-violent resistance and the willingness to serve[1] under foreign domination. Foreign domination was present in Russia only under Mongol rule, but it is perhaps not unreasonable to think that even later certain social conditions (serfdom, totalitarian bureaucracy) may have had a similar effect.

Whether pariah-ethics are the result of resentment, as Nietzsche thought, or simply of the intellectual brooding of outsiders (pariah-intellectuals) who, unconstrained by social conventions and customary opinions, reflect on the meaning of the world, is not the question here, but it should be asked whether the existence of this kind of ethics in Russia did not contribute in any way to the economic mentality.

Some researchers – for example V. Mar'ianowskii (1997) –, have suggested that the Russian economic mentality was formed in the times of serfdom. As a large part of the results of the peasants' labour went to the landowners, this produced, it is claimed, a pernicious impact on the work motivation of the peasants. Similarly under the totalitarian socialist regime, the obligatory work for the State (as opposed to work for oneself) produced a negative attitude toward labour among a large part of the population.

The exterior conditions of life, serfdom and the socialist state, can certainly not be ignored in any explanation of the Russian economic mentality. A precarious legal situation or the absence of individual rights will probably have a negative influence on rationally planned economic activity, but the study of these exterior conditions must be complemented by an analysis of the interior motivations which may have independent origins. In Russia, the pariah-ethics undoubtedly had partially religious origins, although the characteristics may have been intensified and come to the fore by the exterior conditions under which large parts of the downtrodden population lived. They represent a small but not insignificant aspect of the ethos of some of the Russian people. Although physical work was not devalued, the valuation of passive resistance, the willingness to serve, and the passive expectation to become the future elite all tended to direct the economic mentality in a direction which had little in common with the

---

[1] Mühlmann has also found, among pariah-groups elsewhere, a certain art of concealment and of pretending (positively turned: the art of keeping an interior dignity in the context of exterior humiliation). It is far from certain, though, whether the penchant for exaggerating one's own merits (the notorious inflated indicators under Soviet rule) can be interpreted in this context.

world-dominating attitude which developed in Western-Europe after the Reformation. There was, moreover, a high degree of affinity between the exterior conditions of life in Russia and the inner motivations, and it is perhaps from this homogeneity of exterior and interior motivations that the Russian economic mentality derived its strength and durability.

PART THREE

THE PLACE OF INDIVIDUALISM IN THE EASTERN-ORTHODOX TRADITION AND IN THE WEST

CHAPTER FIVE

THE PLACE OF THE INDIVIDUAL IN THE EASTERN
ORTHODOX TRADITION

Introduction

Modernity may not only be characterized by the development of
modern science and a certain economic ethic which Max Weber
attributed to the Protestants, but, even more fundamentally, by individualism. Scholars have described the rise of individualism in the
modern Occident and even its transplantation to the other great civilizations of the world as the characteristic feature of modern development. They have also speculated about its origin and have found it
sometimes in the Renaissance, as did J. Burckhardt, sometimes in the
rise of the merchant class or the modern city. Others again believe
that individualism is in one way or another deeply entwined with the
classical tradition of ancient Greece as well as with the Judeo-Christian heritage and that perhaps the history of the Occident may be
interpreted as its gradual disentanglement and coming to prominence.

   Certainly, there are those with a nominalistic or empiricist scientific outlook, for whom individuals and individualism exist everywhere,
in all cultures and at all times. They do not distinguish analytically the
empirical human being, the individual sample of mankind which is
indeed found in all cultures and societies, from the independant and
autonomous individual to whom a paramount value is attached in
modern society because of its individualistic ideology. Louis Dumont
(1982) has insisted on this distinction and this led him to oppose two
kinds of societies: where the individual is autonomous and a paramount value, he spoke of individualism; in the opposite case, where
the society as a whole is the paramount value and englobes the empirical individuals or particular human beings, he spoke of holism.

   L. Dumont has also suggested that in the search for the origins of
modern individualism one should follow Max Weber's example and
attach prominence to religion. With this in mind, he has advanced
the thesis that in early Christianity the individual as value was conceived as apart from the given social and political organization, out-

side and beyond it, an outworldly individual, as opposed to the inworldly individual in modern society. In traditional holistic societies – as, for instance, also in the Indian instance where the individual as value developed only outside of the hierarchical caste system among the renouncers (samnyasin) and in the sects –, Dumont has argued, the individual or individualism can only appear in its outworldly form in the sense that the individual has devalued or even abandoned his social rôle, and the transformation from outworldly to inworldly individual or from holistic society to individualistic society and to modernity then needs to be explained.

Dumont has proposed an explanation of this transformation along the following lines: the early Christians first adopted from the Stoics the idea of a relative Law of Nature in order to partially adapt their outworldly values to the social and political world. Very soon, however, the conception by the Church of its relation to the State becomes central, for it indicates clearly the relation between the bearer of value, the outworldly individual, and the "world". The conversion of Constantine and then of the Roman Empire to Christianity forced upon the Church a closer relation to the State. The first clear result was Gelasius' formula about the relationship between the priest's *auctoritas* and the king's *potestas*, but the dramatic change occurred in the eighth century: the Popes broke their ties with Constantinople and claimed supreme power, not only *auctoritas* but also *potestas*, in the West. This claim was then based on the forged so-called Donation of Constantine (*Donatio Constantini*) and later justified in the theory of the two swords. The final stage is found in Calvin who suggests that the task of the individual is to work for God's glory in the world rather than taking refuge from it, and where the Church is not a holistic institution any more but a society of individuals and a mere instrument of discipline.

The inworldliness of the individual will then continue in the Protestant sects, the Enlightenment and further on, but we leave this Western line of development, which began with the outworldly Christian individual, and shall ask ourselves what happened to this outworldly individual in the quite different context of another Christian tradition: Eastern Orthodox Christianity or, to describe more precisely the range of this chapter, the Byzantino-Russian tradition. As the relationship between Church and State, which Dumont considered to be a major contributing factor in the emergence of the inworldly individual in the West, was quite different in the Eastern Roman Empire and later in Muscovite Russia, and as, moreover, there was no Reformation and no Calvin in Eastern Orthodox Christianity, the question arises as to whether the individual in Byzantium and later in Russia has perhaps always been outworldly and whether modernity, therefore, has never taken hold there, or whether there have been other mechanisms in the Eastern Orthodox tradition which have led to inworldly individualism. In order to deal with this question, some of the material of the previous chapters will be taken up again and interpreted from this new angle.

Individualism and holism among Outworldly Monks

It is possible to start with Dumont's thesis about Christianity's outworldly individualism, encompassing recognition of and obedience to the powers of this world, or with Troeltsch's well-known statement that the early Christians were "individuals-in-relation-to-God" who, though they remained detached from and indifferent to the sociopolitical order, nevertheless accepted it at its level, according to Christ's saying "Render unto Caesar the things that are Caesar's" (Matthew 22, 21). The State and its ruler, private property and slavery were not simply refused or negated; run-away slaves, for instance, were not accepted as members of monastic congregations and were sent back to their masters (it is interesting to note here a similarity with another equally outworldly tradition, described in the Buddhist pali canon, for slaves were also not accepted in the Buddhist *sangha*), but the laws and traditions of the "world" were relativized and not given the dignity that belongs to God. The Christian position was similar to and perhaps influenced by the Stoïc teaching of the relative law of nature, for the Stoïcs taught that the wise man should practice renunciation and self-sufficiency and that the socio-political order has only a relative value. This teaching was the result of their distinction between a Golden Age when free individuals obeyed only Reason, and the present social order which, under conditions of life directed by human passions, necessitates political power, *patria potestas*, slavery and laws. Similarly the Christians taught that all social institutions which from their point of view were intolerable, were due to Original Sin; that, once lawlessness, avarice and violence have penetrated society, the law of nature has been transformed and must of necessity become evident only in the form of compulsion and of the laws of the

State and thus react against corruption. This is the relative law of nature, at once the result of sin and a remedy for sin (*poena et remedium peccati*). Thus, both Stoïcism and Christianity taught an outworldly ideal or, as Troeltsch also said, religious individualism.

The outworldly Christian individual could be either a simple member of the Christian Church or, since approximately the fourth century, if he did not wish to compromise with the world, an anchorite or monk. In fact, monastic life was to a high degree synonymous with the Byzantine ideal of authentic Christian life. The world-fleeing anchorites and monks did not reject the Church, as the Montanists and Enkratits had done before them. In fact, they acknowledged its right to exist, they never lost contact with it and, since the Council of Chalcedon, their monasteries were submitted to the authority of a bishop of the Church; but they relativized its value and strove to achieve the vision of God and eternal life, beyond family and profession, in the deserts of Egypt and elsewhere. The anchorite, the renouncer of life in traditional holistic society with its laws and constraints – the *saeculum*[1] in theological parlance – was even more a religious individual than the simple Christian church member, but he was an outworldly individual[2], like the Indian *samnyasin* about whose renunciation of life in the caste society and of the wheel of rebirths, in

---

[1] In the Christian tradition, the *saeculum* is the period of time which precedes the return of Christ. It is not a cosmological concept, nor is it synonymous with *mundus* or *kosmos*, but it designates the socio-political order. It was the teaching of the Church that the 'world' (*saeculum*) is a result of the Fall, and that the State, together with marriage, slavery and the other legal institutions, is the underlying principle of the 'world'.

[2] The outworldly individual may be described as someone who relativizes his social role or, if he is a monk or anchorite, who leaves his social role in order to adopt a role which has no equivalent in society and which is both personal and universal.

It might be argued that the concept of the outworldly individual cannot capture the deeper meaning or the essence of man's real nature in Byzantine theology, since the Cappadocian Fathers developed the theory of the person and of *theosis* according to which man is not "autonomous" but destined to share divine life, and where his role in the created world can be fulfilled only if he keeps intact the image of God (Meyendorff, 1975, p. 4), – and it is certainly true that most modern social science does not distinguish clearly enough between the two concepts of the person and of the individual (the concept of the person has, since Antiquity, generally implied a relationship, e.g. the actor's role on the stage, the social role in Rome, the relationship of the three divine *personae* in Augustine's Trinitarian theology).

Nevertheless, it is in relation to modern society that today's individual and the early Christians have something in common; and it is solely for our understanding that it is useful to speak of the early Christians as outworldly individuals who, although very different from us in other respects (their concept of the person and of *theosis*), felt, like the modern inworldly individual, relatively autonomous in relation to society.

order to find liberation outside the world, we read in the ancient Indian texts. And, like the Indian renouncers, the Christian anchorites might live as hermits or join a group of fellow anchorites. This development started with Pachomius, the initiator of a tendency towards cenobitic (communal) monasticism, and came into full flower with Basil the Great who preconised communal living in a single monastery and provided the inner biblical and theological foundations for the cenobitic living of the outworldly Christian individuals, the monks. His monastic rule merits closer examination, not only because his way of seeing the relationship between the individual and the community was original, but also because it portended developments within the Russian-Orthodox religion and, in fact, in Russian society, more than a millennium later.

According to Basil[3], the anchoretic ideal falls short of the demands of Christ for, apart from the love of God, Christ demanded the love of our neighbour. The specific charismatic gifts of the anchorite remain fruitless for all others, and he himself, as he does not possess all charismatic gifts, cannot raise himself to the complete fulness of spiritual life. He lacks, moreover, the necessary critical stance with regard to his own mistakes and shortcomings as well as all support in spiritual matters. On the other hand, many individuals living in common can more easily fulfill a large number of commandments than a single individual, for often the fulfillment of one commandment prevents the fulfillment of another. Basil maintains, in fact, that the *charismata* of every individual have been received for the benefit of others and that in the cenobitic life the energy of the Holy Spirit, which is given to a single individual, is the common good of the whole community. Therefore, not only our own shortcomings necessitate the communal life: it is the essence of the Christian ideal that it can only be attained by a community, for only a community can fulfill all demands of Christ.

While Pachomius had left open the question as to whether the monks could leave the community and return to the "world", Basil considered such an act as a desecration of the *koinobion*.

In Basil's Rule we have the first instance of the idea that individualism, be it inworldly or outworldly, is the little path, that the *koinobion* is not only a useful means of physical protection and material

---

[3] A commented résumé of Basil's Rule can be found in K. Holl (1898). pp. 160 sqq.

comforts which the renouncer or anchorite can join and leave at his
will, but the necessary precondition to a full spiritual life and the
high road to salvation. It is also worth mentioning that Basil's *koinobion* has little in common with Tönnies' *Gemeinschaft*, which is
described as organically grown, based on the naturally given conditions, the ties of blood and location, the traditional unity and whole-
ness of family, tribe and *Volk*, for the *Gemeinschaft* does not know of
the individual, it has not yet conceived and experienced it, whereas
the *koinobion* is the result of the joining of independent individuals at
a higher level of community.

Basil also required the monks to work, partially as an ascetic means
of combatting idleness and passions, but mainly for social reasons, i.e.
in order to support the indigent. This, however, introduced an inner
contradiction into Basil's ideal, for the obligation to work in the service of others and the rule of complete obedience cannot completely
be harmonized with the highest goal of the monks and of Basil himself: the concentration of all thoughts in God and the contemplation
of divine beauty. Only the anchorite could hope to attain completely
the uninterrupted devotion to God which even Basil recognized to be
the highest goal, and it is, therefore, not surprising that the anchoretic
life, in spite of Basil's efforts and in spite of the renewal of his Rule by
Theodore Studites in the eighth century, continued to be regarded as
superior to the cenobitic life (Holl 1898:198). The outworldly individual kept his preeminence, and particularly the ideal of *laborare* (in the
formula '*ora et labora*', later attributed to the Benedictines) did not prevail in Eastern Orthodox monachism (Savramis 1966). The idio-
rrhythmic movement and hesychasm later on reinforced this tendency. It is not surprising that even later in Russia the outworldly monks
were considered superior to the priests (Harnack 1913:170).

Revealing for the struggle between the outworldly individualistic
ideal of the anchorite and Basil's cenobitic ideal was the distinction
which started to be made even within the monasteries between the
regular monks and those monks who, after thirty years (in Russia) of
unblemished ascetic life, were allowed to take a higher vow (μεγα-
λοσχημοι)[4]. While the regular monks looked after the economic
aspects of life in the monastery, the *megaloskhimi* were freed from all
work and from some of the common prayers and liturgical chants in

---

[4] Heiler, op. cit. p. 258 & 272; I. Smolitsch 1953, p. 264.

order to devote themselves completely to a secluded *vita contemplativa*. Bishops who took this vow had to resign from their position.

Karl Holl regrets that Theodor Studites who is our first source regarding the distinction between the monks of the *mikroskhima* and of the *makroskhima*, did not tell us anything about the motives which led to it (Holl 1898:200). From a sociological and comparative perspective, however, the motives are quite clear: like in India[5], where the brahmanic theory tried to integrate the outworldly renouncer and to represent renunciation as a mere stage in the life of the brahmin, the defenders of the cenobitic ideal tried to integrate the option of an anchoretic life into the monastery, to accept the anchoretic life-style as merely a moment at the end of a long cenobitic life of service to the monastic community. The adoption of the anchoretic ideal as the last stage of life within a cenobitic monastery which, apparently, was generally accepted since the time of Eustathios in the twelfth century[6], seems to have been an attempt to limit the outworldly and individualistic anchoretic ideal, as it could not be negated, for the *koinobion* continued to be considered as the elementary school of world renunciation while the anchoretic life remained the high road to perfection.

Later, in Russia, the anchoretic and cenobitic ideals as well as the attempted reconciliation of them in the theory and practice of the *megaloskhima* lived side by side since the beginnings of monasticism in the caves near Kiev. The cenobitic Rule of Studion, itself based on Basil's Rule, was again adopted as model by Sergius of Radonezh in the fourteenth century and, in the fifteenth, by Joseph of Volokolamsk, the founder of the Josephite movement which achieved considerable influence at court and in the Church. The Josephite movement, however, which stressed the importance for the cenobitic monasteries to own land, succeeded by political means, as will be seen later, in repressing the anchoretic monachism of Nil Sorsky and the "Trans-Volga Elders" who lived in groups of two or three in small skits under the direction of a πατηρ πνευματικος (spiritual father) and who strongly stressed non-possession and the hesychastic prayer. In thus raising

---

[5] The similarity to the Indian theory of the four *asrama* is striking. The brahmins tried to show that renunciation, the life of the samnyasin, which in principle was open to everyone, was merely the last stage in the life of the brahmin who is successively novice, householder, hermit and then, at the end, when his worldly obligations have been fulfilled, samnyasin. This is at least the most common view about the *asramas* (see: Kane 1974 Vol. II, p. 424).

[6] J.P. Migne *Patrologiae Cursus Completus, Series Graeca*, 1864, T. 135, ∫ 194.

the value of the *koinobion* and largely reducing the importance of outworldly individualism, the Josephites have given the cultural development of Russia its characteristic aspect.

It is perhaps interesting to note that in the West the discussion
about the ownership of lands by the monasteries had produced different and very new ideas in the writings of William of Ockham. While
Joseph of Volokolamsk talked about the necessity that the *koinobion*, as
opposed to individual monks, should own property (Goldfrank
1983:49), Ockham's nominalistic philosophy, almost two centuries
earlier, would not even have attached any reality to the monastic
community. In his dispute with Pope John XXII concerning the
estates of the Franciscan Order which, in spite of the vow of poverty,
had become rich, Ockham had, in fact, maintained that 'universals'
like man or Franciscan Order have no real being and that there are
only individuals. He concluded, therefore, that the Franciscan Order
was not bound by any positive law to accept the ownership (*proprietas*)
of its estates, as the Pope wished, although he held the individual
monks entitled to the enjoyment of these estates, the *ius utendi* (Villey
1975:243 sqq.).

Church-State Relations in Byzantium

When, under Constantine in the fourth century, Christianity had
achieved a respected and leading role in the Empire, the Church had
to react and to reconsider its relationship with the State and the
Emperor. The conception which the Church developed of its relationship to the State would be central in the evolution of the relationship between the outworldly individual and the 'world'.

In this context, it will be unavoidable to refer to the concept of caesaro-papism which has in the past often (although in recent times with
more hesitation and more sparingly) been used to denote the
State/Church relationship in the Byzantino-Russian tradition. Sometimes, the concept simply denotes the ancient sacral kingship of
archaic societies where the idea of the unity of religious authority and
political power was never lost; at other times, however, and particularly in the case of historical religions (which tend to be associated
with the emergence of differentiated religious activities and at least
partially independent religious and political hierarchies – e.g. by R.
Bellah in his ideal-typical scheme of religious evolution), the term

tends to be used whenever a political leader, an Emperor or Tsar, has 'arrogated' to himself spiritual functions or, more often, an influence on the religious organization. This may happen either on the factual level or because of the personal dispositions of an Emperor, and contrary to the prevailing ideology, or it may be that the prevailing ideology does not exclude or prevent this possibility or that it even justifies it.

The discussion about caesaro-papism in Byzantium has sometimes been confusing because it has not always been recognized that there were two theories on the relationship between Church and Empire which cannot easily be reconciled, – a fact, it may be noted in passing, which probably led Troeltsch to think that the Roman-Hellenistic State, with its ancient laws and ancient culture, only compromised with Christian thought but never inwardly became united with it; that there developed no inwardly uniform Christian society, as in the West, but that the whole system became a parallelism whose component parts could only be kept in right relation with each other by the Emperor.

On the one hand, ideas of Hellenistic sacral kingship as well as the memory of the Emperor's role as *pontifex maximus* always survived in Byzantium, and the old Roman legal statement that *publicum ius in sacris, in sacerdotibus, in magistratibus consistit* (public law is centered on sacred ceremonies, priests and officials – Ulpian, Dig. I, 1, 1, 2), indicating that religious matters are part of public law, was not forgotten. Eusebius called Constantine the overseer of external Church matters, and the Emperors did indeed appoint the patriarchs, they defined the borders of the ecclesiastical provinces, they might decree certain ecclesiastical legislation, and synodal decisions needed their approval. Moreover, the Christian Emperors were thought to be 'spirit bearers' (Beck 1959:36), although not in the same sense as bishops or priests, and their right to govern was based on their *pneuma*. Therefore, when Justinian, in his Sixth Novella, talked of the *symphonia* between the priesthood and the imperial dignity, he did not mean a harmony between two powers or two distinct societies, but the internal cohesion and unity of purpose of a single human society.

But frictions with the Church arose around points of doctrine and of liturgy. For the sake of political unity there were imperial interventions in connection with Arianism and in the monophysitic and monotheletic debates but, as in the case of the ensuing iconoclastic controversy, where the political interests of the Empire seemed to be

on the side of iconoclasm and also later when, again for political reasons (for help against the Turks), a union with Rome was attempted
at the Councils of Lyons (1274) and Florence (1439), the Emperors
were not able to impose their will on the Christian population. There
were explicit denials of doctrinal authority to the Emperors by anti-
iconoclastic writers like John of Damascus and Theodore Studites.

The doctrinal debates centered mainly on the question of how to
understand and formulate the union of the other-worldly and the
this-worldly, or of God and man in Christ[7]. During the iconoclastic
struggle the question was rather if and how the unity of the sacred
and the material, or of the other-worldly and the this-worldly, can
occur in the icon. In the thinking of early Christianity, there was, in
fact, a whole series of similar oppositions – the Pauline pairs, according to Caspary[8] – which were fundamental to Christian thought. As
in letter/spirit and old dispensation/new dispensation or also other-
worldly/this-worldly, two poles were opposed to each other and yet
united by their complementarity. There was, moreover, a hierarchical relationship between the poles in the sense that one of them was
thought of as better than or as superior to the other. In an analogous
way, the outworldly individual and the world were two such poles,
and the attempts by the Church, the concomitant of outworldly individualism, to clarify the proper relationship between itself and the
State, must be seen in the same context.

Gelasius, pope in Rome at the end of the fifth century, taught that
the Church is superior to the Empire regarding things divine whereas

---

[7] According to the dogma of incarnation, developed since the fifth century, Christ
was thought to be an icon of God and still a living being. He had rendered the divine
visible in a human body. During the iconoclastic struggle this led to the further idea
that a unity of the sacred and the material, of the other-worldly and the this-worldly,
may also occur elsewhere, and particularly in the icon itself. On the basis of Aristotle's distinction between matter and form Theodore Studites taught that in the
authentic image (icon) we have the real Christ or a real Saint – only the matter is different (Harnack 1991, p. 275). Louis Dumont has ventured the idea that the core of
Christianity itself lies in the assertion of an effective transition between the outworldly
and the inworldly, in the incarnation of value. On the concept of icon, see chapter 7.

[8] The 'Pauline pairs' have been analyzed by Caspary 1979, p. 113 sqq.
The view of a hierarchical relationship between the pairs is perhaps not surprising
in a society where the concept of hierarchy itself – a divine and sacred order which
needs to be clearly distinguished from a political order or an order imposed by force
– was formulated (by Pseudo-Dionysios). This concept was, however, complemented
by the view that, as a divine hierarchical order can only be established imperfectly in
the material world, considerations with regard to 'economy' (κατ'οἰκονομιαν) always
need to come into play (Ahrweiler 1975, p. 132 sqq).

the religious individual as a member of the Church is subject to the Emperor in worldly matters. According to him, the religious individual has not entered the "world" but is seen in a hierarchical relationship with it.

Photios, patriarch in Constantinople after the end of the iconoclastic struggle in the latter part of the ninth century, was the probable author of the Epanagoge (Eisagoge), an introduction to a planned publication of a revised Byzantine law collection. The Epanagoge is remarkable not only because it attributes jurisdictional primacy in the Church to the patriarchal seat of Constantinople, but also because of its statements on the relationship between the Emperor and the Patriarch, the Empire and the Church. On the basis of Aristotle's teaching, Photios maintained that the substances are composed of form and matter, living substances of soul and body, and that the Church directs the *politeia* as the soul directs the body, as its formal and final cause, giving it unity and purpose. Similar to an icon, the *politeia* and the Church are combined in a higher unity in which, however, they remain perfectly distinct (perhaps a reference to the distinctiveness of the divine and the human in the person of Christ, as established by the Council of Chalcedon), and this higher unity is again called a *politeia* by Photios.

According to the Epanagoge, the Emperor is not only the head of this new *politeia*, but also the first representative of the Church which is conceived as a mere department of the Christian *politeia*. One of the Emperor's functions is the creation and the preservation of morality among men by the proclamation of laws. The Patriarch, on the other hand, has no claim to superiority, although morally he stands besides the Emperor. He interprets the dogma and the Tradition, but should be "crucified to the world" (Epanagoge III,3). Any interest in socio-political matters is denied to him; he is an outworldly individual.

On the basis of these theories it was possible for the Church to resist most attempts by the Emperors to impose their views or their political agenda in matters of doctrine and liturgy, at least since the iconoclastic crisis.[9] At the same time, monasticism, reflecting ideal-typically the attitude of the outworldly individual or of those who are,

---

[9] Most scholars seem to suggest that there was more independence of the Church after the iconoclastic struggle (Ostrogorsky, Barker) while others (e.g. Svoronos) point out that the Emperor acquired more influence over the Church as an institution after the iconoclastic struggle as the patriarchs now had to take an oath of allegiance to the Emperor.

in the terminology of the Epanogoge (and also of Galatians 6, 14), "crucified to the world", acquired more influence, because mainly monks had led the resistance against the iconoclastic policies. This trend received new support when the Athos monk Gregory Palamas, in his dispute with the philosopher Barlaam, had rejected secular humanism and the implicit nominalism which underlay Barlaam's affirmations about God, and had led the hesychastic movement to victory at a Church Council in 1351.

Outworldly individuals, having left their rôle in society, tend to accept a personal and, at the same time, a more universal rôle. It is therefore not surprising that the monks who directed the Church during the last phase of the Empire, had, according to Meyendorff, a more supernational outlook and attitude than the State which, in difficult political circumstances, tended more and more to withdraw to an interpretation of the *politeia* in terms of its Hellenic heritage and culture. In conformity with the Epanagoge, though, the Church did not presume to be able to stand alone. This was clearly stated in the often quoted letter of the Patriarch Antonios to the Grand Prince Basil of Moscow in 1397: It is not possible for Christians to have the Church and not to have the Empire; the Empire and the Church have a great unity and community, and it is impossible to separate them from one another (Meyendorff 1981:103).

Whether one takes Gelasius' hierarchical order or Photios' Aristotelian distinction between form and matter, or whether one simply considers the succession of historical events, it is clear that in early Christianity and in Byzantium the line between the *sacerdotium* and the *regnum* was not drawn in the same way as in the Occident. It is possible to talk of caesaro-papism in Byzantium in the sense of imperial domination of external Church matters or of the legal aspects of the Church's structure; it is, moreover, possible to talk of caesaro-papistic inclinations of some Emperors with regard to doctrine and liturgy, supported by the old Hellenistic theory of sacral kingship, but questioned and resisted by the theories which the Church itself had developed of its relationship with the State. But never did the *sacerdotium* usurp the functions of the *imperium*, at least not on the ideological level, and no effort was made by the outworldly individual to enter and to rule the 'world'.

It has been possible to talk of the spiritualization of the Church in Byzantium (Esser 1963:74), while in the West, with the papal assumption of a political function and with the claim to an inherent right to political power, the Church became inworldly and the formerly out-worldly Christian individual became more intensely involved in the world since the so-called Papal Revolution which had its main sources in Cluny and in the Gregorian Reform, long before the Reformation[10]. A short insertion about these Western events will be useful here for comparative purposes; they will be discussed in more detail in the following chapter.

The Cluniacs were the first monastic order in which all the monas-teries, scattered throughout Europe, were subordinate to a single head, the Abbot of Cluny – and in this respect they served as a model of a single translocal organization and of a corporate unity for the Roman Catholic Church as such and particularly for its clergy. A clear distinction between the clergy and the laity was now drawn, the formerly holy Emperor becoming a simple layman, lower than the lowest priest. The Cluniacs also got involved in the political move-ment of *pax terrae* (Landfriede) and they attacked simony and nico-laism (clerical marriage) and thus furthered the independence of the Church from the feudal structure.

Building on these ideas, Pope Gregory VII, in his *Dictatus Papae* (1075) declared the political and legal supremacy of the papacy over the Church and the independence of the clergy from secular control – while earlier emperors and kings had invested the bishops not only with their civil and feudal authority, but also with their ecclesiastical authority, similar to the situation in Byzantium. Gregory VII went even further and declared the ultimate supremacy of the Pope in sec-ular matters, including the authority to depose and to excommuni-cate emperors and kings. The papacy thus assumed a political and inworldly function, and we can speak from now on, with regard to it, of spiritual power (*potestas*), rather than of spiritual authority (*auctori-tas*).[11]

---

[10] It is becoming more widely recognized that the Gregorian Reform or what Berman calls the Papal Revolution in the eleventh and twelfth centuries, was the first great turning point in the history of the West, the source of major aspects of Western social thought, because of the violent separation of the ecclesiastical polity from the secular power and then the subordination of the secular power.

[11] Taking our concepts from the Western tradition and from Political Science which analyses it, we tend to think and to speak of the temporal and of the spiritual 'power' and of the 'struggle' between the two almost in the same way in which we talk of a war between two secular powers. This way of thinking has been common since the time when the Popes claimed not only religious authority but also political power and thus introduced a fundamental ideological change in Western society. It

The result was not only a civil war between the imperial and papal parties throughout Europe until the concordat of Worms (1122), and further the crusades which increased the political power and the influence of the papacy, but, on the ideological level, and more importantly, the complete separation of secular and ecclesiastical jurisdictions and the arrangement of the various sources of law in a hierarchical order by Gratian in his *Concordance of Discordant Canons*, where customs and the laws and enactments of princes were considered as subordinate to Natural Law and to the ecclesiastical *leges* and *constitutiones*. On the whole, according to Berman (1983:158), the Church started to be viewed as a visible, legal, corporate identity. The emphasis shifted from sacredness in the sense of outworldliness or otherworldliness to the incarnation of the sacred, to its claim to rule the world through the Church, and this meant its manifestation in the political, economic and social life of the times. The outworldly individual had stepped into the world and now acted in it.

Church-State Relations in Russia

In Russia, on the other hand, after more than two hundred years of Mongol rule by the Golden Horde had come to an end, the Byzantine ideal of the *symphonia* between Church and State which cannot exist without each other, was remembered again. The Muscovite princes had already begun to consider themselves as the protectors of Orthodoxy, and when the Metropolitan Isidoros had signed the decree of the Union of Florence (1439) between the Eastern and the Western Church, he was immediately arrested after his return to Moscow. Later, after the fall of Constantinople in 1453, the Orthodox Church, and particularly the Josephite monks, saw in the Muscovite ruler, who began to call himself Tsar, their sole support, and they revived the political theory of Agapetos (6th century), according to whom "the emperor in body is like all others, yet in power of office he is like God." But the study of Byzantine writings, including the Eis-

would, however, be a mistake to believe that the Byzantinians also thought in terms of two powers. When Ostrogorsky (1968, p. 294) translates a passage by Leo Diaconus (101), a Byzantine historian, in the following words: "I acknowledge two powers in this life, the priesthood and the Empire", he commits what might be called a westernism. A better translation, in view of the term ἀρχη—would be: "I acknowledge two principles (or: realms) in this life, the priesthood and the Empire".

agoge, did not preclude a development of the relationship between Church and State, and of the status of the individual, in which the accents must be put differently.

Two different conceptions of monachism and of the Church developed at that time. The already mentioned Joseph of Volokolamsk, founder of the Josephite movement, stressed the necessity of landownership for the Church with the argument that it was needed for charitable causes, furthermore he argued that, if the monks had to work for their living, they would not have the time to acquire the knowledge and experience required to become bishops (the Orthodox Church draws its bishops from the ranks of the monastic clergy), and finally that the socially higher elements of society would not wish to enter monastic life at all. Nil Sorsky, on the other hand, a monk of the hesychastic tradition and with strong ties to Mount Athos, had settled as a hermit in the wilderness of the Upper Volga, envisaging an ideal church, unencumbered by worldly responsibilities, as the moral conscience of the country. He denounced the monasteries for owning land and insisted that only a poor Church can be the moral conscience of the country and will be able to face up to the Tsar. At the same time, the followers of Joseph and Nil were opposed on the question of how to treat heretics in general, and in particular the so-called Judaizing sect which had gained some influence in Novgorod.

Nil's movement of the "Trans-Volga-Elders", who wanted to live hidden from the "world", represented more than others the tradition of outworldly individualism in Russia. When it was repressed with the help of the Muscovite princes (Nil's disciples were persecuted, imprisoned, sometimes killed, and it is suspected that certain of Nil's writings of which only the title is known today, were intentionally destroyed), and when the Josephites gained the upper hand, at least at the official level, this represented a break with an important aspect of the Russian-Orthodox church ideology. After this, outworldly individualism survived only in the northern forest regions of Russia (Kapiton and his followers may serve as examples) and later in certain sects, but its importance was reduced, and the official church ideology gradually integrated the individual into the *koinobion*.

Moreover, on the basis of the prophecy of Daniel, the Josephites developed the theory of Moscow as the Third Rome. The Rome of Peter and the Rome of Constantine (Constantinople) have fallen, the monk Philotheos wrote, but the Third Rome (Moscow), the only pure Christian empire in the world, stands, and a fourth there will not be.

These words could be interpreted as an appeal to the Tsar to accept
the role of sovereign and universal emperor in the Roman tradition
(this view was adopted by the so-called Stoglav, a synod held in 1551),
but also as the appeal to accept the responsibility for the continued
existence of the world (Nitsche 1991:94), for Rome, according to this
theory, was the last of the four empires in Nebuchadnazzar's dream.
In any case, the Tsar was seen as the head of the Church to whom the
clergy owed obedience and who sometimes even superseded canoni-
cal and ritual considerations.

There was no separation and hierarchical ordering of secular and
ecclesiastical jurisdiction, as it had developed during the Papal Revolution in Western Europe. Nothing had changed since Justinian had
declared in Novel 131 that the canons of the Oecumenical Councils
are to be observed as laws of the Empire. The Tsars did not feel
bound by Natural Law and Ecclesiastical Law; they, in fact, sanc-
tioned ecclesiastical legislation, convoked synods, designated hierarchical candidates and sometimes judged clerical personnel and thus
completely dominated the external aspects of the Church. While it is
true that judicial immunities were often granted to 'church people'
and that the inhabitants of ecclesiastical estates were mostly under the
jurisdiction of their clerical superiors, these privileges could also be
revoked by tsarist fiat, as happened in the State Code (Ulozhenie) of
1649. But the Tsar's authority went beyond the purely external
aspects of the Church.

Ivan IV, for instance, insisted that the autocratic Tsar's will is
God's will, and he did not hesitate to order the killing of a metropolitan who, in defense of ecclesiastical law, resisted his wishes. Any
attempt to show that the *sacerdotium* is greater than the *imperium* (as the
case of Maximus the Greek, who denied the religious nature of the
Tsar's autocracy and was incarcerated, shows), was considered heretical. The fact that in 1589 Moscow became the seat of a patriarchate
did not change the situation. Even the so-called Donation of Constantine was evoked by the Russian Church only in support of the
claims to its landed estates and other economic privileges, but never
to point to the superiority of the *sacerdotium*, contrary to the situation
in the West where it had been used to justify the Church's claims of
political superiority.

It is true that during the "Time of Troubles" (*Smuta*), the Church was
the sole element of socio-political cohesion and even fulfilled political
tasks (the Patriarch Job convoked and chaired a *Zemskii Sobor* in order to

determine who could qualify as a ruler), but this was undertaken with the intent of stabilizing the State and not in order to acquire lasting political influence. Not much later, Tsar Alexis did not hesitate to intervene in matters of ecclesiastical discipline and Church ritual (e.g. the *edinoglacie* discussion, relating to "single voice" in chants and liturgy).

While Medlin (1952:146/8) argues that Tsar Alexis may have come closer than any of his predecessors to imaging the ideal prince of East Rome and that Moscow was a direct reflection of the Byzantium of Justinian I, others[12] have suggested that the Byzantine ideal of harmony between Church and State had largely disappeared since Ivan IV and even that Moscovite political ideology was always more influenced by Asiatic despotism than by Roman or Byzantine law. It is clear, in any case, that, contrary to the situation in Byzantium where the Church with the help of outworldly monks became more independent in regard to dogmatic and liturgical questions after the iconoclastic struggle and later after the victory of the hesychastic movement, Russia remained more caesaropapistic. According to Kapterev, the decisive word in both ecclesiastical and secular affairs belonged to the sovereign, particularly after the metropolitan began to be appointed independently from the patriarch in Constantinople. This was mainly the result of the repression of the outworldly individualism of the hesychastic Trans-Volga-Elders by the Josephite movement.

Only the Patriarch Nikon in the seventeenth century, motivated perhaps by the fact that he had been asked to look after the administration of the state in the absence of the Tsar in times of war, tried to establish the superiority of canon law and ecclesiastical law over all civil law; only he tried to attribute to the spiritual authority an ultimate supervision over secular matters when he stated that the bishop has a certain interest in secular jurisdiction for its better direction, while the Tsar has none whatever in ecclesiastical and spiritual administration, and when he added that in certain cases it is in the power of the bishop to issue a censure or excommunication against the Tsar.[13] Nikon's ideas were perhaps influenced by Western thought. But not only were his personal ambitions in the end not supported by the Tsar, but the ecclesiastical council of 1666/67 flatly refuted the political philosophy

---

[12] Benz 1971, p. 147; Pipes, 1974. Kapterev (Vol. 2, p. 104) has even gone so far to state that the Muscovite Church Councils of the 16th and 17th century were simple advisory panels before the sovereign and that the sole source of the law, be it ecclesiastical or civil, was the Tsar.

[13] Palmer 1871, Vol I, p. 251 sqq.

of this Patriarch who, like the Tsar, liked to assume the title of *velikii gosudar'* (great lord of the land). The Byzantino-Russian political tradition resumed immediately after Nikon, although the Tsar at first renewed the clergy's rights and privileges.

But in the West it was the time of Absolutism and of the revocation of the Edict of Nantes (1685) by Louis XIV, and absolutistic ideas now started to penetrate Russia. Peter the Great abolished the patriarchate and the ecclesiastical courts; the newly established Department of Monasteries appropriated to itself the administration of all church properties and an obligatory oath of allegiance of the clergy to the Tsar was introduced[14]. The supreme jurisdiction in ecclesiastical matters (with no clear distinction between the *ius circa sacra* and the *ius in sacra*, in the terminology of Pufendorf whose writings then entered Russia) resided, more than ever before, in the State.

It was a State which did not see its purpose any more in the creation of the conditions for morality and religious salvation, but which saw in the interests of the State itself the ultimate standard for judging all actions; a State in which the Emperor or Tsar was considered to be above the laws (*princeps legibus solutus*) and which was not kept in check by anything resembling the modern tradition of thought which considers the State to be made up of autonomous individuals.

The Raskol and the Russian Sects

Outside of Russia schismatic movements and sects have often been found to have a close affinity to individualism. In Calvinism, for instance, the Church had been dissolved as a holistic institution, as an institute of grace and salvation, and had become a mere instrument of discipline for the individuals of which it considered itself to be composed. Max Weber underlined that disillusioned and pessimistically inclined individualism which, according to him, can be identified in the national characters of the peoples with a Puritan past, and Louis Dumont has analysed the outworldly individualism of the Indian renouncers and their close connection with Indian sectarian movements. Was there a place for individualism and of what kind was that individualism in the schismatic and sectarian movements of Russia?

---

[14] Nikol'skii 1983, p. 220. Such an oath had also existed in Byzantium, at least for the higher levels of the Church hierarchy (Svoronos 1951).

Superficially seen, the Russian Raskol (schism) resulted from the reaction of the uneducated sectors of the population who clung to unimportant or even trivial aspects of the Church ritual, attaching magical forces to them, when the Patriarch Nikon tried to assimilate Russian rituals to those of the Greek tradition. Particularly Protestant interpreters, viewing the essence of religion in dogma rather than ritual, have shown little understanding for the 'superstitious accentuation of trifling points of ritual' by the Old Believers. Kartashov has shown, however, that the Russian-Orthodox people consider the icons as not created by human hands (*nerukotvornyi*) and the Church ritual as sacred, and that through them it is thought possible to attain already in the present, although temporarily, the true life and a glance at salvation. These ideas, moreover, were related to the ideology of the Third Rome which underlined the mission of Moscow to conserve the pure truth of the Orthodox religion, especially at a time which feared the impending arrival of the Antichrist. Nikon's reforms and, soon afterwards, Peter's Absolutism appeared to many to be the result of the arrival of the Antichrist.

Those who decided on a break with the official Church, the Old Believers, faced the difficulty that no bishop had joined the Schism and that therefore no new priests could be ordained. Soon they were deprived of priests and of most sacraments (communion and marriage in particular), except those sacraments which, according to ancient ecclesiastical usage, laymen can perform (baptism and confession), yet they had nothing in common with Protestants who believe that sacraments are '*magis opinione quam re*' (are effective through the opinion of the believers rather than in themselves). Not out of the conviction that the sacraments are useless, did they reject them. On the contrary, they believed them to be necessary, but they thought it impossible to have them because of the lack of priests.[15]

There were those who tried to attract the priests of the 'Nikonian Church' to their cause, the so-called priestists (*popovtsy*), but the group which grew most, the priestless (*bezpopovtsy*), rejected this compromise and all other contacts with the world of Antichrist. The life of layper-

---

[15] The distance of the early Raskol from protestant and especially calvinist individualism is striking in the autobiography of Avvakum, one of its most revered leaders in the seventeenth century, for it always stresses the congruence of the author and his social position in a world which remained, in Weberian terminology, an 'enchanted garden'.

sons in a Church directed by priests was not available to them any more, and out of the whole Christian tradition only the lifestyle of monks, but of "monks without vows", in S.A. Zenkovsky's words (1970:442), remained to them.

Some of them broke all ties with society and lived homelessly as so-called Wanderers (*stranniki* or *beguni*) an outworldly individualism, although they might be supported by members of their group who continued to live in the world but had taken a vow to become Wanderers one day[16].

Most Old Believers, though, cut loose from the holistic ties with the Church and unable to marry, because the sacrament of marriage was unavailable to them, lived the life of "monks without vows" in the world, the life of a certain inworldly individualism perhaps, but of an individualism which was considered to be only the low path to salvation. For it was an individualism accepted by necessity and not by choice or as an ideal, accepted only because of the loss of the holistic Church. Moreover, the Old Believers continued to live within the Russian-Orthodox tradition which, since the Josephite movement, had preferred the Basilian concept of the higher importance of the *koinobion*, of the community, of what was soon to be called the *sobornost'*.

Everywhere the Bezpopovtsy who, by fate and circumstances, found themselves divorced from the traditional Church, adopted the Basilian and Josephite idea that the communal life is the higher road to perfection. The leader of the Pomorcy group of the Bezpopovtsy, A. Denisov, ignored the idea of Moscow as the Third Rome and of the Tsar as the spiritual and autocratic leader of the Church; he introduced the idea of the primacy of the Russian people as the bearer of spiritual authority and, for the first time in Russian literature, used the terms *sobor* and *sobornyj* with the particular connotation of communal organization blessed by God[17]. Like most Russian monasteries, Denisov's Vyg community also applied the principle of common ownership and, according to S. Zenkovsky, became a miniature

---

[16] According to Conybeare (1921), the organization of the Wanderers closely resembled that of the Cathars, for the Elect Cathar cut himself off from the world, while the other adherents continued to live in the world, fed and sheltered the Elect and cherished the hope of being themselves elected one day.

[17] S. Zenkovsky 1957. It is true that Zenkovsky is more interested in the 'democratic' aspect of the social life of the Old Believers, considering that the prevailing majority of the Pomorcy were the "spiritual descendents of the free citizens of the democratic republics of Novgorod and Pskov" (p. 60).

socialist state, based on a collective economy. Also the communal rules of the Theodosians, another priestless group, were similar to those of the monastic rule of Joseph of Volokolamsk. They also lived like monks without vows, had common property, worked for the community, had common prayer halls and common institutions for the invalid and the old.

Because of the loss of the sacrament of marriage various solutions were discussed for those who felt unable to live without a wife. For some, marriage consisted in a simple agreement of the parties, a dissoluble union, others considered marriage part of natural law and independent of any sacrament or rite – certainly an individualistic position – but marriage was nevertheless always considered as an evil to be tolerated, and married couples were not generally accepted as full members of the community and during religious services were given a place behind the congregation (Conybeare 1921:200-205). Clearly, in this case also the individualistic position was the low path to salvation. Individualistic considerations based on the idea of natural law were accepted at an inferior level and were englobed by the ideal of *sobornost'* of the "monks without vows".

While the schismatic movement of the Old Believers insisted on the importance of ritual and liturgy even when some rituals were not available to them, the Russian sects rejected all ritual and all icons as means of salvation.

The Khlysty who tried to achieve an ecstatic vision of God or the Holy Spirit, the so-called *radenie*, at the end of ecstatic dances, and who prepared for it by the total suppression of physical urges and desires (fasting, complete interdiction of sexual relations), were religious and outworldly individuals who, however, hid their outworldly individualism to the 'world' by means of their *disciplina arcani* (the practice to keep the rules of their sect as well as individual religious acts and accomplishments a secret).

The Skoptsy, for whom castration was the basis of the *certitudo salutis*, also followed the *disciplina arcani*, but theirs was an icy individualism without illusions. Castrations were private events, the castrated individual was separated from family life and from the ties of community. The address 'orphan', sometimes used among them, indicated the separation of the individual from traditional holistic society. At the same time, among all Russian sects, their individualism seems to have been the most inworldly, for they tried to get involved in worldly affairs and even proposed a restructuring of the Russian State (Nikol'skii 1983:363).

The Dukhobors, whose ideology may best be studied in their 'Ekaterinoslav Confession' of 1791, believed that the 'people of the world',
craving for pleasures, would fight each other like dogs if there were no
laws and no ritual. Only they themselves, God's people, who had
attained spiritual wisdom, had no need for human laws. On the surface, their view of the world may have been individualistic, similar to
Hobbes' or Kautilya's, but the Dukhobors also taught, following the
philosophy of Skovoroda, that that which is genuine and true, the
essence of every man, as compared to the many empirical beings, is
numerically one in all, and they thus robbed individuality of all meaning beyond the limits of the phenomenal world. Their own life-style
was outworldly, in an utopian community which rejected government
authority and military service.

The Molokans, finally, although they may have been slightly more
adapted to the 'world' than the Dukhobors, nevertheless, in their
principled rejection of worldly authorities and laws and military service, and in their insistence that there is a law of God in the conscience of every man which has got to be obeyed, remained outworldly individuals.

On the whole, it may therefore be said that the Russian schismatics
and sectarians, except perhaps for the severely persecuted Skoptsy
whose numbers, moreover, were very small, were either outworldly
individuals or placed inworldly individualism at a hierarchically lower
level than the englobing *sobornost'*. Modern individualism has not been
produced by them.

Slavophiles and Populists

When the Crimean war broke out in the middle of the nineteenth
century, it was seen by many, in Russia as well as in the West, as the
result of a struggle of two essentially different worlds which opposed
each other not only as political enemies, but as the embodiments of
two disparate spiritual principles or ideologies[18]. There was no unanimity as to whether the hostile and aggressive mood which then

---

[18] This interpretation of the Crimean War as the result of a struggle between two
basically different ideologies has been advanced by von Schelting (1948). In a similar
way, the First World War has been interpreted by Louis Dumont (1991) as a struggle
between the individualistic and cosmopolitan ideology of the French and the holistic
ideology of the Volk in Germany.

resulted in war, originated in Russia or in the West. The Western powers saw themselves in an inescapable struggle against a totally different barbarian world, as the representatives of rights and freedoms against tyranny and slavery, while Russia saw itself as the true and only defender of Orthodoxy against Enlightenment and revolution.

Not only those in nineteenth century Russia who felt that their own culture was threatened by the modern individualist culture of the West, but Westernizers and Slavophiles alike had in common the conviction of a basic ideological and spiritual difference between Russia and Europe, and that the key to understanding Russia must be sought in the Orthodox religion. The Russian minister of culture, Uvarov, had in 1832 formulated the foundations of Russian cultural policy as autocracy, Orthodoxy and *narodnost'*. *Narodnost'*, a term which perhaps was derived from German romantic thought (for it denotes what in German is called Volkstum), suggested, in combination with Orthodoxy, the importance of the social whole. But the Russian cultural policy did not request a complete turning away from Europe, it only condemned any infatuation with the West; only the "so-called European ideas", those which questioned the autocracy of the Tsar and the Orthodox religion, were to be rejected (Schelting 1948:25).

A few years later P. Chaadaev, in his First Philosophical Letter (1836), had found in Byzantino-Russian Orthodoxy an "idée défigurée" of Christianity, he had criticized its caesaro-papism and its passive-contemplative ethics and had proposed the total reeducation of the Russian people in order to imprint on them the same inner predispositions and the same attitude towards life which in the West, according to him, were the result of a long education in the Catholic tradition. But even Chaadaev abhorred the "so-called" Europe, the revolutionary and individualistic Europe of the French Revolution and ideas of a social contract (Schelting 1948:170). He accepted and preconised individualism, but only to the extent that it did not endanger the englobing social whole.

Slavophilism was at least partially a reaction to Chaadaev's Philosophical Letter as well as it was an answer to the encroachments of the culture of the Enlightenment. It rejected all foreign influences and proposed to return to Russia's own sources, to the true Orthodox religion, for only in Russia true Christianity was thought to have been possible because its traditional social organization, the village commune (*obshchina* and *mir*), supposedly had an affinity with the Christian community.

Particularly Khomyakov underlined the importance of the Orthodox religion for understanding Russia. The Orthodox Church,
according to him, emphasizes the primacy of the social whole, and
only in the Church, in brotherly love for others, he suggested, does
the individual human being find his talents. The concept of the
'Church as a whole' did not mean for Khomyakov the total sum of
individual adherents of Orthodoxy. What he called *sobornost'*, denoted
a perfect organic fellowship and togetherness of people united by faith
and love. Incidentally, *sobornost'* was the Church Slavonic translation
of the Greek *ekklesia* (church). It was the home of the person[19] in the
Orthodox sense and the condition of its development – whereas the
individual in the modern sense had no place in it.

Khomyakov's epistemology is particularly interesting. According to
Walicki's interpretation of his writings, possession of truth is not a
function of individual consciousness, but is entrusted to the Church.
Truth is inaccessible to isolated individual thinkers who are condemned to partial knowledge, or to 'rationality', while the organic fellowship of *sobornost'* makes true understanding possible. It should be
mentioned in passing that V. Soloviev later elaborated the idea that
truth and integral religious justice cannot be attained in isolation, but
are given only to the universal Church (Soloviev 1947:70).

In this context, Khomyakov formulated the Slavophile criticism of
the West: Catholicism was to him blind submission to authority, and
Protestantism a picture of lonely individuals in an atomized society,
and he suggested that the sole measure of truth was not the Pope or
the Scriptures, but the extent of harmony that was achieved within
the collective consciousness of the Church. The Western Church,
having accepted a new dogma (the dogma of the *filioque*) without the
consent of the Eastern Church, had undermined the moral conditions
of knowledge and thus had succumbed to 'rationalism'. Rationalism
is here understood as logical knowledge isolated from moral principles, while the attainment of true knowledge was to Khomyakov a
common cognitive effort, illuminated by love.

Kireevsky, another major Slavophile writer, criticized with regard
to the West its ancient Roman heritage, especially the rationalism of
Roman law and jurisprudence[20], and its impact on the Western

---

[19] More on the term *persona* or person can be found in the following chapter.
[20] This as well as other Slavophile insights have later been corroborated by Max
Weber who talked about the rationalism of Roman law and its profound impact on

churches and the bureaucratic State, further the Enlightenment and industrialism, all leading to the 'Social Contract' which, according to him, was not an invention of the Encyclopedists but an ideal towards which all Western societies strive unconsciously. In ancient Russia, however, the basic social unit seemed to him to have been the village commune (*obshchina*) which was founded on the common use of land and governed by the *mir*, a council of elders. There was no social contract but solidarity and faith; in fact, all holy Russia was one great *mir*[21], while in the West, he thought, private and social life are based on the concept of an individual and separate independence that presupposes the isolation of the individual.

Kireevsky opposed the Western trend towards formalization and the universality of knowledge, the democratic demand that truth should be the same for everyone[22], and he spoke of truths which are recognized only by concrete collective bodies. Moreover, he maintained that not all individuals possess the capacity for true understanding to the same degree. Kireevsky's epistemological elitism, – to use Walicki's words – placed at the apex of the spiritual hierarchy those who were illuminated by a superior light and an unusually strong faith. Such people, he wrote, owe their 'integral personality' (*tsel'naya lichnost'*) and their integral reason – a harmonious unity of all psychic powers –, as opposed to logical reason which is shared by every man, regardless of his moral worth, to the organic ties binding them to the community and the Church or to a supra-individual consciousness. They are not isolated individuals who, because of a one-sided accent on rationalism, suffer from a disintegration of the psyche and of social bonds. Kireevsky formulated these ideas in conformity with the Orthodox tradition in which rational deductive methods,

---

European history, e.g. the Western Churches and the bureaucratic State (*Economy and Society*, p. 828). On the other hand, there was indeed a relative lack of legal rationalism in the Orthodox tradition, for instance in the Church's approach to sin. Sinful acts were considered as manifestations of man's internal disease which can only be overcome by *theosis* (deification), while in the West Anselm taught that actual sins may be expiated by temporal punishment and that Redemption can be explained in terms of a legal transaction which leads to justification.

[21] Kireevsky Vol. I, p. 192; Obshchina, in the technical sense, refers to the village commune as an economic unit, whereas mir refers to the social and judiciary aspect. In nontechnical literature, the two terms tend to be used interchangeably.

[22] Mannheim (1936) has shown that the democratic cosmopolitanism of the capitalistic bourgeoisie was closely connected to the demand that truths should be the same for everyone and universally valid. In traditional societies it is often assumed that there are different levels of truth.

although they were not completely eliminated, have always represented the lowest and the least reliable level of theology[23]. Since Byzantian times, it was mystical *theoria* (contemplation) – which does not imply emotional individualism but rather a continuous communion with the Spirit that dwells in the whole Church – by which one attained the highest truth (Meyendorff 1975:9 sqq.).

Walicki (1963 : 9) has suggested that the Slavophile antithesis of Russia and Europe, of *narod* (people, *Volk*) and society, of integral personality and isolated individual corresponds exactly to Toennies' distinction between *Gemeinschaft* and *Gesellschaft*, perhaps because of the deep influence which German romanticism exercised both on the Slavophiles and on Tönnies. The very problem of the antithesis, however, as Walicki also acknowledges, is older. It does not, however, lie in the question of whether *Gemeinschaft* should be taken as an historical ideal-type, based on the patriarchal family, or rather in an anhistorical way; it must rather be seen in the fact that *Gemeinschaft* and *Gesellschaft*, holism and individualism, can exist in the same society, although, as has been shown in the previous pages, they will then exist at different levels, one of the two being superior to or englobing the other. The Slavophiles themselves, in their perhaps excessive or one-sided insistence on the *sobornost'*, neglected this fact.

The populist movement (*narodnichestvo*) did not distinguish itself from the Slavophiles by new ideas on the historical differences between Russia and the West but rather by ideas on the future development of Russia (they advocated that Russia could by-pass the capitalist stage of development and idealized the self-sufficient peasant economy). Their most influential theorist, Mikhailovsky, rejected the division of labour and maintained that in tribal society, based on simple co-operation, man lives a primitive but full life, developing an integral personality (*tselostnaya lichnost'*), while the division of labour and social differentiation destroy the integral personality and turn men into specialized monofunctional organs of a larger whole. Individual progress and social evolution are therefore mutually exclusive;

---

[23] Besançon (1977) has, like others, insisted on the fact that the Slavophiles borrowed all their major ideas from Western Europe, and particularly from the German romantics, rather than from the Greek Fathers, as Kireevsky had stated. This observation is, however, much less surprising, if one keeps in mind the similarity in the historical circumstances, for the German romantics, like the Slavophiles in Russia after them, represented the reaction of a basically holistic society (Dumont 1991) to Western individualism.

in fact, "progress is the gradual approach to the integral individual (*k tselostnosti nedelimykh*), the fullest possible and the most diversified division of labour among man's organs and the least possible division of labour among men" (Mikhailovsky 1896, Vol. I, p. 150).

It is true that Mikhailovsky also talked of a struggle for 'individuality' and that the simple social organization without impersonal mechanisms was to him simply a means to achieve more individuality, but Mikhailovsky's struggle for individuality had but little in common with modern individualism. While an individualistic aspect cannot be denied, as Mikhailovsky never abandoned the ideals of intellectual and moral autonomy and of the rational choice of common values, he stressed evoking Durkheim's mechanical solidarity, factual mutual independence and, at the same time, a "longing to be drowned in the mass of the people", and a perception of oneness with the folk, the peasants, in the sense of *sobornost'*. This is quite different and, in fact, opposite to the modern situation where each person is very dependent on the material level, but where the ideology makes us believe that we are autonomous individuals. Mikhailovsky's model has sometimes been called a hybrid (Walicki 1979:263) because he idealized a precapitalist communal economy and at the same time insisted on the value of the human individual. However, this common interpretation neglects Mikhailovsky's distinction between the level of social development and the type of social development, his suggestion that Western society and its individualism have attained a higher level than Russia's, but that Russia's 'integral personality' in the peasant commune is of a higher type. It is perhaps possible to say that Mikhailovsky tried to place individualistic and holistic ideas within a hierarchical order.

Mikhailovsky's remarks on the uniqueness of the Russian word *pravda* – truth and justice designated by the same word – are revealing about the tension between individualism and holism in his own mind and in the Russia of his time. "I could never believe, he said, that it is forbidden to find a point of view in which *pravda* as truth (*pravda – istina*) and *pravda* as justice (*pravda – spravedlivost'*) could not go hand in hand, one enriching the other" (Billington 1958:34). Mikhailovsky is here trying to keep together what in the modern individualistic world has fallen apart. In 'Science as a Vocation' Max Weber reminded us that something can be sacred in so far as it is not beautiful (as in the fifty-third chapter of the book of Isaiah), and beautiful in so far as it is not good, as in Baudelaire's *Fleurs du Mal*; that it is in fact a common-

place today that something can be true although it is not beautiful
and not holy and not good. While Socrates may have believed in the
unity of knowledge and virtue or that true knowledge is the source of
morality, modern man separates the True and the Good, science and
morals, what is and what ought to be, judgements of fact and judgements of value, and he can do so only because he stresses the
supremacy of the individual as a value, and because he finds morality,
as Dumont says, exclusively within the individual's conscience instead
of finding the Good within society as a whole. Mikhailovsky, in any
case, was unwilling to accept this modern view.

The intellectual history of Russia in the nineteenth century may be
described as a clash of its holistic cultural identity with the Western
individualistic configuration[24] and the almost desperate attempt to
integrate the value of the individual which could not be completely
denied, into the holistic view. The result among Slavophiles and Populists was a sometimes excessive holism, but also the concept of the
"integral personality" which admitted aspects of Western individualism at a subordinate level.

It should at least be mentioned in passing that in the Russian literature of the same period both L. Tolstoy and Dostoyevsky condemned
Western individualism and called for humility in the face of "the peoples' truth" (Karataev in Tolstoy's *War and Peace* and the critique of
the Russian "wanderers" in Dostoyevsky's *Address on Pushkin*), and
Tolstoy taught that the division of labour in society should be
replaced with the principle of the division of each individual's daily
work into different 'harnesses': each man should occupy himself, successively, with all kinds of labour, thus exercising all his capacities.
The 'integral personality' comes to mind.

More Recent Social Upheavals

It has been shown that the Eastern Orthodox tradition never produced the idea of inalienable rights of the individual as part of a system of natural law or as the foundation of a contractual concept of
the state; it rather was a tradition of holism, of the *koinobion*, of

---

[24] The term individualistic configuration includes not only individualism but also
its concomitants, as, for instance, liberty, equality, the separation of values and facts
and the separation of knowledge into different disciplines.

sobornost, of the *obshchina*, of a relatively outworldly individualism, of an individualism which was considered as the lower path to salvation, and, finally, of the integral personality. Although, after this short survey of the history of the place and the kind of individualism in the Eastern Orthodox tradition one is perhaps reminded of Ranke's suggestion that not states, but cultural and religious traditions may be conceived of as "thoughts of God" which outlast all political revolutions, the process of acculturation to the Western individualistic configuration became inevitable in the nineteenth century.

Marxism, which had made inroads in Russia almost solely among the deracinated intelligentsia and the proletariate of the cities, was of course a completely Western system of ideas, with sources in the Enlightenment and in the individualistic tradition. From its economic perspective, it did not proclaim collective ends apart from the ends of the individuals, as L. Dumont (1977) has shown.

Lenin[25] embraced Marxism, but adapted it to an idea which had captivated the minds of the Russian intelligentsia since Chaadaev and Herzen and which more recently has been called the theorem of the privilege of backwardness, namely that it is possible for a backward culture to avoid the mistakes of other or more advanced cultures and to preserve earlier forms of social life which contain the germ of a future synthesis. Thus he led Russia directly from tsarism to socialism, trying to repress the individualism which had infiltrated into the country, by the principle of partiinost' (party-mindedness) and thus imposing an artificial holism: a totalitarian regime and a totalitarian bureaucracy (Davydov 1995:163).

---

[25] Alain Besançon (1977) has compared the ideology which dominated Russia during most of the twentieth century to the gnosticism of the beginnings of the Christian era. According to gnostic teaching, only *gnosis*, the true knowledge about the destiny of the cosmos and of the self, can end man's state of ignorance, only *gnosis* can tell man what is right and wrong in the cosmic plan and free the pneumatic self from the bonds of the world, in order to contribute to the *apokatastasis* which will come at the end of times.

Gnostic structures of thought have indeed never been absent in Russia. The Chlysty, the Dukhobors and some Old Believers probably were connected with the Bogomils, a neo-Manichaean movement which flourished in the Balkans and ultimately had gnostic origins. But what characterized gnosticism was the idea that the innermost or pneumatic man is not of this world, that he wishes the release from the bonds of the world and to return to his native realm of light. Lenin's "new man", however, described by Besançon as an image of Rakhmetov, the hero of a novel by Chernyshevsky, far from resembling the pneumatic man of the Gnostics, wanted to act within the world and to reconstruct it artificially by technical and political means.

The process of adaptation of the Russian Orthodox tradition to the Western individualistic configuration continues until today, but it is an acculturation, a complicated process which combines the traditional and the modern, and not a simple replacement of the old by the new. In this context it is perhaps useful to remember that the inworldly individualism of the newly proclaimed capitalism in Russia, while it may be accepted on the level of facts, has no basis in the Eastern Orthodox traditional ideology, except at an inferior level.

But before we can finally turn to the process of the acculturation of the Russian tradition to the West, it will be helpful to analyse the development of Western individualism or of modernity in the Occident itself in order to show more clearly what characterizes it.

CHAPTER SIX

THE OCCIDENT'S SEPARATION FROM THE ORIENT, ITS UNIQUE PATH OF DEVELOPMENT

Introduction

In the previous chapter, many references have been made to the concept of Western individualism. It is now possible to turn the mirror around and, with the help of what we have learnt about the place of individualism in traditional culture, to study the historical evolution of this new kind of individualism in its own right and its own context.

The concepts of the individual and of the person, and also of individualism, individuality and personality, which are so often at the centre of discussions about modern life and society, are frequently used indistinctly and with a certain lack of clarity and precision. The fate of many discussions in which these concepts occur in all their vagueness and imprecision, sometimes even interchangeably, tends to give rise to a feeling of apprehension.

Already in the first version of his study on the Protestant Ethic, Max Weber (1905, vol. 20, p. 12) noted that the expression "individualism" combines the most heterogeneous ideas imaginable. Jakob Burckhardt's brilliant ideas, he pointed out, are today at least partly out of date, and a thorough analysis of the concept in historical terms would be highly valuable to science. Although Weber repeated this opinion in the final version of "The Protestant Ethic and the Spirit of Capitalism" (PE) fifteen years later, he never undertook such an analysis. The difficulty of having to deal with the different meanings of the term individualism has also been referred to by Troeltsch (1960, vol. II, p. 744), although this did not prevent him from using it frequently.

It has been mentioned earlier that much more recently, and clearly on the shoulders of Durkheim's earlier article on individualism, Louis Dumont has rejected the nominalistic and empiricist scientific outlook of those for whom individuals and individualism exist everywhere, in all cultures and at all times. He opposed those who fail to distinguish analytically between the empirical human being, the individual sample of mankind found in all cultures and societies, and the independent and autonomous individual to whom a paramount value is attached in modern society because of its individualistic ideology. Thus, Dumont has distinguished two kinds of societies: Whereever the individual is autonomous and is the paramount value, as in modern society, he spoke of individualism; whereas in the opposite, traditional case, where society as a whole is the paramount value, englobing the empirical individuals or particular human beings, he spoke of holism.

Dumont's theory of the origins of modern individualism needs to be recapitulated here (Dumont 1982). These origins need to be explained, he believed, because from a traditional point of view, it is difficult to understand how the individual, rather than society as a whole, can become the bearer and embodiment of ultimate values, and, correlatively, how society came to be thought of as merely a collection of such individuals. In this search for the origins of modern individualism, he suggested that one should follow Max Weber's example – he could have added Troeltsch's name – and attach prominence to religion. With this in mind Dumont advanced this thesis: while in the Axial Age civilisations and in early Christianity the individual as value was conceived of as being apart from the given social and political organisation, among religious renouncers outside and beyond the holistic society, a transformation towards inworldly individualism gradually started to take place as the Church developed, from the eighth century, a new conception of its relationship to the State, or the "world". The representatives of the Church, being outworldly bearers of value, now claimed power in the world and thereby entered it. The final stage of this transformation came with Calvin, who suggested that the task of the individual was to work for God's glory in the world rather than to take refuge from it.

Dumont's main argument that modern individualism could emerge from traditional holistic society only as a transformation of the 'outworldly' individualism of the religious renouncer must remain a major reference point and guideline for any attempt to understand the evolution of Western individualism and modernity.[1] This chapter, while accepting the fact of this transformation as well as its rootedness

---

[1] Some anthropologists would claim that there was and is individualism, even extreme individualism, in primitive tribal societies and that therefore the whole question must be restated. But the individualism of primitive societies seems to exist on the level of factual behaviour or self-sufficiency rather than on the level of ideology or representations.

in religion, will attempt to reinterpret the way in which it took place. In the process of weaving nuances and modifications into Dumont's account, both by moving the point of origin of the unique occidental path of development backwards and by extending it further into the present, it reveals not only that it is necessary to distinguish, as Dumont did, between the empirical human being and the autonomous individual, be it inworldly or outworldly, but that the concepts of person, personality, and individuality, seen in the social and religious context which first shaped them, also play a definite role in the understanding of the transformation from traditional society to modernity.

When we refer to the 'Occident' as opposed to the 'Orient', we tend to attach to this contrast two different meanings. On the one hand, we sometimes oppose the Judeo-Christian tradition to Asian religions and cultural traditions, such as Islamic, Hindu, Buddhist or Confucian; on the other hand, we also refer to the Western European religious and cultural tradition which has been separated from the Eastern Orthodox tradition since the schism of 1054. As we will see, the special historical path of the Occident, its *Sonderweg*, has both these meanings for its first stage was characterised by a particularly Christian concept of the human being – the concept of the *persona* – in contrast to the concepts of the other major traditions, whereas the second stage was perhaps a *Sonderweg* within the *Sonderweg*, the Western European reinterpretation and transformation of the concept of the individual, a path which separated Western Europe from the Christian tradition surviving in Russia and elsewhere, and which provided the basis for its development towards modernity.

The Axial Age

During what Karl Jaspers called the Axial Age, c. 800-200 B.C.E., when Confucius, the Buddha, Heraclitus and the Israelite prophets were contemporaries, thoughts and ideas emerged which became important for the whole of humanity. Mythical thought and magical practices were relegated to the past or at least rejected by those who were about to become the new religious and intellectual elite within their societies. The monistic worldview of the archaic religions, in which social order was harmoniously grounded in a divine cosmic order and in which there was little tension between religious demand

and social conformity, was replaced by a dualistic worldview, characterised by a basic tension between the transcendental and the worldly
orders, between religious and intellectual demands and the empirical
cosmos (Eisenstadt 1986:3 sqq.).

Max Weber has shown that there existed only two consistent conceptions of a divine and transcendental order : the idea of an impersonal and uncreated order and the idea of a personal creator god ; he
has also shown that there have been only three coherent resolutions
of the tension between the worldly and the transcendental orders : the
theodicies of karma in India, of Zoroastrian dualism, and of Calvinist
predestination. But, whatever these conceptions and theodicies, the
chasm between the transcendental and the worldly orders can be
characterised by the development of three phenomena which have
had continuing importance in the context of the development of individualism.

First, the political and the religious domain started to drift apart on
the ideological as well as on the institutional level. Rarely was it possible any more since the Axial Age for a divine king to monopolise religious leadership without being challenged: the rift between the Confucian scholar and the Chinese ruler, between the Israelite prophet
and the king, between the brahmin and the ksatriya in India, and
between the traditional *polis* and the philosopher in Greece made this
impossible. There was now a conception of the accountability of
rulers to a higher order or even to the community and its laws.

Second, based on the precepts of a higher metaphysical order,
there was the gradual emergence of religious ethics out of a world of
magic. The formation of the human personality was taken beyond the
needs of daily activities towards considerations connected with 'salvation' as Max Weber called it. While in pre-Axial Age civilisations no
differentiation had been made between success orientation and value
orientation, or between technical and normative rules, there now
appeared ethical concepts which could be contraposed to magical
techniques. Such normative ethics were sometimes disconnected and
fragmented, although not in ancient India and Israel, and their survival generally depended on external guarantees like disapproval or
punishment (Schluchter 1996:69 sqq.).

But by no means, as Weber (ES:438) stressed, did all these ethics
complete the shift from magical ethics and achieve a total systemati-
zation of ethical concepts, leading to a conduct of life based entirely
on inner motivation. While the opposition between the transcenden-

tal order and the world certainly existed in all Axial Age civilisations, an opposition between an ethical God and sin did not develop everywhere; moreover, Confucianism, as well as the religions of Greece and Rome lacked, among other things, the phenomenon of prophecy which generally produces an inner systematisation and rationalisation of ethics by commanding that an individual's entire conduct of life be oriented to the pursuit of a single sacred value rather than to the pursuit of disconnected single norms or various worldly goods; in India, prophecy was not absent, but it was of the exemplary rather than of the ethical kind. In all these cultures, therefore, the ethics remained of the ritualistic or of the legal-ethical kind which generally has a stereotyping effect on the conduct of life as ceremonial, legal, and ethical norms are not clearly distinguished.

Third, in some Axial Age civilisations the realisation developed that within the 'world', i.e., within holistic society, the tension between the transcendental and the worldly order cannot be overcome satisfactorily. This prompted some men to leave the 'world' and thus led to the institution of outworldly individualism. In India, for instance, for more than two millennia, society has been characterised by two complementary features : the tight interdependence, based on hierarchical relationships, of the caste system, and the institution of world-renunciation for those who choose it.[2] The renouncer (*samnyasin*) who seeks ultimate truth and salvation, forgoes society and his role in social life and devotes himself, as a hermit or with a group of fellow-renouncers who may advocate a particular discipline of liberation, to his own progress in the liberation from the fetters of life in this world. Certainly, to leave society does not involve ceasing to have any relationship with its members (e.g. living from alms, teaching), but it involves renouncing the role given by society in one's family and one's caste, and it also involves a relativisation of life in the world and of worldly ethics. As distancing from the social world is generally a precondition for entering the path of salvation in India, sects of renouncers never tried to change the world or to initiate revolutions. The Indian renouncer is self-sufficient, concerned only with himself, and in several ways he is similar to the modern individual, except for one basic difference : the modern individual lives within the "world", i.e. within society, whereas the *samnyasin* lives outside it. The *samnyasin*

---

[2] This account of the outworldly individual is largely based on L. Dumont (1966).

may therefore be called an individual-outside-the-world, an outworldly individual, in contrast to the inworldly individual of the modern world. In the Aggañña Suttanta of the Buddhist pali canon, a story is found of a kind of contract among these outworldly individuals,
similar to modern theories in which society is not seen as a whole, but
as composed of autonomous individuals who conclude a contract
among themselves. If it seems surprising that the *samnyasin* is called an
individual although his aim is to rid himself of self in one way or
another – the Buddhist concept of *anatta* comes to mind –, we should
remind ourselves that it is precisely this endeavour which gives his self
a reality and makes him an individual, albeit an outworldly one.

The purpose of the following pages is to describe the transformation from the outworldly individualism found in Axial Age civilisations to our modern inworldly individualism, to emphasize the religious roots of this transformation, and to see how it was related to
changes in the other two characteristic aspects of the Axial Age: the
relationship between the religious and the political domain, and the
emergence of religious ethics, i.e., of the idea of a personality.

Individualism in Antiquity

At first glance, the situation in Greece was rather different from that
in India.[3] There was the self-sufficient city state, the *polis*, and the presumption that a good life implies participation in it. In Pericles' funer-
al oration, according to Thucydides, the individual derived value and
gratification from fully participating in the *polis* which he thought to
be greater than he himself; outside it and without submission to its
laws, Socrates could not imagine human life worth living, and Aristotle[4] remarked that the whole must be prior to the parts, that the *polis* is
both natural and prior to the individual, and that the man who can
live without the *polis* is either a beast or a god. Glaucon's suggestion in
Plato's *Republic* that the *polis* is the result of a kind of social contract
among egoistic individuals, although it foreshadowed future developments, did not conform to the prevailing holistic ideology. Nor can

---

[3] The individualism of the prophets in ancient Israel, described by Gunkel as
"exemplary individualism" under the heading "Individualismus und Sozialismus im
AT" in: *Religion in Geschichte und Gegenwart*, Vol. III, Tübingen 1912, column 493-501,
will be left aside here.
[4] *Politica* 1253 a.

individuality as an ideal be discerned in classical Greece. When Socrates talked of the psyche on his deathbed, he meant an impersonal entity, the psyche within him, rather than his own psyche, to which the lower passions and pleasures are to be submitted by means of *paideia* and *askesis* (Vernant 1989:228 sq.). This was possible only by submission to a universal conception of reason and by truthfulness to a typical model[5], not to individual concerns.

During the twilight of the *polis* after the Peloponnesian War, however, and later when Alexander had established his world empire, the ideal of the sage who defines himself in opposition to worldly life, became accepted in the teaching of the Epicureans, the Cynics and, to some extent, of the Stoics. Their philosophy of renunciation and of escape, as Sabine (1963:137) has called it, fostered the development of the ideal of outworldly individualism. Epicurus started from the atomistic assumption that individuals first exist by and for themselves and then enter voluntarily and with design into societal relationships, and Diogenes went so far as to proclaim homelessness as a pleasure and to call himself απολις (without a polis). Clearly, a chasm had opened up between the holistic concept of the *polis* and that of the self-sufficient outworldly individual[6].

The Stoics' particular kind of outworldliness, perhaps best described as a relative outworldliness, allowed them to accommodate themselves to a large extent to life within society. According to their teaching, participation in social life is prescribed by nature; the wise man may not need the state, but the Roman Stoics often assumed heavy duties in the world, for they saw virtue in such involvement, particularly if it was combined with indifference to the solicitations of pleasure. Self-sufficiency, formerly attributed to the *polis*, now became an attribute of the individual sage who, while fulfilling social duties,

---

[5] Daraki, 1981, p. 99. Greek identity was always a model to be attained. The title of άνθρωπος was given, as Daraki writes, only to those who submitted themselves to the norms of society.

[6] To argue that no (outworldly) individualism existed in hellenistic times because the individuals joined new subcultures where membership was conferred by invitation or instruction (L. Martin 1994), results from a misunderstanding of the sociological concept of individualism which certainly does not exclude the possibility of individuals joining groups.

In fact, it was in the more atomistic society of late Antiquity, among Christians and others, that the relationship with the sacred, with the gods, was no longer achieved by society as a whole, but by exceptional individuals – ascetics, anchorites, "friends of God" – as Brown (1978) has argued.

nevertheless must remain detached and in inner isolation; one might feign sympathy, but must take care not to feel it (Bevan 1913:67 sqq.). The Stoics did not renounce possessions, but their guiding principle was to be without attachment to them: to have as if they did not have.[7] To have done the right thing, to have acted according to an inner conviction and the demands of reason was preferable to external success, as can be gleaned from Lucan's dictum : *Victrix causa diis placuit, sed victa Catoni* (The winning cause pleased the gods, but the lost cause pleased Cato – *De bello civili* 1, 128).

This apparent partial accommodation to social roles within society must receive a new interpretation perhaps from the time of Seneca on when, under the emperors, there was little room for political involvement. Cicero had still thought that political service to the *polis* or the state was the crown of human activity, but there now appeared the idea of a divided allegiance in which another loyalty might compete with the claims of the state. This divided allegiance resulted from the doctrine that every man is a member of two communities, the civil state to which one belongs and the *cosmopolis* of all rational beings. Seneca also thought that the sage, although he may not have a political role, can still render service within the *cosmopolis* of humanity by virtue of contacts with fellow men or even through contemplation alone.

The Stoics distinguished between relative ethical actions (*kathekonta*), conformity to duty, fulfilled externally by the average man, and absolute ethical actions (*katorthomata*), the fulfilment of the demands of reason solely from the intention to do the Good. Perhaps, because of these high ethical demands, Windelband (1893:168 sqq.) has suggested that for the Stoics the idea of personality, a rationally guided consistency in the conduct of life, became a determining principle. Living according to Nature (in the sense of Reason, λογος) and in opposition to his sensuous inclinations was a duty which the wise man had to fulfill. The Reason referred to was not individual reason which modern man regards as a human construct, but Reason as a transcendent

---

[7] One is reminded of the *Bhagavadgita*, the Indian paradigm of world-renunciation accommodated to the world, where the hero, Arjuna, receives as an answer to his question whether one is allowed to give oneself up to the pragmatics of violence and of inworldly action that one can, if one fulfills one's worldly duties with inner distance, a distance provided by knowledge. It is not necessary to leave the world physically, one can leave it mentally, remain inwardly detached and without wish for the fruits of one's endeavour.

order, as the ultimate principle of the universe to which human beings subordinate themselves. W. Cantwell Smith (1984:270 sq.) has interpreted man's participation in this ultimate principle, insofar as his ideas are true and his behaviour is rational, as characteristic of the Greek *religious* tradition, as that in which the Greeks (and later, the Roman Stoics) had faith. If one accepts this interpretation, it is possible to suggest that it was the Greek religious tradition which brought about the relative outworldliness of the Stoics and the beginnings of the idea of personality. This tradition was all-pervading in Hellenistic times and under the influence of Rome; it can be found even in the attitude of Philo of Alexandria, a Jew who preferred his early monkish isolation to the political service into which he was forced.

While the teachings of the Stoa had to a large extent permeated the *weltanschauung*/religion of the upper classes of the Roman Empire since Cicero, Christianity, which had an equally ambiguous attitude towards outworldly individualism and developed similar ideas of a divided allegiance of the individual was, at least in its early stages, restricted to the lower classes. It was within Christianity, however, that a new concept, that of the person, would give more prominence to these ideas.

Imperium and Sacerdotium in Early Christianity

The earliest Christians had doubtlessly been outworldly individuals, similar to the Essenes. While some lived as anchorites according to the ideal of Athanasius' *Vita Antonii*, others internalised all their efforts and gave to biblical and social events the tropological interpretation which Origen used in his exegesis.[8] After Constantin's turn to Christianity, however, the Christians were looking for integration into the empire, and their relationship with society needed to be reevaluated, – and here the old concept of divine kingship of the Hellenistic tradition conflicted with the new situation. It would be inappropriate in this context to refer to the relationship between church and state, because on the one hand, the early *ekklesia* cannot be identified with

---

[8] Origen's "tropological" exegesis interprets biblical events as if they happened in the internal life of the Christian (e.g. the trumpets at the fall of Jericho represent the joy of the individual Christian whenever he receives Jesus within the city of his soul – *vide* Caspary 1979).

the later bureaucratically organised office church (Schluchter 1988:226) and, on the other hand, because the empire considered itself as a universal political and social structure which englobed religious life as far as possible.

The attempts at integration were perhaps facilitated by the idea, inherited by the Church Fathers from the Stoics, of a relative natural law, as opposed to the absolute natural law. According to this idea, more prevalent in the West through the Roman Stoa (Cicero, Seneca) than in the Orient[9], political subordination and even slavery had to be accepted after the Fall as facts of life and served as *poena et remedium peccati* (punishment for and aid against sin).

In Constantinople, Eusebius developed a political theology, in the West sometimes criticized as "caesaropapistic", which saw the Christian emperor as God's representative on Earth and "as if" he were a bishop[10]; the emperor was the principal architect and the guarantor of the unity of the *ekklesia*, he convoked the Church Councils, proclaimed the canons, and set the borders of ecclesiastical provinces, so that even in the fourteenth century, at the very end of the Byzantine empire, the patriarch of Constantinople could write to the Grand Prince Basil of Moscow arguing that it was not possible for Christians to have the Church and not to have the emperor, that the emperor had an important function within the Church, and that he could not be assimilated to local sovereigns (Dagron 1996:322). And yet, in spite of the seemingly all-englobing position of the emperor, the *sacerdotium* alone was responsible for nominating bishops and for defining the *credo*, and it jealously defended its autonomy in this regard. There remained a structural duality, a logical opposition between two principles, clearly discernible in words the Byzantine historian Leo Diaconus attributed to the emperor John Tzimisces : "I acknowledge two principles (αρχαι) in this world, the priesthood and the *imperium*, one of which is responsible for the souls and the other for the bodies" (Niebuhr 1828:101 sq.).

The relationship between the two principles (which must not be confused with the relationship between the two powers – the ecclesi-

---

[9] See: 'Das christliche Naturrecht im Orient und im Occident' in Troeltsch 1925, p. 724 sqq.

[10] This is, according to Dagron 1996, p. 146/7, the rhetoric of the "as if" : the Christian emperor is an *episkopos* in a metaphorical sense, and particularly he is ἐπισκοπος των ἐκτος (the translation of this expression is uncertain, as the Greek article των may be masculine or neuter).

astical and the royal – in the sense which later developed in the Occident) was described as a *symphonia* by Justinian, and, a few centuries later in the *Eisagoge*, the patriarch Photios interpreted this relationship as similar to that between matter and form or body and soul. But it must be added that it was not possible to completely integrate the outworldly Christian individual with the socio-political whole, for, on the one hand, the orthodox tradition required that only outworldly monks be appointed as bishops and, on the other hand, orthodox religiosity itself, characterised in comparison with the West by its more mystical tendencies[11], fostered a certain relative outworldliness. Max Weber wrote that the activity of the contemplative mystic within the world is characterised by a distinctive 'brokenness', as he resigns himself to the orders of the world but also constantly strives to escape from this activity to the quietness and inwardness of his god (ES:543).

In the western part of the empire, following the capture of Rome by the Visigoths in 410, an answer needed to be found for the old reproach that the dissolution and inner self-destruction of the *civitas Romana* was due to Rome's acceptance of Christianity. The challenge was taken up by Augustine who, according to Ernst Troeltsch (1915), intended to provide what he thought was the sole possible synthesis of antique culture and Christianity, and who in *De Civitate Dei* refuted every argument which treated Christianity as a threat to the survival of the State by insisting that Christians did attach a relative value to most of traditional Roman culture and institutions (Troeltsch 1915:95). These Roman values could be embraced in humility and self-renunciation as part of an attitude related to the *civitas Dei*, but they should not be enjoyed with pride and independently from God, or with an attitude related to the *civitas terrena*, according to the formula *"uti non frui bonis terrenis, frui non uti Deo"* (To use but not to enjoy earthly goods; to enjoy but not to use God).

It is apparent that *civitas Dei* and *civitas terrena* cannot simply be identified with Church and State respectively, as long as the term

---

[11] Max Weber opposed the mysticism of Orthodox Christianity to the asceticism of western Christianity; he referred to the secret belief among orthodox Christians that our social, political and family life in this world is meaningless against the 'acosmistic' background of absolute love which provides the door to the timeless and divine (Weber's comments on Troeltsch's conference on 'Das stoisch-christliche Naturrecht' in : *Gesammelte Aufsätze zur Soziologie und Sozialpolitik*, Tübingen 1924, p. 467). It is possible to mention as an example of such mysticism the hesychastic tradition within Orthodoxy, its methodical contemplation and visions of divine light.

Church implies ecclesiastical hierarchy and priesthood, but that they are of a different order. Augustine did accept the relative ideal of a state in which the emperor and the bureaucracy had been influenced by Christian ideas, and he even approved of its intervention against heretics.

But while, according to Augustine, both *civitates* are inextricably intermingled within the world so that the true Christian, whether priest or layman, lives in both "cities", there is no alliance or complementarity between them; and, while a Christian life in the world, i.e., within the social life of the *civitas Romana*, may be theoretically possible, it generally fails because of temptations and resistance. Therefore, for Augustine the true manifestation of the *civitas Dei* remains the monastery[12], the realm of the outworldly individual, the depoliticised *vita contemplativa*, as in the later Stoa. Troeltsch (1915:157) believed that, in the last analysis, Augustine was unable to bring together antique culture and Christianity, and that there remained in his ethics an inner "brokenness" (*Gebrochenheit*) or mixed attitude, the attitude of an outworldly individual who takes a very hesitant half-step into the world.[13]

The theory of Pope Gelasius (492-496) was built on Augustine's work, but went a step further. While it is often thought to contain no more than a simple juxtaposition of priestly authority (*auctoritas*) and royal power (*potestas*), Louis Dumont (1983:52) has offered a more complete hierarchical interpretation. According to it, religious leaders must submit to the imperial power in inferior, worldly matters, whereas the imperial power is submitted to the religious authority in superior, spiritual matters. Thus, priests are superior, for they are inferior only at an inferior level. In more general terms, that which, at a higher level, is considered superior, may become inferior at an infe-

---

[12] This is true at least for Augustine himself, as he returns again and again to this subject. See also Troeltsch 1915, p. 136 & 153.

[13] According to Troeltsch (1915), Augustine's *magnum opus* really represents the terminal point and the completion of Christian Antiquity and not, as has often been assumed, the beginning of the Middle Ages. Since that time, however, it has been used as a quarry in order to support the most different insights and sociological constructions. Louis Dumont, with good reasons, finds in it a subtle advance of individualism, but, as Troeltsch has shown, there is in Augustine not only the abstract individualism of the absolute natural law and the religious individualism of the elect, but also the supra-individual value of the community in the context of the relative natural law and the supra-individual concept of the Church – a most varied array of concepts.

rior level. These two different levels of consideration are often confused, for the modern mind is not used to such an hierarchical view. There is, as Dumont has also noted, a close resemblance between Gelasius' formula and the ancient Indian situation in which priests (*brahmins*) regarded themselves as religiously superior to the political representatives (*ksatriyas*) yet materially subject to them. Given the vast differences in the respective backgrounds of Gelasius' formula and the brahmanic teachings in India, Dumont was even led to talk of the logical formula of the relationship between the two functions. If one assumes that Gelasius tried to formulate a coherent distinction by assigning two key words of terminological precision, *auctoritas* and *potestas*[14], to the two respective principles, one has here a coherent hierarchical configuration in which the higher principle englobes the lower principle while neither of them loses its identity, its superiority in its own domain, and its inner logic (*Eigengesetzlichkeit*).

On the whole, it would be anachronistic to describe the relationship between the *sacerdotium* and the *imperium* in the early centuries of the christianised Roman Empire as a struggle between two "powers" which somehow needed to find their equilibrium. Rather, two categories or principles (αρχαι) were thought to exist, and a concerted attempt, more or less successful and repeated in various ways, to combine the spiritual with the temporal, the religious with the socio-political category, into a hierarchical whole can be found. Except for Gelasius' formula, these incomplete or tentative hierarchical combinations remained 'broken' in Weber's and Troeltsch's terminology, as the religious individual remained partially or inwardly an outworldly individual.

---

[14] Gelasius' distinction between priestly *auctoritas* and imperial *potestas* is perhaps not part of a coherent and developed theory, for in other texts he seems more uncertain about the use of these terms and writes about *regale et sacerdotale genus, uterque ordo* and even *utraque potestas* of kings and priests (Thiel 1867, p. 568). But it is perhaps possible to say that the hierarchical distinction between *auctoritas* and *potestas* was the clearest expression of Gelasius' thought, an expression towards which he was tending. Theodor Mommsen's thesis of a dyarchy during Augustus' reign, consisting of the imperial *potestas* and the *auctoritas senatus*, can perhaps be interpreted in a similar way. A different view of the relationship between *auctoritas* and *potestas* can be found in A. Magdelain (1947).

Early Christianity and the Concept of the Persona

A basic ingredient of human nature is the capacity, and indeed the necessity, to live in terms of one or another human culture[15]; in other words, human nature is not a given to which the various cultures of the world have been added; it is better to say that the concept of human nature within a given society should be seen in a relationship of elective affinity with the view that is held of society itself. In the early Christian period when the two categories or principles, the religious and the political, remained "broken" and qualitatively different, the view of human nature was discussed in relation to the new concept of the *persona*.

While originally the *persona* was probably the mask of the actor in classical tragedy and then the actor himself – that which conceals and that which is concealed –, and while in Roman times it often referred to the social role as well as to the human being who played that role – perhaps with all his legal rights and duties[16] –, the term was also used in a grammatical sense and, furthermore, in the analysis of literary dialogues and in biblical exegesis, for – to take an example – God's monologue in Genesis "let us make a man, someone like ourselves", led to the observation that at least one other person must have been present. Thus, the term *persona* found its way into theological discussion and gained importance in two different but related contexts. The intensity of early Christian discussions about dogmatic questions related to the concept of *persona* is evident in the fact that the path of its development was soon littered by many abandoned attempts to resolve the issue: Arianism, Apollinarianism, Eutychianism, Monenergism, Monothelitism.

---

[15] Clifford Geertz "The Impact of the Concept of Culture on the Concept of Man" in: C. Geertz 1973, pp. 33-54.

[16] Although Schlossmann showed as early as 1906 that in Roman legal thought the concept of *persona* was not used, as Harnack had suggested, in the sense of someone who has legal rights and duties and that, in fact, it was not a legal term at all (the grammatically correct translation of the often quoted passage '*servum personam non habere*' is: servants do not play a role in legal matters – Schlossmann, p. 65), more recent authors, for example Marcel Mauss in his influential study of the person as a category of the human mind, have continued to maintain that the notion of *persona* was a basic concept of Roman law and as such contributed to the development of the modern concept of the person. Here is an example of an idea which, although shown to be erroneous, continues to reappear in the scientific literature perhaps because it fits well into the accepted scientific framework, for the more general idea that Roman law had a profound influence on the development of Western civilization continues to be widely accepted.

On the one hand a theological controversy resulted from the difficulty of reconciling Christian monotheism with the adoration of Christ and with the conception of the Holy Spirit as a separate entity. While the ramifications of the controversy over the Trinity and the formula "una substantia, tres personae" need not be detailed here (in particular the rejection of subordinationism), the λογος/τροπος distinction, introduced by the Cappadocian Fathers, is of interest in this context. It provided the opportunity to distinguish between the mode of existence (*tropos*) of persons and their essence or principle (*logos*), between the way they are and what they are. Thus the three divine persons (Father, Son and Holy Spirit) were thought to be modes of existence of the same Godhead, and they were characterised or defined by their mutual relations (the Father was said to be father only in relation to the Son, etc.). The Cappadocian Fathers initiated perhaps the idea that persons can be characterised and must be defined by their relations to other persons[17], Augustine also mentioned it, although he remained sceptical[18] with regard to the use of the term person in this context, and the idea was repeated in modified form by Thomas Aquinas[19] (*distinctum relatione subsistens in essentia divina* – that which is distinguished in the divine essence manifests itself in a relationship) and again and again until modern times.

On the other hand, a related controversy was concerned with the question of how Christ could be both God and man at the same time. The solution of the Council of Chalcedon (451) was to affirm that in Christ there are two natures in one person. This affirmation drew upon the distinction made by the Greek Fathers (for example, by Gregory of Nyssa in the Epistula 38), between nature or essence (ουσια) which is not limited and cannot be circumscribed, and hypostases (subsisting beings; manifestations) which are clearly defined and have distinctive characteristics[20]. "Man" or "human

---

[17] v. Schönborn, 1976, p. 38 and p. 125; equally Heinzer, 1980, p. 43 sqq, who discusses the innertrinitarian relations where the mode of existence (τροπος) coincided with its relationships (σχεσεις).

[18] *De Trinitate* 7, 11.

[19] *De potentia Dei*, 9, 4c.

[20] The word hypostasis had two different ranges of meaning, for it was sometimes derived from the middle voice and sometimes from the active voice of the verb ὑφιστημι. Thus it could mean sediment, matter, substance, but also solid fact, independent objectivity, concrete existence. When Latins translated it into their language, they used the exact philological equivalent of the Greek hypostasis, namely *substantia* (substance), imagining incorrectly that words philologically identical in the two

being" referred to (human) nature; Peter or Paul to a hypostasis of this nature. The term hypostasis was then, since the fourth century, identified with the term *atomon* (*individuum*, the individual) and the Latin term *persona*.[21]

This distinction between hypostasis (or *persona*) and nature was perhaps the most basic issue of patristic theology and philosophy. It was, for instance, pivotal in the various attempts to resolve the Iconoclastic Controversy. This point becomes quite clear in the study of Christoph v. Schönborn on the theological foundations of the adoration of the Christian icon, where he shows that an icon did not represent the nature of the one who is represented – this would have been quite impossible and even blasphemy in the case of Christ –, but his hypostasis. To arrive at this conclusion, which was later formulated in its definitive form by Theodore Studites, v. Schönborn relies heavily on a text[22] by Maximus Confessor (580-662), the most eminent theologian of his time and, in H.-G. Beck's opinion (Beck 1959:436), the most universal mind of the seventh century, who provided a succinct analysis of the difference between nature and hypostasis as it applies to Christology and to man.

Few attempts to solve some of the major questions of early Christianity were as subtle, as consistent, and as logically rigorous as Maximus', and the solutions which he proposed may therefore be regarded as quite influential[23], for, as can often be noticed in the study of the history of ideas, what is rational in the sense of logically consistent has some degree of 'power' over man; thus, we can best understand the specific historical effect of a complex of ideas, if we study it in its most consistent and logical form. Max Weber knew this when he chose as the centre of his study of the Protestant ethic the Calvinist doctrine of predestination, which was certainly not

languages must have the same meaning. In fact, the meaning of the Latin word *substantia* is more closely related to the Greek οὐσια. Numerous misunderstandings resulted, because it was not realised that hypostasis also has an active sense (to be translated approximately as concrete existence or manifestation), and that this active sense was in fact the sense in which the term was being applied to theology by the Greeks (comp. Prestige 1936, p. 163 sqq.)

[21] For instance in the text of Leontius Byzantinus in *Patrologia graeca* 86, 1306 C.

[22] J. Migne: *Patrologia graeca* 91, 552B-553A.

[23] Boethius' definition of the persona (*rationalis naturae individua substantia*) has often been regarded as quite influential, but, as P. Hadot (Meyerson, ed. 1973, p. 130) has indicated, Boethius may simply have wanted to say that, in the case of beings endowed with reason, one used the term persona rather than hypostasis.

accepted by all protestant sects although all of them breathed the air
of its logic.[24]

Maximus wrote that things may be united either according to
their nature or essence (οὐσια), or they may be united in a common
hypostasis or person. In the first case, when several beings or things
are united in one nature, they must at least be numerically distinct,
and then one can speak of them as hypostases, as particular manifestations of a common nature (or species), such as particular horses
belonging to the species *equus*. These things or beings, while having
the same nature, will show certain differences in their hypostases or
manifestations. Paul may be distinguished from Peter by the form of
his nose or by the colour of his hair, while both are human beings
and therefore have the same nature. Likewise, the unity of the three
persons in the Godhead falls into this category. In the second case,
Maximus went on to explain – and this case is central to the argument here – , while two distinct natures cannot be combined according to their essence without losing their inner principles or without
resulting in a *tertium quid*, they may be combined in a common synthetic hypostasis or person. Such unions are, in Maximus' terminology, con-hypostatic and hetero-essential. This is the case with Christ
who is both God and man, and this is also the case with every human
being, who is both body and soul. The hypostasis of Paul, for
instance, receives its identity from what distinguishes his body from
other bodies and his soul from other souls, but his body and soul nevertheless constitute one single identity on the level of their common
hypostasis. They do not exist separately, for they have come to life
together; the different natures of body and soul remain united on the
level of the hypostasis or the person without admixture, but also
without possibility of separation or division, – and as such they participate in the common form (εἶδος) of man. Thus, human hypostatic, that is, personal being differs radically from natural or physical
being. It may be characterized by distinguishing marks, but it is also

---

[24] Weber thought that in the Calvinist doctrine of predestination the Protestant
idea of proof (*Bewährung*) appeared in the most consistent form although it reoccurs as
a framework for the connection between faith and conduct in the other denominations (Weber 1958, p. 126). He also insisted that in various Protestant groups an
alignment with the most consistent expressions of Protestant asceticism almost always
took place – and that therefore the mere number of pure Calvinists among the
Protestants cannot be used as an argument against the significance of their ascetic
conduct of life (Max Weber: *Kritiken und Antikritiken* 1978, p. 313).

the καθ έαυτο είναι, the being-for-self, of two different natures in one person.

If we take Maximus' analysis as the most developed and as representative of his time, it becomes perhaps clear that the idea of the person as a synthetic hypostasis provided a new paradigm which was based on the definitive breakthrough of the distinction between what is natural and what is personal. The early Christians had now left behind the outworldly individualism of the Epicureans and early Stoa and had formalised the idea of the dual nature of the human being.[25]

Maximus' nuanced understanding of the human being must be set apart from many commonly accepted concepts: neither was man conceived as an individual in the sense of a mere sample of mankind within a social whole which englobes him, nor was he thought of as an autonomous individual in the modern sense, for autonomous human life was not thought to consist in following one's own will (this, in Maximus' terminology, would simply be called 'gnomic' willing), but in acquiring similitude to God, in deification. Even the concept of outworldly individualism, in the sense in which it has been applied to India, is not applicable here. The *persona* accepted the socio-political order as a relative value, it relativised the social roles, but it did not forsake them. Man was thought to have two natures, to be a *homo duplex*, belonging to two worlds. Dumont (1970:141) has suggested that the subject of institutions in India (e.g. the joint family) should be viewed as empirically multiple, but ontologically one, in order to solve some false problems like "ownership of land". In Maximus and in early Christianity we find the opposite: the human being as a person, as a hypostasis or manifestation, is one, but ontologically man is double, both inworldly and outworldly. He becomes a person by the way in which he lives out this inner tension within a "broken" world.

The Papal Revolution

While in the Ancient World the *sacerdotium* did not attempt to regulate the conditions and institutions of the "world", and while the early Christians adjusted themselves more or less to State and society

---

[25] The conception of man as two natures in one is confirmed in the Prooimion of the Eisagoge (ninth century). *Vide* Schminck, 1986, p. 4-5.

through the theory of relative natural law and had a "mixed" (*gebrochen*) attitude towards them, so that it was impossible to talk of a uniform Christian civilisation, fundamental changes occurred from the eighth century on and led to what may well have been a major turning point in Christian history.

After loosening its ties with Constantinople, the papacy ceased to conform to Gelasius' formula, for it assumed political functions, first by transferring political power from Constantinople to the Frankish kings and, soon after that, by claiming political power for itself in parts of Italy, basing itself on the so-called Donation of Constantine, a forged document. This document did not refer any more to the *auctoritas* (authority), as Gelasius had done, but to the *potestas pontificum* (the power of the popes).[26] From the previous attitude of passive toleration of the "world" the *sacerdotium* now moved forward, within the setting of the new and simpler medieval conditions of life, and established a papal theocracy, the legal supremacy of the Pope over all Christians, and particularly over the secular (political) leadership, in all religious questions, with the proviso that it was for the Church to decide what problems concern religious salvation. The emperor was demoted from his position of quasi-sacerdotal splendour to the status of a simple layman. Excommunication now also entailed the civic consequences of exclusion from society and loss of legal rights.

While the political success of the papal claims and ambitions must be evaluated separately – for instance, Gregory the Seventh's claim in his *dictatus papae* that the pope is entitled to depose the emperor, as well as that no law is valid without the approval of the pope – it is clear that a significant ideological change occurred here, for the *sacerdotium*, the spiritual function, now sought to rule in worldly matters and had thus entered the "world". The difference between the two realms, the *sacerdotium* and the *imperium*, was now conceived as one of degree, not of kind, so that the spiritual power, as it was now called, was deemed to be superior to the temporal power even in temporal or worldly matters, for instance, in the claim of Innocent III that *occasione peccati* (in case of sinful actions) of kings or emperors the Church must get involved in politics, or in the doctrine of swords which now was interpreted as referring to the relations between ecclesiastical and lay authorities in the "world" rather than to the relations between the

---

[26] Fuhrmann 1968, p. 93, line 267.

earthly and heavenly spheres of Christian living.[27] The two principles (αρχαι) of which Leo Diaconus had spoken in relation to Byzantium, were now thought to be two powers.

Whether this transformation was connected to a change in the nature of law as it turned into a disembedded and autonomous legal system (developed by Gratian and his successors in Bologna, as Berman has suggested), is not the question here, but the Church now came to be viewed as a visible, legal and corporate unity, with the emphasis shifting, to use Berman's words, from sacredness in the sense of otherworldliness to the manifestation of the sacred in the political, economic and social life of the times (Berman 1983:158). The Church was also considered as the only whole, as englobing society, while all other groups or associations were seen as fictitious and without "real" life, according to the doctrine of the *persona ficta*, enunciated by Pope Innocent IV (Gierke 1977:32).

A concomitant phenomenon – not without elective affinity to the first one – took place in theological thought. While in the Eastern Orthodox Christianity of Byzantium the crucifixion had no significance apart from the resurrection, so that much emphasis was placed on man's *theosis* or deification and his otherworldly aspects, the Western Church now shifted the emphasis to the incarnation of the sacred in the world, and to the crucifixion which, according to Anselm, was necessary for man's justification. Anselm's theory of satisfaction that the God-Man, Jesus Christ, had to sacrifice himself, pay the price of man's original sin, and thus reconcile him to God, gave Western theology its distinctive character,[28] while it was considered legalistic in the East.

In this new world where the State was simply the political department of the Church, the term hierarchy took on a new meaning, dif-

---

[27] Clearly, the separation of social life into different spheres – religious, political, economic etc.- which all have their own inner logic (*Eigengesetzlichkeit*) was absent from the doctrines of the medieval Church which was part of a unified culture.

[28] The striking difference between these conceptions of Christ's mission was manifested in religious art: since the eleventh and twelfth centuries, Roman Catholic religious art has emphasized Christ on the cross while the icons of the Eastern Church have typically shown the resurrected Christ.

The concept of original sin in Western theology provides the opportunity to note that the path from early Christianity to Western Christianity seems to have been littered with incorrect translations. Ὑπόστασις became substance (*vide* footnote No 20 of this chapter), αρχη became *potestas* or power (Niebuhr 1828, p. 101-102) and the harsh Western interpretation of original sin was justified by an incorrect translation of Romans 5:12, as explained in detail by J. Meyendorff, 1979, p. 144.

ferent from the hierarchical organization of castes in India or from
Gelasius' hierarchical formula. It was no longer a value-related order
in which the whole encompasses the contrary, and which also may be
defined as the relationship between a whole and an element of that
whole. Rather it foreshadowed the modern bureaucratic organisation: the simple chain of command or the units of successive orders,
different with regard to the degree of their power or responsibility,
but not different in kind. This is also how Gratian organised the various sources of law in his *Concordance of Discordant Canons*, starting from
divine law and then descending through natural law, ecclesiastical
law, the laws and enactments of princes to, finally, customs. Referring
to the Church itself, Max Weber (1972:480) talked of the first rational
bureaucracy in history. Moreover, the social organisation and the
division of labour were no longer thought to be the result of the Fall,
but something which had been willed by God for the harmony of the
world because of the natural inequality of men. Compared with the
theory of the relative natural law, this social philosophy implied a
strong turn to a positive valuation of the world. Berman has even suggested that the Papal Revolution introduced a sense of progress in
time towards achieving the preconditions for salvation, a belief in the
reformation of the world in contrast to the older view of secular history as a process of decay, so that for instance Gothic architecture was
planned to be built over generations and centuries.

  Not only did the Christian person who had formerly relativised the
world without, however, leaving it completely, now become more and
more involved in it, but even those who could truly be considered
outworldly individuals, the monks, now were made to enter the world
as well. While the Indian *samnyasin* and many Eastern Orthodox
Christian monks may have been living an anchoretic life alone in the
forest or the desert and while the Buddhist monk renounced his social
roles, anchorites were not even mentioned in the *Codex Juris Canonici*
(Mantzaridis 1981:66). Instead, many monastic orders, e.g., the Tem-
plars, the Hospitallers and the Teutonic Knights, became the "auxiliary troupes" of the Pope, with well-defined roles in the world, and
some of them may even have injected into the world their individualistic ideas and customs about representative and deliberative assem-
blies, about electoral techniques and majority votes which had been
used in the monasteries (Moulin 1964:176 sqq.). Monasticism was not
an end in itself any more, but a method used by the Church for the
common purpose of the Church. This did not exclude the possibility

that subjectively the *contemptus mundi* might prevail (Bultot 1963). Later on, as will be seen, the idea of monasticism was further altered, for after the Reformation – at least as Sebastian Franck saw it (PE:121) – every Christian had to be a monk all his life in his mundane occupation; monasticism now strode into the market place of life and slammed the door of the monastery behind it.

As the *sacerdotium* or the Church became more and more involved in the "world" and even pretended to rule it, the Christian *persona* who in the past had been standing with one foot in this world and with the other foot outside it, now lost the traditional footing in a double or "broken" world and turned increasingly to the social and political scene of what had become, according to both Troeltsch and Max Weber, a unified culture[29] (*Einheitskultur*). The *persona* thus took the initial step towards evolving into an inworldly individual. This unified culture was also described as a *corpus mysticum* in which individuals were not only members of an organic whole but also entities with a final cause of their own (Gierke 1913:7). Certainly, there already existed what Troeltsch (1960, vol. I, p. 251 & 328) called anarchistic or concrete individualism, for instance the personal contract in the feudal system; there had also developed a heightened interest in the individual human being in, for example, Abelard's ethic of individual intention or in the newly imposed practice of individual confession[30], and there was, since the eleventh century, the growth of cities which developed as corporations of individual human beings and not of sibs (Weber 1972:745), but there had still not developed the autonomous standing of the individual, the bearer of value, in relation to the Church, and therefore autonomous individualism in the modern sense did not exist yet.

In this new unified culture, the human being belonged to one world only: this world – and the old concept of *persona* had lost its inner necessity. The inner preconditions for the development of inworldly individualism had thus been created. Moreover, with the move towards formalisation of an autonomous legal system and

---

[29] The English reader should note that O. Wyon's translation of Troeltsch's authoritative account (*The Social Teaching of the Christian Churches* 1931, many reprints) is sometimes less than satisfactory for today's ears. The all-important term *Einheitskultur*, rendered by Wyon as "unity of civilization", is probably better translated as "unified culture".

[30] These and other interests in the individual human being are described in Morris 1972.

towards modern bureaucratic organisation some exterior or institutional aspects of inworldly individualism had also come into being.

New legal concepts such as those of William of Ockham (1285-1349?) whose earlier mentioned dispute with Pope John XXII regarding the properties of the Franciscan Order will be remembered, were symptomatic of this development.[31] Whereas Thomas Aquinas had attached the notion of 'right' to the hierarchical social order which he saw as a reflexion of nature and eternal Reason, Ockham denied the existence of universals, whether genus or species: such terms as 'man' or 'tree' or even 'Franciscan Order' were, according to him, not ontologically real; while they might be useful conventions they signified nothing in themselves. It would therefore not be correct, he argued, to infer a normative conclusion from a universal term, to derive a natural law from the nature of man or from an ideal order of things, for example. Law (*ius*) signifies *dominium*, power ; and there is only one source of the law : the individual will, be it the will of God or the will of individual men. Natural law (*ius poli*) is of divine origin and, as no Reason can limit the power of God, it is a command beyond human understanding. But in those areas of human life for which no commandments were given by God, a moral no-man's land, man posits his own human law (*ius fori*). Human law cannot be derived from natural law, and there is no necessary correlation between them, because the two kinds of law are born of two different wills rather than of a common principle. Thus, law for Ockham is not any more the just relationship among human beings, but the expression of the will and power of individual legislators; the term is used to designate the social recognition of the power of the individual, and no natural order exists beyond that upon which the individuals decide. Power has become the functional equivalent of order and hierarchy.

The modern conception of the individual as a value comes to mind here, but within the englobing inworldly Church, the individual was not yet autonomous. This last step was left to the Reformation.

---

[31] Ockham's work may have been little known by jurists, as Villey (1975) states, but it is highly suggestive of the times to come.

The Decisive Step of the Reformation

If one follows the account of Troeltsch (1960:357) and then of Dumont (1982), the really permanent attainment of individualism in the modern sense was due to a religious movement, to the Reformation, rather than to the Renaissance as is often thought. The decisive step was perhaps taken by Calvin, although in many respects he was only making Luther's stand explicit. While in early Christianity the *persona* had lived in a broken world the parts of which could perhaps be hierarchized but not subjected; and while in the unified culture of the Middle Ages the human being was thought to be both a part of the *corpus mysticum* and a whole, with Calvin there are only individuals: they are in society and, in fact, they create society and dominate it. This is best understood in conjunction with Calvin's concept of God as supreme will. While Luther had removed the Church as an intermediary between God and man, God had remained accessible *sola fide*. But the distance between God and man became unbridgeable with the accentuation of the dogma of predestination, interpreted to be the outcome of God's majestic and inscrutable will.

According to this dogma, some men are invested with the grace of election, others are condemned to reprobation, but the task of all, as nobody can be certain of his election, is to work for God's glory in the world or, as Troeltsch (1911:622) put it, to enter the world and, while inwardly rising above it, to shape it into an expression of the Divine Will. The faithfulness to this task is the only proof of election.

As the Church cannot provide salvation, Troeltsch (1960:590) referred to the independence, although unintended, of the individual with regard to the Church, and he quoted Schneckenburger : "The Church does not make the believers what they are, but the believers make the Church what she is."[32] In fact, Calvin's Church was dissolved as a holistic institution; it had become a mere instrument of discipline and an institution of sanctification (*Heiligungsanstalt*) rather than an institution of salvation (*Heilsanstalt*), created for the systematic endeavour to mould the life of the family, the state and the economy.

But while Troeltsch (1960:598) also thought that it might be superficial simply to interpret Calvin in terms of atomistic individualism where the community is believed to consist merely of the sum of the

---

[32] Troeltsch, 1911, footnote 320; Schneckenburger Vol. 1, p. 157.

individuals composing it, because to him the individual completely depended on the grace of predestination and all his actions flowed from it rather than from his own initiative, it is Louis Dumont's opinion that the Calvinist subjection to God's will and grace was the necessary condition for legitimising the shift towards inworldly individualism (Dumont 1983:21). While Troeltsch was concerned with the theological doctrine, Dumont is more interested in the result which follows from the psychological motives of the individual to gain proof of his election.

Instead of being straddled between this world and the other, the Calvinist, according to Dumont, has decided that he should embody the other world in his action upon this one, or rather, that he should apply to the things of this world an extrinsic, imposed value – not a value derived from our belonging to this world or its traditions, such as harmony, but a value rooted in our partial heterogeneity in relation to it. In Troeltsch's words, the Calvinist permeates the life of the world with the spirit of world-renunciation (Troelsch 1960:605). The relativisation of the world is now centred in the individual's will, and thus he is able to participate in it and to dominate it. Tönnies' *Kürwille*, as opposed to *Wesenswille*, comes to mind.

There is a further aspect to this new inworldly individualism, resulting from the particular form of religious experience in Protestantism. As Luther's soul stands freezing and lonely before its all-powerful and infinite God, as all its peripheral and outlying regions are cast off and it is reduced to its innermost core, a single numerical point without particular qualities and not distinguishable from other souls, one may speak of quantitative individualism (Schmalenbach 1919). But in Luther this is a transitory situation and, as soon as divine grace has been obtained *sola fide*, the joy overflows and warmth, affection and emotion return to human relations. With Calvin, however, this quantitative religious individualism becomes permanent, and it is also transferred to the life in the world. As the soul cannot in total self-abandonment unite with God and cannot be certain of divine grace, it will also not abandon itself to emotional contact with creaturely things, and friendship becomes sin. Rather, the soul remains reduced to its innermost core and thus permanently quantitative.

Protestant Individualism and Personality according to Max Weber

An analysis of Max Weber's work on the Protestant Ethic will widen this view, and it will make it possible to distinguish more clearly between a purely configurational view of the ideology of Protestant Christendom and the practical-ethical conduct upon which premiums were placed. For Weber too, inworldly individualism was one result of the Reformation. He underlined that the inner isolation of the individual was a consequence of the doctrine of predestination (PE:104) and he associated a pessimistically inclined individualism (PE:105) with the national characters and the institutions of peoples with a Puritan past; more important, he described how the protestant individual separated himself from the 'natural ties' of the community[33] and how this led to an individualistic critique of all institutions, not only of economic ones, so that all Calvinistic social organisations turned into unbrotherly and depersonalised structures and came to be based on individualistic motives (PE:223, fn. 27). Predestination, as Bulgakov (1911, vol. I, p. 192) once described Weber's view, separated the human beings like a transparent but impenetrable wall. This was not the world-fleeing individualism which Weber (PE:22, fn. 23) connected with Pascal, but rather the forerunner of the political individualism of the Western European human rights which he attributed in part to the religious convictions of the protestant sects[34]. But not only did the Reformation produce inworldly individualism, according to Weber, it also created what he called the ethical personality.

Whereas for Kant personality had meant the capacity of the person, belonging to the world of the senses as well as to the intelligible world, to follow the principles of reason and the categorical imperative, Weber did not see practical reason as the hallmark of the personality, but ultimate value-judgements. He thought that man could have a constant relationship to values and that empirically he develops a personality as a consequence of a type of conduct which results

---

[33] Max Weber 1958a, p. 237 (footnote 91). Parsons did not translate this sentence and its meaning correctly. It should read: ... how the individual became loosed from the communities based on "natural" feeling.

[34] Max Weber 1971, p. 62. In his essay on India, Weber (1921, p. 300) explains that the contractually fixed feudal relationship in Japan could also provide a basis for "individualism" in the occidental sense, but, on the whole, he more and more eliminated, over the course of his later years, the terms individual and individualism from his vocabulary.

from the type of his system of values and meanings and from its social transmission.

Weber fitted his own idea of the personality to achievements of the Protestants, to their particular kind of personality. Certainly, personalities were not absent before the Reformation or in other Axial Age civilisations: self-control, as Weber noted, was found among Confucians, Buddhist and other types of monks, Arab sheiks and Roman senators, and there were rationalisations of life of a very different kind[35] among the Japanese samurai, the cortegiano and the Stoa (Weber 1978b:53), but in Protestant Europe the self-control and the constancy of motive of the Puritan arose from the necessity of his subjugating all animal impulses to a rational and methodical plan of conduct so that he might secure the proof (*Bewährung*) of his own salvation in his worldly calling.[36]

Whereas the Confucian conduct of life involves ritualistic adaptation to the external order, to the conditions of the 'world', well-roundedness and not specialised calling; whereas the Buddhist karma doctrine bases itself on individual acts and whereas Catholicism is ethically unmethodical according to Weber because actions are evaluated and credited singly, the Puritans tried to achieve a unified ethical personality within the world and within the institutions which they viewed as material to be fashioned according to coherent norms. They abandoned the ritualistic and often disconnected norms of the Axial Age, based on external guarantees; by systematising their norms of conduct and relating them all to the goal of salvation, they created an ethic based on principles or on conviction, they separated legality from morality and they strengthened the inner conditions of motivation.[37] Their life was the result of a constant intrinsic relation to ultimate ethical values and meanings of life (Weber 1968:132), directed

---

[35] Weber's Kantian model of the personality is not being transformed into a Durkheimian model when it is suggested that the personality was related to a cultural and religious context. The prior existence of the ability to become a personality was, in Weber's opinion, a transcendental precondition of being human at least since the Axial Age (Weber 1968, p. 180), but the form which the personality took in different religious and cultural contexts obviously varied.

[36] Admittedly, not only the pragmatic desire to secure the certainty of salvation played a part in the shaping of the Puritan personality, but also the desire to achieve logical consistency of the dogma and the desire to achieve legitimation of the distribution of non-religious goods like power and economic goods.

[37] That there were also institutional motivations, in particular the mutual control and penitential discipline, – the organisational scourge, as Weber said, – is another matter.

methodically from within – and not just a combination of useful particular qualities.

The *persona* of early Christianity had belonged to two worlds, but these two worlds were now combined into one, and this single world, that is society, was now thought to consist of autonomous individuals who favoured certain kinds of social organisation. The other world was now centred in the will of these individuals who saw themselves as instruments of God, who conducted their life according to systematised ethical values, and who thus became ethical personalities. The ethical personality may thus be seen to be in a relationship of elective affinity with inworldly individualism; it even requires the presence of individualism and cannot develop in a hierarchically organised society. At the same time, it intensifies inworldly individualism as it implies the inner unity of the individual's will and conduct over time and provides the motivation to act as an autonomous individual. It is this relationship of elective affinity, and not of causality, which is decisive for the consolidation of inworldly individualism.

According to Weber's famous study, the influence of Protestantism on the spirit of capitalism and on the development of modernity lay, in fact, in this particular view of man: he was considered to be an inworldly individual, logically prior to social life, and he was also an ethical personality who applied outworldly values to this world in a consistent manner. The discussion on the "Protestant Ethic thesis" and on the related studies of the economic ethics of world religions has not generally advanced to the point where it is realised that the ethical personality of the Protestants could achieve its full potential only in an individualistic world in the modern sense and that Neo-Confucianism, for example, as it was not characterized by individualism in the modern sense (Metzger 1977:42), was not a fertile ground for the kind of ethical personality which Weber attributed to the Protestants.

The coexistence of inworldly individualism and the ethical personality was not permanent, however. When the religious spirit, the basis of the ethical personality, which lived in the individualistic social structure, declined in succeeding centuries, all that remained was egoistic individualism. The social structure turned into an 'iron cage', as Weber said, and the individuals turned into 'specialists without spirit and sensualists without heart'.

Natural Law Theory and Individualism

In the following centuries, the idea of natural law dominated social thinking and contributed to the further development of inworldly individualism. Natural law theories are sometimes divided into classical and modern : in the classical version man is a social being and the basis of law is the social and political order in conformity with the order of nature, whereas in the modern version (since the seventeenth century) the principles of state and of society are deduced from the inherent properties of man taken as an autonomous being, endowed with natural rights. Modern natural law theory thus does not involve social beings but instead self-sufficient individuals, whose state of nature is conceived to be logically prior to social and political life (the logical priority sometimes blends into historical anteriority). Otto v. Gierke (1958:135) has recorded the increasing preponderance of this individualistic view in natural law theory, a view which starts with the autonomous individual and which uses as its main device the idea of contract or compact; the earlier conception of the independent existence of an organic social whole was rejected and the priority of the individual over the community was emphasised with an ever increasing intensity.

This view of the difference between classical and modern natural law is incomplete, if one does not take into account the distinction between the 'absolute' law of nature and the 'relative' natural law, for, as mentioned earlier, in Stoic and early Christian times the *ius naturale* was thought to have applied to equal and free individuals in a golden age or before the Fall, whereas positive laws, organic social structure, government, slavery – aspects of the relative natural law – were interpreted as adaptations to man's nature and situation after the Fall. Thus, there was individualism in the idea of natural law in Antiquity, but it was at best a relative or outworldly individualism, referring to an eschatological age and accepting at the same time the holistic political and social conditions of the present, whereas the individualism of modern natural law is complete and inworldly.

But it was not the modern natural law theory alone which furthered the system of human rights and of inworldly individualism. England had quite successfully resisted the influence of Roman law, its public law had developed on Germanic foundations and it had rejected the late-Roman concept of an omnipotent State. On the basis of this tradition there developed, especially among American

Puritans, as Jellinek has shown, the religious ideas of inalienable subjective rights of the individual, in particular of the liberty of conscience (perhaps the first human right[38]) and of religion, and this led
to Bills of Rights in a number of American States (Jellinek 1919:42
sqq.). The "Pilgrims of the Mayflower" had drawn up a pact between
themselves, and others followed; it was thus the desire of religious
freedom which turned the earlier theories of modern natural law into
positive law and political reality. Objective rights of freedoms were
now reinterpreted as inalienable subjective rights of man, of the individual, and prior to the State (Jellinek 1919:67). Religious sects thus
formed one of the important foundations of modern inworldly individualism.

Whether the French Revolution itself was at bottom a religious
phenomenon, as Tocqueville thought, will have to remain unan-
swered, but there is no doubt that the idea of the French 'Declaration
of the Rights of Man and of the Citizen', the apotheosis of the doctrines of modern natural law and of inworldly individualism, was tak-
en over from the Bills of Rights of certain American states, especially
that of Virginia, as Jellinek has shown. Thus, its implicit sociology
which viewed all biological, cultural and historical differentiations as
unreal or irrelevant, and which suggested that society was a mere collection of inworldly individuals, was at least partially rooted in the
religious ideas of the Puritans.

The Rise of Individuality

The inwordly quantitative individualism of the French Revolution
was not hailed everywhere as an ideal and adopted into the political
reality. Germany's Lutheran tradition, and Pietism which had reinterpreted it, had asserted individualism in the Church alone, for it
rejected hierarchy and the division of labour on the religious level,
but not in the 'world', and it did not oppose, as the French Revolution did, the social and political hierarchy. This was an almost outworldly or rather an interior individualism which subordinated everything else to the inner life of the Christian but which, while subordi-
nating it, left the holistic socio-political community intact and recom-

---

[38] Weber: *Wirtschaft & Gesellschaft*, p. 725 (referring to Jellinek).

mended obedience to established and traditional political powers. Louis Dumont (1991) has described, based on an analysis of authors from W. v. Humboldt to Thomas Mann, how out of this Lutheran tradition – especially its pietistic branch – there emerged the German ideal of *Bildung* (self-education, inner self-cultivation), which, however, always remained tied to the traditional devotion to the state as a superindividual entity or, to use Tönnies' term, to the *Gemeinschaft*. On the level of literary forms it may be interesting to note that, while the French or English *Gesellschaft*, based on inworldly quantitative individualism, produced the novel of social criticism, Germany with its very different kind of individualism invented the novel of personal cultivation (*Bildungsroman*) which describes the shaping and perfecting of an incomparable and unique individual as almost a work of art within the social whole.

A prime example of this is Goethe's *Wilhelm Meister* which presents a world that is based on the personal peculiarities of its individuals and which is, in a way, a discussion on *Bildung* concerning Meister. In this *Bildungsroman* par excellence, the connection between Pietism and *Bildung* is obvious, especially in a chapter on a pietistic lady, entitled 'Confessions of a Beautiful Soul'. What is interesting though, and has been underscored by Dumont, is the fact that in the end Meister joins a higher collective whole, the Society of the Tower[39], which, without his knowledge, has been involved in most of his previous undertakings. The Piestist, although internally an individualist, sought the community of the like-minded.

In his autobiography, *Dichtung und Wahrheit*, Goethe presents his own education as having been in conformity with the doctrine of *Bildung*, as resulting from the encounter both of his own natural tendencies and the impact on him of those men and women with whom he had contact. Weintraub, in a study of individuality which culminates in Goethe, shows how Goethe rearranged selected facts of his life and thus superimposed a new truth on the truth of past events, in the opinion that the narration of a whole necessarily modifies the narration of parts. A fact of our life, he said, counts not insofar as it is true, but insofar as it means something[40]. Thus, the activity implied in *Dichtung*, at least insofar as Goethe's autobiography is concerned, is the act

---

[39] Goethe had been a member of a secret society related to the Free Masons, and the Society of the Tower is perhaps an allusion to this.

[40] Goethe : *Gespräche mit Eckermann*, March 30, 1831.

of placing isolated facts in relation to others so that a meaning is formed that is wider than that of any single component part. Also, in *Dichtung und Wahrheit* we do not simply encounter the unfolding of a given nature, but the formation of an individual within a specific historical context ; not simply uniqueness but a unique way of making oneself part of one's world. This is clearly different from the autobiographies of the past, for example Augustine's *Confessions* which offered the story of his life not as the story of an individuality but as a typical story, as an *exemplum* for all Christians.

Bildung became almost an institution in Germany, while the educated German, the *Bildungsbürger*, generally had only contempt for the political dimension of life with its divisions and struggle for particular interests, – and this may also be the reason, as Dumont (1991:43) has suggested, for the weakness of the Weimar Republic: because of its democratic and individualistic formula it was unable to arouse the identification with the whole which the German "ideology" requires.

In the German ideal of *Bildung* we have an alternative to the individualism of Calvinism and of the French Revolution : not a quantitative or formal individualism in which all individuals are fundamentally identical and equal, but a qualitative individualism which stresses the uniqueness, the incomparability and irreplaceability of each human creature as it must represent its society in a particular manner; not individualism of singleness, but individualism of uniqueness. It is this particular kind of individualism which Weintraub, in his above-mentioned book, has termed individuality, – a particular kind of personality which shapes the individual into a work of art and so is very different from the ethical personality of the Reformation. In fact, there is a tension between the ideal of *Bildung* and the necessity of one-sidedness and specialisation in modern bureaucratic society. While the Puritan attempted to reconstruct the world or its institutions in order to secure the proof of his salvation, the German individual was required to attempt the continuous reconstruction and perfection of self in order to achieve *Bildung* – and neither the work of the Puritan nor the self-cultivation of the German *Bildungsbürger* was ever considered to be complete.

There was, moreover, a deeper meaning to the uniqueness of the individual than that which results from a mere comparison with others: the uniqueness implied that the individual as a totality should and does develop according to its inner laws and logic. While Max Weber coined the term *Eigengesetzlichkeit* to indicate that the different societal spheres (e.g. the religious or the political sphere) follow their own inner laws or logic and that this results in tension between them, it may here be possible to talk of the *Eigengesetzlichkeit* of the individuality which is centred in the individual itself.[41]

What Thomas Aquinas had attributed to the angels, namely that there cannot be two individuals of the same species, can almost be said here of human beings. (Did not Leibniz suggest this when he talked of the human individual as an *infima species?* [42]). But, at the same time, another insight of Thomas must be recalled in this context: Where there is difference, *disparitas*, it refers back to a higher order (Gierke 1913, fn. 88). The qualitative individual of *Bildung* did not simply seek to acquire uniqueness according to its own inner logic, but rather sought a unique way of making himself part of his world, of the social whole. Simmel who compared Shakespeare's and Goethe's dramas, expressed it in the following way : In Shakespeare's individuals, the metaphysical element is located between their heads and their toes, while Goethe's characters appear to be fruits from a single tree or members of a metaphysical organism (Simmel 1912:261).

Another view of Simmel, namely that qualitative individualism originated in some way from quantitative individualism, perhaps as a sort of intensification, needs to be complemented : it is better to say that qualitative individualism was the answer or the reaction to quantitative individualism in a holistic society which had gone through the religious experience of the Reformation and was therefore, as Thomas Mann has suggested (Mann 1983:505 sq.), immunised against the ideas of the Enlightenment and the French Revolution. In the process of acculturation, the pietistic inner self-experience turned into a qualitative individualism, with some affinity to outworldly individualism. At one point, Goethe had even considered the possibility of letting his Faust end on Mount Athos.[43]

---

[41] An example of this inner *Eigengesetzlichkeit* (termed *Selbstgesetzlichkeit* by Schmalenbach, 1919, p. 385) can be found in Schiller's *Über Anmut und Würde*.

[42] Discours de Métaphysique ∫ 9, 13.

[43] See: Erhart Kästner 1956, p. 280. The opposition between the individualism of mysticism and the individualism of the sects, as elaborated by Troeltsch comes to mind.

Concluding Remarks

From outworldly individualism in the Axial Age civilisations to the divided allegiance of the *persona* in early Christianity, then further to the slow rise of certain aspects of inworldly individualism since the Papal Revolution and to its blossoming in the Reformation – these latter phenomena combined with the concomitant development of the ethical personality and the later appearance of the idea of individuality – , this was the special path, the *Sonderweg* of the Occident. It had three stages, closely connected to religious developments. The first stage was attained by the development of the religious concept of the *persona* which transcended the purely outworldly individualism of the Axial Age. It was a precondition for all further development and impregnated it with the underlying idea of two natures in man[44].

The second stage was prepared in the Papal Revolution. At least since Max Weber it has been generally taken for granted that the Reformation was responsible for one of the major contributing factors of modern capitalism and of modernity in general. But it now seems possible to agree with some of the Russian thinkers of the nineteenth century, such as P. Chaadaev or the Slavophiles, who attributed to the influence and the leadership of Rome around and immediately after the time of the schism the 'indelible furrows' which were created in the Western European mind, and which became the basis for Western Europe's development towards modernity (Schelting 1948:36). Only because Western Europe had already been impregnated by ideas of inworldly individualism since the Papal Revolution, could Calvinism and the Protestant sects have the impact which they had, whereas sects with a similar ethic in Russia remained relatively marginal. Russian Orthodoxy created a different set of sect-types and of schismatics than the Western Church. They did not become heterodoxies, with a chance to take hold of the religious center, for both Church and sects in Russia were part of a wider social setting in which a development towards modern individualism did not take place.

---

[44] Carrithers (1985), in a critique of Mauss' influential article on the category of the human person, has tried to disentangle the two natures of the *persona* (its relationship to the world or society and what he calls the *moi*, the physical and mental individuality), without concern for the fact that it is precisely the tension between the two which constitutes the Christian and occidental *persona* and which underlies all further development.

The third stage was not simply the development of qualitative individualism or of individuality as such in traditional Lutheran and pietistic Germany as a reaction against the individualism of the Enlightenment, but rather the incorporation of this new kind of individualism into the dominant modern ideology of the West. In fact, modern Western ideology is characterised by individualism in its two meanings, quantitative individualism and qualitative individualism, and by the tensions which inevitably result between them.

CHAPTER SEVEN

ORTHODOX RUSSIA'S ACCULTURATION
TO MODERNITY

Theoretical Considerations

There is no doubt that modern civilization or modernity appears to be spreading everywhere. But, whereas there may be increasing uniformization in all societies to some extent, the situation is more complex, for what can often be seen is a mixture of two modes of being, the traditional and the modern. Some peripheral cultures have completely endorsed modernity and have thus practically disappeared as separate cultures, others have closed in upon themselves and developed counter-modernization ideologies, and still others interact with modern civilization, they integrate some aspects of modernity and accept acculturation. The following lines will be concerned with this process of integration or of hybridization which produces subcultures within the culture of modernity, and it will then be asked what kind of response the Russian traditional culture has given since it was submitted to the onslaught of modernity.

The point of departure should consist of a clarification of the difference between modern and traditional society. In order to avoid a sociocentric viewpoint, it may be best to identify the Western configuration of ideas and values, our own ideology. The modern culture of the Occident, i.e. modern civilization, stresses the value of the individual human being. This primacy of the individual is exceptional in the history of humanity, for in traditional cultures we find a holistic ideology which valorizes society as a whole and subordinates the individual human being.

There are two major concomitants of the modern ideology. One is its artificialism, or the idea that man can distance himself from the given social and natural environment of which he is a part, and that society can be artificially constructed or remodelled according to the wishes of its elements, the individual human beings. The other is the separation of facts and values, the chasm between what is empirically given and valid norms. Whereas in holistic traditional societies the everyday routine or what has been traditionally handed down is an

inviolable norm of conduct, and whereas the epistemological difference between *is* and *ought to be* generally does not appear within a
world-view which is regulated by a mythical order, as the normative
and the narrative contents of myths are not separated in the perception of the adherents, the rise of (inworldly) individualism in a world
in which society as an englobing whole ceases to exist any longer, has
led to internalizing morality, to locating it exclusively within the individual's conscience while it is distinguished from social, political or
economic ends. Modern individualistic culture is faced by an
unbridgeable chasm between *sein* and *sollen*, by the impossibility to
deduce what ought to be from what is.

What happens if the individualistic ideology comes into contact
with a holistic society? Germany provides an early example of a culture which did not agree to a wholesale adoption of the dominant
individualism and rationalism of the Enlightenment and the French
Revolution. At least until the beginning of the twentieth century it
appeared to retain a holistic ideology, as Louis Dumont (1991) has
argued, although the present ideology of *Verfassungspatriotismus* tends to
point in a different direction. According to Thomas Mann, Luther's
Reformation had immunized Germany against the French Revolution, it had produced a purely religious individualism and thus had
enabled the Germans to resist the socio-political individualism of the
years after 1789. Under the influence of Western cosmopolitism,
however, the religious individualism of Luther and pietism turned
into the ideal of self-cultivation (*Bildung*), a qualitative individualism
which has been so prominent in Goethe, W. Humboldt and later.
Thus, the German acculturation to the modern ideology was limited,
and the concomitants of modernity, artificialism and the separation of
facts and values, remained less developed. Goethe's *weltanschauung*, for
instance, was based on the unity of being and value; God was for him
but another name for nature, and he talked of the universally-human
(*das Allgemein-Menschliche*), being and value at the same time (Simmel
1912:271 sqq).

On another level, J. G. Herder's 'Auch eine Philosophie der
Geschichte' (1774) was a polemic against the Enlightenment and a
defence of the existence of equal but different cultures – or perhaps a
defence of the rights of cultures or *Völker* as opposed to the Rights of
Man. The modern ideology is different from traditional ideologies in
that it attaches a fundamental value to the Individual rather than to
society as a whole. And yet, while in purely traditional and holistic

cultures society is exclusive, and all those individual beings or strangers who do not belong to it are devalued or even despised, there is something modern in Herder's defence of holistic cultures: they are recognized as equal in principle or, in the words of Herder's interpreter Louis Dumont, as individuals of a collective nature. Herder's conception was a Janus, for he accepted a feature of the modern ideology even while attacking it: he accepted individualism on the global level – all cultures are individual entities of equal value, – but rejected it on the subordinate level, for he considered each culture as a whole, a collective *Volk*. This combination of holistic and individualistic traits is characteristic of acculturation to modernity. In this particular case, it resulted in what has been called the ethnic theory of nationalities (the nation as a collective individual), frequently encountered in the Third World today, as opposed to the elective theory of nationalities (the nation as a collection of individuals).

The Russian Intelligentsia

If we now turn to Russia, we encounter the history of a people torn between traditional cultural identity and the modern individualistic configuration, and we find that the impact of modernity and the subsequent acculturation produced a synthesis of traditional holistic and modern individualistic traits. The development of the Russian *intelligentsia* in the nineteenth century is characteristic in this regard. Surely, their philosophical activity, their sustained exercise of rational inquiry into the foundations as well as the ideals of social life, must have had a close affinity to individualism. And the premise of their inquiry and their disputes, namely, the opinion that the world is an arena of choices, that human societies can choose to remain traditional or embrace modernity or opt for a third path – all this is, of course, highly individualistic. But the members of the *intelligentsia* were not simply intellectuals in the modern sense, they were, as I. Berlin (1979:117) has written, like a dedicated order, devoted to the spreading of a specific attitude to life, something like a gospel. They were expected to be morally upright and conscious that they were under public scrutiny. In the West, an artist's or a writer's private life may be of no more concern for the appreciation of his œuvre than the private life of a carpenter. Indeed, it is possible to characterize modernity by the fact that there is a large number of independent and specialized activities or disciplines (economics, arts, family life, etc.), each with its own inner logic or rationality, whereas there is much less rationality in the distribution or comprehensive ordering of these disciplines. This was impossible to accept for the Russian *intelligentsia*. In spite of all their 'individualism' they considered social life and individual life as coherent wholes, and they maintained that man cannot divide what he does as an expert or a professional from his activity as a human being, that one cannot have one kind of personality as a citizen, another as a writer, and a third as a husband: whatever man does, he does with his whole personality.

The social whole and social justice were for them – as for the average Orthodox Russian – more important than individual freedom and yet, they often had a utilitarian and individualistic morality; many were willing to accept any means which appeared to advance their goal of social justice and others, like Mikhailovsky or Bulgakov, insisted on the importance of individuality (*lichnost'*) or integral personality, a kind of qualitative individualism which refers to the unique set of features of an individual and leaves the holistic worldview intact. Only individuals who possessed well-developed moral and intellectual qualities were worthy of this title (although some authors, e.g. Chekhov, seem to have attributed it to every single person in the street), and there often was the presumption that, in order to have a *lichnost'* one had "to work on oneself" (*rabota nad soboi*) in order to achieve self-improvement by self-renunciation. Even Lenin wrote of the need for a long methodical manufacturing of a professional revolutionary out of oneself [1]. This qualitative individualism had made its appearance in Germany – as has been shown in the previous chapter – and it then crossed over to Russia [2] and developed, under similar circumstances but with some different characteristics – particularly the interest in the *narod* and in social justice –, as a reaction against the quantitative individualism elsewhere in the West.

[1] Quoted in Kharkhordin 1999, p. 231 from Lenin's *What is to be done?*
[2] Billington (1966) has even ascribed Tikhon Zadonsky's ideas of self-renewal and "attending to oneself" to German pietistic influence. The writings of this eighteenth century leader of monastic revival were read by Dostoevsky, and the monk Zosima in *The Brothers Karamasov* may be a reflection of these readings.

Changing Concepts of Nationality and Sovereignty

On another level, the ideas which N. Danilevsky, the defender of Pan-Slavism, advanced in *Russia and Europe* were the result of a similar synthesis. It is true that he advocated a federation of Slavic nations and ultimately the conquest of Constantinople, but he also stated that Russian or Slavic principles have no absolute or universal value, that they are simply a historico-cultural type, simply different. To claim for the Slavic culture a universal significance would be just as absurd, he said, as to ask whether palm or cypress or oak better express the concept of plant. There could be no such thing as universal values shared by all human beings as the individualistic ideology of the West proclaimed and as also the Russian *zapadniki* (Westernizers) as well as the Slavophiles tended to believe (although they obviously did not agree on what these values were). The relations between states or cultures, each belonging to a historico-cultural type, could only be based on self-interest and on the natural laws of evolution. But within the nation, or within a historico-cultural type, social harmony must prevail and particular interests must be subordinated to the general good. And there may be evolutionary levels within these types, but the types themselves cannot be arranged in an evolutionary scheme.

Just as Herder had done in Germany, Danilevsky adopted a feature of the modern ideology: he insisted that all historico-cultural types are equal collective individuals – but he rejected individualism on the intra-cultural level as it was the collectivity which was valued, and not the individual human beings.

The coexistence of individualism and holism in Danilevsky's thought represents another kind of interrelatedness of these two features in nineteenth century Russia. But there was another feature which will round out the picture of the specificity of traditional Russian culture. It concerns political ideology and it might explain Pan-Slavism or the belief that a federation of Slavic states under the direction of Russia would constitute not just a larger state but an empire.

Henry Sumner Maine (1887) has distinguished between three types of sovereignty: tribal sovereignty, universal dominion (where the chieftain is not any longer king of a tribe but claims to be emperor of the world), and, finally, territorial sovereignty, an offshoot of feudalism and implying, as Kantorowicz (1957) has shown, a transfer of values from universal sovereignty to a particular territory – as in the for-

mula *rex imperator in regno suo* (the king is emperor in his own kingdom)
–, which predominates in the modern world.

The Roman emperors, of course, as well as those of Byzantium,
claimed to be universal sovereigns. After the fall of Constantinople in
1453, the universalist consciousness of the Empire was mainly voiced
by the monastic circles in Russia and found its most famous expression in the letters of the monk Philotheos of Pskov, written to Grand-
prince Basil III in the early sixteenth century and formulating the
idea of Moscow, 'The Third Rome'.

Some scholars have advanced the idea of the *translatio imperii* (the
transition of world-sovereignty from Constantinople to Moscow), but it
is true that the Muscovite Grand-princes did not formally claim the
succession of the Byzantine emperors, in spite of the marriage of Ivan
III with Zoe-Sophia, the niece of the last Byzantine *basileus*, or even
when Ivan IV assumed the title of tsar in 1547 (the word *tsar* derives
from Caesar and is clearly related to the Roman Empire) or when Boris
Godunov had succeeded in pressuring the Patriarch of Constantinople
to establish a patriarchate of Moscow in 1590. In the sixteenth century,
the "Holy Roman Empire of the German People" (*Heiliges Römisches
Reich Deutscher Nation*) was still strong, and the Muscovite empire could
not be compared to it. Later, in the nineteenth century, when the Holy
Roman Empire of the German People had disintegrated in fact
(although the concept of a *Reich* may still have lingered on), the ideology
of world sovereignty had been replaced in Western Europe by that of
territorial sovereignty. Russia, one of the members of the 'Holy
Alliance' and imbibing Western ideas and knowledge, became Janus-
headed: on the international level – in its relations with the other European 'Great Powers' – it wanted to be a national and territorial State
among equals (interrelated by the delicate mechanism of the European
'balance of power'), whereas on the level of internal representation it
was not only a holistic culture, but the Byzantine idea of the empire
and the ideology of the 'Third Rome' had not been replaced: universal
sovereignty continued, perhaps unconsciously, to be part of the politi-
co-religious self-definition and probably can also account for the spec-
tacular growth of the Russian empire since the sixteenth century[3].

---

[3] To be sure, the Russian tsars were also internally caught in the contradictions
between ethnic nation-state and empire; they were rulers of the empire, but they
draped themselves in the cloth of Great Russian national ethnic culture. The recent
break-up of the Soviet Union and the surviving dream of rebuilding the empire are a
result of the tension between the two concepts.

Moreover, a major Byzantine inheritance possessed by Russia lay in the Tsar's relations with the Orthodox Christians *in partibus infidelium* (in countries governed by non-Christians), resulting perhaps from a modified view of universal sovereignty. The Byzantine emperor had considered himself, and was considered by the Muslims, in a manner for which modern international law and the concept of territorial sovereignty make no provision, as head of the Orthodox peoples, in whosoever's domains they might dwell. The Tsar took over the Emperor's role. His intervention on behalf of the Orthodox inhabitants of the Ottoman Empire, which so often troubled the chanceries of Europe during the eighteenth and nineteenth centuries, was an expression of this heritage (Runciman 1957).

The combination of the concept of universal sovereignty with the modern idea of territorial sovereignty was perhaps impossible to achieve without creating tensions on the international level. L. Dumont (1983:260) once mentioned that there is much talk today concerning the recognition of those who are different – and that there is no theoretical problem involved if recognition simply means equal rights and chances, but that, if it implies recognition in a more subtle way, the recognition of the other qua other, this would lead to a contradiction in terms, for such recognition is impossible without integration and hierarchization or subordination. In any case, the Western powers were unable to accept the archaic Orthodox concept of universal sovereignty at the same level as their own concept of sovereignty, and Russia had found no way to completely acculturate the modern concept of territorial sovereignty, and it is therefore not surprising that the Crimean War was seen by many contemporaries not so much as a war between political enemies as between essentially different ideological concepts.

Some of those who realized that universal sovereignty was out of the question on the political and economic level, transferred it to religion. Against the depravity and degeneracy of the West, the Russian people were seen by them as bearers of superior values and of a unique religion, so that for instance Prince Myshkin in Dostoyevsky's *Idiot*, presaging Berdiaev, could proclaim that the renewal of the whole of humanity will come about solely through Russian religion and the Russian idea. Had not, in a comparable way, the Germans, when the Holy Roman Empire had disappeared and Germany was divided into small princely states, lived in the conviction that their culture, as opposed to Western 'civilization', was culture par excellence and destined to dominate all others? (Dumont 1991:39).

Russian Socialism

Individualism and holism were also combined on the economic level. When serfdom was abolished in 1861, the *obshchina*, the holistic village commune to which the former serfs had belonged, was nevertheless retained. In fact, it may be said that socialism in any of its versions represents a combination of collective solidarity and individualistic development, of community and modernity. Socialists believe, as Peter Berger once said, that one can have one's cake and eat it, too. It reintroduces a concern for the social whole, but it nevertheless believes that the real being is not the social group but the individual human being, and it thus replaces the hierarchy within the social whole by equality: one element from holism (concern for the social whole) and one element from individualism (equality) are combined into a new form: socialism.

What has more recently been called the theorem of the privilege of backwardness took shape gradually in the nineteenth century, and not all Russian authors attached an identical meaning to it. It refers to the possibility of a better future than that of the Western nations in spite of Russian backwardness at the time, to something that would be neither traditionally holistic and Russian nor simply individualistic, and that would have its own inner logic. Chaadaev had prepared the terrain, and the theorem then became an essential element in Herzen's Russian Socialism. History is unjust, he wrote (1919 : vol 8:151) for it gives to late-comers the privilege of knowledge and experience (particularly regarding what happened with regard to capitalism in the more advanced countries). Herzen rejected the Russian Westernizers' conviction that Russia must pass through the same historical evolution as Western Europe, for the Russian people had not been corrupted, according to him, by the Roman juridical heritage or the individualistic view of property relations. The future of Russia depended on whether it would prove possible to fuse the communitarian views and autochthonous traditions of the common man with the universalism of the *intelligentsia*, to synthesize holistic Russian principles with modernized ideas.

Yet not only the privilege of better knowledge and experience was referred to in the theorem, but also, as in Chernyshevsky's writings, the greater proximity of late-comers (*tarde venientes*) to idealized earlier forms of social life, e.g. the *obshchina*. The probably last version of the theorem, however, belonged to Lenin.

Lenin was perhaps much more a product of Russian reaction to the West than of Marxism. In some respects he resembled certain professional agitators of the *narodnichestvo* movement (e.g. Tkachëv) and he willed himself, as Besançon (1977) observed, to incarnate Rakhmetov, the revolutionary hero of Chernyshevsky's novel *What Is to Be Done?*. He believed that a Russian socialist could not completely accept the correctness of Marxian theory to the extent that it was based on a presumed law of historical development, for he would then have to admit the need for capitalist development in Russia and the ruin of his own ideal, at least in the short term. Out of the predicament of backwardness he deduced the possibility of a third path: neither Russian traditionalism, as the Slavophiles and the Populists wanted, nor Western capitalism, as the *zapadniki* wanted, but immediate Socialism. In fact, Lenin pretended to nothing less than overstepping one historical stage: a small group of conspirators (the Bolsheviks) would be able to make Russia skip the capitalist stage of economic development and lead Russia directly from Tsarism to Socialism.

If an example were needed of modern artificialism, Lenin provided it. Not only did he undertake the total restructuring of Russian society, but he wanted to re-engineer even the human soul, as he explained during a visit to the laboratory of the great physiologist Pavlov (Figes 1996:732). But, at the same time, the other aspect of modernity, the clear distinction between values and facts, was cancelled as pointless by Marxist-Leninist theory, for theoretical and ethical consciousness was thought to be just an expression of social interests or an aspect of the world under investigation. Whereas modernity had separated conscience and consciousness, the Russian revolutionaries brought attention to the concept of *soznatelnost'* which refers to moral as well as to factual judgement.

The totalitarianism which resulted from Lenin's revolution, did not spring from 'the Byzantine heritage of caesaropapism' (Donskis 1995:20), nor was it simply the old Russian holism in a new guise, but it was the result of an effort to impose or to reimpose the priority of the social whole by individualistic means in a society in which this priority, under the influence of Western individualism, had become

---

[4] It would be possible to see here an intensification: What previously had been, in Kantian terms, a regulating idea, unattainable but needed to direct one's thought in

dubious. As the social whole as a value had become questionable, an excessive emphasis[4] was now placed on it and its promoters resorted to violence. The totalitarian bureaucracy, as Davydov (1995:162) has described it, was characterized by its ubiquity (it permeated the whole of social life so that there were no social relations independent of it), by the fact that it shaped everything anew, and by using armed force not only for war, but for the permanent terrorization and physical destruction of designated social groups within the State or society. Thus, it effaced the dividing line between war and peace.

This synthesis of holism and individualistic artificialism was complemented by a surviving element of the old ideology of universal sovereignty: the Soviet Union was seen not only as the first socialist society, but as a pioneer in the liberation of mankind from exploitation.

On the whole, the phenomena discussed here (the Russian *intelligentsia*, the ethnic theory of nationalities, the tension between two concepts of sovereignty, and the theories and practices born out of the theorem of the privilege of backwardness, especially totalitarianism) were Janus-faced hybrids, local modifications of modern values, resulting from the interaction of modernity and non-modernity. Some, for instance the idea and the ideal of an *intelligentsia* in the typically Russian sense, have largely remained Russian phenomena. Others are examples of a phenomenon which is present in many contemporary non-Western cultures and which has even been reintegrated into the dominant Western culture: the tension between the idea of equal rights of individual entities (be they individual human beings or individual nations) and the recognition of the other qua other, exemplified with regard to Russia by the tension between two concepts of sovereignty. It is perhaps this tension which lies at the heart of what sometimes is called post-modernity. Still others, finally, for instance totalitarianism, are examples of a disease of modernity.

From Byzantine Icons to Modern Russian Art

The acculturation to modernity can also be studied in the field of Russian-Orthodox art. Exodus 20,4 and Deuteronomy 5,8 expressed

---

a traditional order where the distinction between facts and values was blurred, now became a well-defined political goal, to be imposed by political means. It thus became part of modernity.

the interdiction of the making of images of any sort, but this did not prevent early Christian paintings and even individual portraits in the Roman catacombs since the early third century. Although theological leaders often disapproved, the image-friendly hellenistic tradition in which most newly converted Christians were rooted, was perhaps responsible for the fact that images of martyrs and saints were venerated very early. Before these images could turn into icons during the Iconoclastic Controversy, however, a new religious attitude towards them, founded on a new theological understanding, needed to be developed.

The Iconoclastic Controversy in the eighth and ninth centuries, whose importance and scope within Eastern Orthodoxy can be compared only with the Reformation in Western Christianity, erupted when some reform-minded emperors attacked the use of images within the church. Iconoclasts based their criticisms on the Old Testament as well as on John 4,24 and they advanced theological arguments especially against the image of Christ as it can in no way circumscribe or represent the divine prototype. In fact, it was the image of Christ which was at the heart of the controversy.

The Iconophiles countered that the interdiction of images in Exodus and Deuteronomy was not in force any longer since God had appeared in the flesh, and they drew further arguments from the long philosophical tradition. The One or the Good of Plotin which produces hypostases in a descending succession of levels of being gave rise to the thought that, in reverse, man can also ascend to higher levels of being, and attain deification or *theosis*. These Neoplatonic ideas were introduced into Christianity by Pseudo-Dionysius the Areopagite in his treatises on the celestial and ecclesiastical hierarchies (Pseudo-Dionysius coined the term hierarchy), and John of Damascus applied them in his discussion of the veneration of images. John thought that the resemblance of images consisted in their more or less intense participation in the model or prototype, and he also suggested that there is a hierarchy of participation, starting from con-substantial identity (the Son as the image of the Father) to painted images of Christ which reflect and participate only in a limited way in the divine realities although the model is present even in them. Because of this grace-providing presence of the model in the images, they must receive veneration (*proskynesis*), but not adoration (*latreia*) which is reserved for God.

These Platonic or Neoplatonic arguments were not sufficient to defeat the Iconoclasts, but the situation changed when Aristotelian categories were introduced. Aristotle had thought that not ideas as such are the real being, but that reality is created or formed when a form shapes or imprints itself on matter, and that therefore only individual human beings exist in a true sense and not the idea of man. As long as the Platonic view that the ideas are the true being and the highest reality was accepted, the question could be asked if and to what extent an image resembles its model – and here the Iconophiles were in the defensive and open to the charge of heresy, at least insofar as the image of Christ was concerned. For if they argued that the image represents Christ's human nature, they implicitly separated the two natures of Christ (which was against the rulings of the Council of Chalcedon of 451), and if they argued that the image also represents Christ's divine nature, they conflicted with the principle of the same Council that Christ's two natures cannot be confused.

With the help of Aristotelian categories, however, the patriarch Nicephorus could argue that the image is of a different nature than its model, that there is a relationship of similarity but not of substance (which would include a kind of magical presence of the archetype in the image), or, in his words, that the icon is not a natural but an artificial image. Nicephorus' interpretation resulted in what Schönborn (1976:209) has called a demystification of sacred images. It was Theodore Studites, though, who completed the argument and who combined the developing theology of the icon with the christological dogma.

Icons do not represent somebody's nature, he wrote, but his hypostasis or manifestation, his personal way of being. Peter, for instance, is not represented as a mortal or as a being endowed with reason, for to this extent he is not different from Paul (mortality and reason are common human characteristics and aspects of human nature), but he is represented with a certain colour of the eyes or a certain kind of nose and a certain complexion of the face. Similarly, it is not the nature of Christ which is represented in an image but the hypostasis or the person in which the two natures of Christ manifest themselves. Christ's icon can be drawn because, in biblical terms, the Word has become flesh. It does not lift man towards the contemplation of a superior reality (λογος), as the Platonists would have said, but of a divine mode of existence (τροπος). While it is true that the archetype is present in the icon, it is a hypostatic presence – just like the impression of a seal in wax. It can perhaps be said that with this interpretation of the icon Theodore transcended the contrast which is often assumed to exist, on the one hand, between oriental religious art and its close affinity to a mysticism of infinity and a merging into a union with the divine and, on the other hand, the art of the Occident which reproduces the *angst* and the impressions of the individual.

While Theodore's coherent defence of the sacred images may be taken as the epitome of the theological arguments which were finally accepted at the Council of Constantinople in 870, it remains, nevertheless, that the common people ignored these philosophical considerations completely, and that the common practice of the veneration of icons often had more affinity to the Platonic approach. In any case, the icon was an external expression of man's transfiguration, of a person who is on the path of deification or *theosis*.

There were conventional methods of transmitting the state of theosis. The golden background eliminated most spatial perception and provided the dimension of spaceless eternity; illuminating the image from behind, it also provided some justification for the often-used inverse perspective, for instance in the table and foot-stools of Rublev's *Trinity* (fifteenth century). Oversized and wide-open eyes, a thin nose and a small mouth were meant to convey the state of sainthood, and colours, halos, aureoles and gestures all had conventionalized meanings.

As Russian interpreters of the veneration of icons have written[5], the iconographer did not paint his subjective impressions or experiences. The icon had the character of a communal creation, and only those who lived according to the moral demands of the Church and who accepted the authority of the religious and artistic tradition were thought to be in a position to paint it according to accepted norms. This is quite different from the Catholic tradition which does not impose an aesthetic doctrine or a particular style.

While in Eastern Orthodoxy the religious image, the icon, is an expression of church dogma (christology) and of what is thought to be objective truth, in the West, at least since the Renaissance and the Reformation, the images simply have the purpose of decorating the churches and of reminding the people of the stories of the Bible. For Luther the question of images was an *adiaphoron* and he did not include the interdiction of images of Exodus 20,4 into his catechism; reformed churches, though, remain without images.

---

[5] Khomyakov, Vol 1, pp. 143-74 ('Po povodu Gumbol'dta'); also Ouspensky (1983).

The religious image of the modern West expresses a subjectively experienced truth about the history of salvation as interpreted by the artist. Since the fifteenth century when new geographic and intellectual discoveries produced far-reaching changes in the self-perception of people, the disappearance of the golden background and the use of the central linear perspective (which had been known in Antiquity but had been abandoned in favour of a different understanding of reality) implied that the location of the painter determined which aspects of the space and of the objects will appear in the painting; the individual painter became the centre and the judge of what aspects of reality would become visible. Interest in portraits grew, and they were not painted any more according to a cultural model so that Rembrandt's individual models sometimes were afraid to see their portrait (Malraux 1965:66).

In Byzantium after the Iconoclastic Controversy, however, and also in Russia until Peter the Great, there was almost only sacred art; secular objects remained largely unrepresented, as if they were not worth the effort (with the exception of the popular art of wood engraving, the *lubki*). Icons were seen as a path to God, and this explains perhaps why even recently a Russian could claim to feel nauseated at the sight of Rubens' *Bacchanalia* (Besançon 1994:196).

When in the seventeenth century Russian-Orthodox artists and thinkers came into contact with Western views about art, iconographers like Simon Oushakov adopted the central perspective and other Western techniques, although the Old Believers who were committed to the tradition to which Rublev's name is attached, rejected the new ways of painting as unorthodox and founded their own (commercially quite successful) icon-workshops. On the whole, the contacts with Western art formed and strengthened the conviction in Russia that Russian art must be different from western art, and they produced new concepts of art which combined the two traditions. On the theoretical level, Leo Tolstoy's view, expounded in his *What is Art?*, may serve as example.

Tolstoy defined art generally as a means of transmitting feelings to other men; art in the highest sense was, according to him, the transmission of religious feelings so that others are infected by them. On the basis of this view he attacked modern western art as empty, vicious and artificial, resulting not from religious sentiments, but from the desire of enjoyment of the upper classes.

But there was something modern in Tolstoy's defense of traditional religious art. While traditional man generally considers his culture as the only culture and devalues all outsiders so that they are accepted only on an inferior level, Tolstoy accepted individualism on the global level in the sense that he recognized all true artistic cultures as equal individuals, for he considered that there have been many true arts, each of them corresponding to the religious view of life held by the people among whom it arose. But he rejected individualism on the subordinate level, for he considered that an art must necessarily be shared by the whole community and transmit feelings accessible to everyone. This hierarchical combination of individualistic and holistic traits is characteristic of the Russian-orthodox acculturation to modernity.

Kandinsky was a theorizer and a practitioner at the same time. Like Tolstoy, he rejected the moral emptiness of conventional western art. When the artist tries to imitate nature or to interpret it, he wrote, his pictures may be beautiful or sublime, but he nevertheless only tries to satisfy his ambition or greed. But just as Wagner and Schönberg had opened new avenues in music, the art of painting should also lead to a higher level of spirituality. Art should improve and refine the human soul and provide access to the spiritual world; art, in fact, should be similar to religion, Kandinsky believed, and it is perhaps not surprising that he saw the roots of his own art in the Russian icons. To achieve these goals, the artist should paint the invisible, the abstract – the only world which really matters. In Kandinsky's opinion it was not worth the effort to paint the objects of this world, and he demonstrated a total lack of interest in them; but he thought it worth the effort to paint the absolute which reveals itself in colours and abstract forms. This may be characterized as an attempt to escape from the exterior world, as the seeking of unity with the One in Plotin's sense, or as religious individualism.

From Traditional to Modern Russian Music

Music was until recent times considered as the model of beautiful and harmonious being, an image of the eternal harmony of the cosmos. Orpheus tamed the wild aspects of man and beast, for music was thought to contribute to the fundamental attitude or the ethos of all. Plato even wanted to eliminate certain musical instruments like the *aulos* (which was attributed to the ecstatic nature of Dionysos) from the ideal state and to accept only Apollo's *kithara*, and Philo of

Alexandria opposed true ethical and cosmic to sensuous-feminine music, although the music of Dionysos was never suppressed.

Gregorian chant which retained elements from Christian antiquity, excluded musical instruments and cultic dance. Without pulsating rhythms and sensuous elements, it represented an interiorized prayer, while the singing in unison was taken to be a symbol of unanimity.

Russian church music, too, was performed without musical instruments; it was monodic chant in the four authentic and four plagal echoi or modi, written down in Byzantine neumes, called *kriuki* in Russian. From the year 1600 on a certain kind of "polyody" (*mnogoglasie*) began to spread, but it is uncertain to what extent this was the result of Western influences or an indigenous development (Arro 1962:32). The Old Believers, however, continued to insist on monophony and to use only *kriuki*-notation. In all cases, the musical tradition resulted from anonymously transmitted collective rather than individual production.

On the other hand, the central problem of the history of Western music has been the departure from traditional monophony and the development of the specifically occidental contrapuntal polyphony and of chordal-harmonic music. More than other musical traditions Western music is characterized by a specific tendency towards rationalization (Weber 1958 d) and the gradual dissolution of holistic and melodious attributes.

Replacing the neumes of Antiquity, the staff notation and the mensural notation, developed in medieval monasteries, were the necessary innovations without which the production or transmission of modern polyphonic compositions would have been quite impossible.

Musical modernity started when the ancient and medieval modes that had previously served as the basis of melody and harmony, were gradually replaced, during the seventeenth century, by the system of tonality which has dominated Western music until the beginning of the twentieth century. The principle of tonality can be characterized by the fact that it orders the tones of a composition and that it confers meaning and significance to them by placing them in relation to a tonic and to the three common triads. Within this system each voice of a polyphonic composition could be an individual entity and, at the same time, a part of an organic whole.

Furthermore, the equal floating temperament, perhaps determined by the interest in the transposition of melodies, is an example of the technical (means-end) rationality, so characteristic of the occidental 'spirit'. The modern system of musical keys is, in fact, a circle, a closed system of twenty-four keys, which attempts to realize, to a higher degree than in any other musical tradition, a rational tonal system – without, however achieving it completely as it is thwarted by the Pythagorean comma: the chasm between the empirically given and the logically correct has remained unbridgeable.[6]

In more recent times, perhaps since Beethoven, Western music reflected purely individual artistic concerns; since the nineteenth century it even tried to express wild passions (Wagner's Kundry) or the perverse and terrifying (Richard Strauss in *Salome* or *Elektra*). The sharpest dissonances came to be accepted. In the twelve-tone music of Schönberg and others, finally, all tones of the well-tempered tone-system are of equal standing instead of receiving different meanings from their respective relations to a tonic, and dissonances are not resolved any more.

If it is asked what happened to the musical traditions of non-Western societies which were exposed to the influence of Western music, it can generally be stated that everywhere attempts were made to create national musical styles out of a combination of Western and indigenous structures. In Russia, for instance, on the purely instrumental level, the music of Russian church bells can be heard in many modern pieces (the finale of Glinka's 'A Life for the Tsar'; Tchaikovsky's Overture 1812; Rachmaninov's second piano concerto). More importantly, and on another level, Glinka, Rimsky-Korsakov and other composers promoted the idea of a national Russian operatic style: Russian traditional melodies were harmonised in such a way that their modal character was not marred by considerations related to the modern system of tonality which uses concepts such as tonic or dominant. Archaisms such as whole tone scales and augmented fourths were also used. Glinka set up rational patterns of 'creative behaviour' without which modern compositions which include folk themes would result in an unfortunate ethnographic babble.

---

[6] Weber (1958d:3) explained that if one ascends or descends from a tonic in circles first in the octave followed by fifths, fourths..., the powers of these divisions can never meet on one and the same tone no matter how long the procedure be continued. The twelfth perfect fifth $(2/3)^{12}$ is larger by the Pythagorean comma than the seventh octave equalling $(1/2)^7$. Thus, the desire for musical rationalization produces, as Weber saw, inescapable irrationalities. This, in fact, is not different, according to him, from what happens to doctrines and ethics of salvation in the process of rationalization: the more they follow the demand of consistency, the greater the likelihood that their principles come into conflict with the realities of life.

In another area, Taneev's cantatas offered a solution to the problem of how to combine the melodies of the Russian folksong with the Western contrapuntal techniques, and Stravinsky in 'Le sacre du printemps' used irregular metrics and developed a certain harmonic style, filled with dissonances, out of the modal melodies of folksongs. Thus, even in the field of music modernity is not accepted as an unquestioned whole. The rationalizing aspects of Western polyphonic and chordal-harmonic music as well as its individualizing aspects are combined with the melodic and modal principle of traditional Russian music in such a way that a new and perhaps even intensified version of modern music is created, listened to everywhere but nevertheless a typically Russian exemplar of modernity.

TRIALS AND ERRORS SINCE THE OCTOBER
REVOLUTION

The preceding chapters have distinguished between the modern individualistic ideology and the holistic ideology of the Russian-Orthodox tradition. It has become apparent that, whereas within the context of and in close affinity with the rise of inworldly individualism there arose in the West the many other facets of modernity – modern science, law and art as well as particularly the capitalist 'spirit' – , Russia's holistic ideology which preconised *sobornost'* and *obshchina* and accepted individualism only at a subordinate level provided a set of ideas, values and motivations which were not opposed to tsarism and which favoured a 'spirit' or ethos without inner motivation for economic success as it was not considered relevant for salvation.

Even the Old Believers and the sects whose congregational religiosity led to increased methodical economic activity did not produce the world-dominating personality of the Protestants, for the Old Believers retained traditionalistic and ritualistic characteristics, and the sects remained 'broken' and undecided in their attitude towards the 'world'.

But when, under the impact of modernity which seeped into Russia from the West, the traditional Russian ideology began to incorporate some individualistic concepts and values (without, however, completely rejecting holism), ideological hybrids were formed which in some cases had a resemblance to those which another traditional and holistic culture, Germany, had developed in its encounter with modernity: the ethnic theory of the nation and the idea of qualitative individualism or individuality which also manifested itself in the arts and in music. Another ideological Janus was Lenin's idea of the artificial reconstruction of society as a whole. All this led to attempts to reshape the social and institutional structure as well as the Orthodox 'spirit' which traditionally had lived in it.

Some Russian authors, like Chaadaev or Gogol, had already proposed a reeducation of the Russian people, a new discipline of the soul (although Chaadaev found his model in the West and Gogol in Russian antiquity). At the beginning of the twentieth century the authors of *Vekhi* (Signposts or Landmarks, a collective publication)

had in common the idea of the primacy of the moral-religious education of the Russian people over the external social forms, as Gershenzon (1909) stated in the Preface, and even under the Soviet regime
the modern Russophiles, as can be gleaned from Rasputin's novels,
considered moral regeneration to be a major problem. The *Vekhi*-
group later served as a model for Solzhenitsyn whose manifestoes
were rooted in Russian Christianity and a concept of *homo religiosus*;
the new intelligentsia, according to Solzhenitsyn, should be recognized by its spiritual selflessness and by laying aside all material well-
being. Although he had spent many years in Russian prisons and
labour camps, he also tended to reject Western individualism and
democracy and instead favoured the formation of a benevolent
authoritarian regime that would draw upon the spirit of Russia's traditional holistic values and would be most natural and least painful in
the Russian context. He did not propose to reconstruct (*perestroit'*)
Russia's institutions but to revitalize (*obustroit'*) her ethos or soul.

   There was also another trend in which the idea of individuality
(*lichnost'*, a term which had gained prominence among the intelligentsia since the middle of the nineteenth century) was accentuated.
It referred to a qualitative individualism which was shaped in reaction
to the quantitative individualism of the West. The concept of *lichnost'*
(self-fashioning and self-improvement by means of internal control)
remained to a certain extent prominent even after the October Revolution when Lunacharsky, the People's Commissioner of Education,
claimed that the individual (*lichnost'*) is one of the highest aims of
socialist culture for all people even if it must develop all its endow-
ments and its unique set of features only in a harmonic and solidary
society of equals – i.e. in the collective – in order to serve society. But
while Lenin had willed himself from within to be a revolutionary, the
development of individuality was soon submitted to an external discipline of a particular kind. There seems to have been a startling similarity of the practices of the Communist Control Commissions and
monastic disciplinary practices and the practices of ecclesiastical
courts which had followed the tripartite Orthodox canon law process
to denounce, to admonish and, if necessary, to excommunicate.
Among the Josephites the individual monk had been under constant
surveillance by a core group of "bigger brothers" who enforced congregational discipline. Kharkhordin (1999) has suggested that the
Soviet collective was structured on the model of a virtuous Orthodox
congregation and that these practices soon pervaded every social

body so that every *lichnost'* lived under the tyranny of a multitude of sanctimonious bigger brothers. The rejection of the personality cult (*kul't lichnosti*) was just an extreme case of this general tendency.

Although there is a difference between the organically grown *Gemeinschaft* of the Russian tradition and the state-created collective, it was less the imposed discipline in the collective which irritated its members than the suspicions, the informers and the artificial and arbitrary reconstructions of social life. This feeling was poignantly expressed by a number of poets and writers, for instance by Pasternak in the conclusion of *Doctor Zhivago*. Lara, standing at the coffin of Zhivago and looking back at their life together, remembers that they lived in and by togetherness and the compatibility of the whole; the basic principles of an artificial society, transformed into politics, struck them as particularly amateurish. The idea is expressed that "the riddle of life, the riddle of death, the beauty of loving – that we understood; as for such petty trifles as reshaping the world – these things were not for us". Is it surprising that the Soviet government, in opposing Pasternak's Nobel prize, did not tolerate this feeling of individuality which devalues political life and the rebuilding of society in considering them irrelevant and inconsequential, although it was far removed from Western individualism?

Since the breakdown of the Soviet Union the attention has been turned away from the creation of a new 'discipline of the soul' or a new ethos. Instead, many efforts have gone into the creation of new legal institutions in order to set up a democratic regime and a market economy [1]. It has been assumed that there is a link between economic

---

[1] Kingston-Mann (1999) has drawn attention to the fact that Western economic thought never was a uniform entity when viewed from Russia and that there also was the German-Russian school of historical economics which during the *Methodenstreit* at the end of the nineteenth century and in contrast to classical liberalism emphasized the historical aspects of economic life (e.g. that the behaviour of peasants was shaped by loyalty to family and community as well as private interests). However, this should not blind us to the fact that, whereas liberal or neo-liberal economic theory can be criticized because of its illusions of progress and its optimistic assumption that reality can be rationally reconstructed, historical economics, more attentive to cultural trends, was based on the belief that economic policies flow logically from the study of economic history. Max Weber, though to some extent a disciple of the historical school, insisted that economic policies are necessarily based on value-judgements, be they ethical, cultural or political.

Similarly, the present essay, although it draws attention to the deep cultural roots which are the legacy of Russia, would deserve criticism if it claimed to lead directly to a policy option rather than simply to provide sound foundations for responsible decisions.

growth and the introduction of the rule of law as it is understood in the West (Sachs & Pistor 1997), and that the absence of the rule of law leads to corruption, a weakness of the judiciary and the difficulty to enforce ownership rights.

In the Western legal tradition law transcends politics, and a monarch or parliament, although they may make law, may not make it arbitrarily, and they are themselves bound by it. Furthermore, the rule by law is transcended by the rule of law which implies that there are natural law rights of the individual and that the state itself is subordinated to them; they are higher than statutory law and govern the normative acts of society. The necessity to uphold and to defend these individual rights led to the separation of legislative, executive and judicial powers.

Russia's cultural tradition, however, has generally devalued law; the Slavophiles (Kireevsky) even thought that Russia distinguished herself from the Catholic Church and the Western states by the fact that she was not the product of jurists and of Roman law. In peasant communes, as can be gleaned from Leo Tolstoy's stories, matters were decided on an ad hoc basis "according to justice (*pravda*)", rather than on the basis of formal legal norms. There was no movement of obligations "from status to contract" – to use Henry Maine's memorable phrase.

On the level of the state, the autocracy and later the Party stood above the law. Whereas in the collection of statutes of 1832 (*svod zakonov rossiiskoi imperii*) the power of the tsar was still characterized as unrestrained (*neogranichennyi*), the courts became separated from the administration in the Judicial Reform of 1864, and for the first time the idea of state power restrained by the rule of law (*pravovoe gosudarstvo*, derived from the German term *Rechtsstaat*) appeared on the horizon although Weber (1906) still talked of *Scheinkonstitutionalismus* at the beginning of the twentieth century. It disappeared again after the October Revolution, for socialist legality was not designed to restrain state power, and only reemerged during the period of *perestroika* and in the 1993 Constitution. This Constitution created an independent judiciary and made possible the judicial review of administrative acts, but the separation of powers between the *duma* (legislature) and the executive remains blurred, for the President may rule by decree as long as the decrees do not contradict existing laws. With regard to basic rights, it is not clear whether they are granted by the state (which would imply the possibility that they can be revoked) or whether they are considered prior to the state.

Even if one assumes that the constitutional framework for the rule of law does exist to a certain extent, the actual state of affairs is different, for the establishment and the survival of the rule of law requires much more than the mere availability of appropriate legislation. Legal scholars are well aware that it also depends on extra-legal factors such as the existence of a strong state and the prevalence of a certain ethos or certain attitudes in society (Feldbrugge 2000 : 213) without which the path inevitably leads to administrative corruption. Moreover, as Max Weber (1954) has already shown in his Sociology of Law, there is no obvious and clear connection between legal and economic systems in the sense that a particular legal system will necessarily lead to the development of an expected economic system.

Russians have traditionally believed that their country is the land of the one and indivisible truth (*pravda*, which means both truth and justice) which can be discovered only by the community as a whole. There is in their tradition no concept of a relative truth or of the possibility of many aspects or versions of the truth (Mehnert 1958 : 316). Laws or even a constitution achieved by a compromise between independent and autonomous individuals or parties may therefore seem of inferior value to them; they may be useful, but they are not *pravda*.

Neither the modern individualistic ideology nor the spirit of capitalism (in Weber's sense) are the natural heritage and ethos of all humankind; they do not take hold automatically once the institutional "impediments" to their development have been eliminated or replaced by modern legal institutions. Moreover, self-reliance (*samostoyatel'nost'*) and economic rationalism do not have the same intensity or stability if they are not rooted in value-rational action based on a value-rational worldview which directs the actions of its adherents from within.

Just as in Germany after the First World War the Weimar Constitution conflicted with the traditional holistic ideology, one finds in modern Russia the persistence of collectivist sentiment even among state enterprise directors (Brym 1996) but, equally often, crass egoism as the external discipline of the Societ collectives has not been replaced by anything else. There is also individuality (*lichnost'*), a qualitative inner individualism. Whereas on this basis in the arts and music the creation of national styles, combining the traditional and

the modern, has been attempted with some success, it is perhaps rea-
sonable to suggest that on the politico-legal and economic level it is
much more difficult to create new institutions which have an affinity
to the ideology and the ethos of the people and do not produce inner
tension between the form and the 'spirit', and which might thus lead
to a development of unbroken homogeneity. Policies which ignore
the indigenous definitions of reality are likely to fail. Any successful
perestroika needs to take account of and to adapt to the ideology and
the meanings by which the people live, to be aware that men do not
live by bread alone. These deep cultural roots can perhaps be compared to the unheard theme in Elgar's *Enigma Variations* as it influences and shapes the countermelody which one hears.

THE CONCEPT OF ADEQUATE CAUSATION IN COMPARATIVE CULTURAL STUDIES

A study about the economic ethics of Russian-Orthodox Christianity, undertaken in the Weberian tradition, can certainly provide insights into Russian development, but it can also be interpreted as part of a universal history of capitalism and economic development in which similar studies on China, India, Islamic culture or the Russian religious tradition support and complement each other, especially if the economic development within these cultures is seen in comparison with the Western development. In order to achieve this global view, the preceding effort which attempted to characterize the economic ethics of Russia, will be placed in a wider methodological context.

When Max Weber wrote his essays on the 'Economic Ethics of World Religions' and when he planned additional essays on Islam, early Christianity and Russian Orthodoxy (Schluchter 1984:the appendix), he thought that capitalism in a general sense has existed in most advanced cultures. Certainly, when he talked of capitalism Weber did not mean the uncontrolled impulse to acquisition, the simple pursuit of gain or of money, for this pursuit has been common at all times and in most countries among coachmen, dishonest officials, crusaders and waiters, and, as Weber said, this naïve idea of capitalism should be given up once and for all. By capitalism in a general sense Weber meant the pursuit of profit by means of continuous rational enterprise and by formally peaceful exchange (Weber 1958a:17) which can exist among traders and moneylenders and can also take the form of political capitalism, for instance in colonial capitalism or tax-farming.

While being well aware of these different manifestations of capitalism in Western history as well as elsewhere, including Russia, Weber was mainly interested in the particular kind of capitalism which developed in Western society in the last several centuries: modern Western capitalism. He described it as rational-capitalistic organization of formally free labour, based on free market exchange and on the separation of business from the household, for the satisfaction of the needs

of the masses (Weber 1958a:21-2).[1] Within this system may be found
– at least at the time of its early development – the 'spirit of capitalism', identified with the rational tempering of the irrational impulse
of gain, based on calculations in terms of capital and resulting from
the religious doctrine of proof (*Bewährung*). In his *Protestant Ethic* (PE)
Weber mainly, although not exclusively, tried to understand (*verstehen*)
this 'spirit' of capitalism, a certain style and conduct of life which a
century or two after the Reformation appeared to have a close elective affinity with the religiously oriented ethical rationalism of the
Protestants.

Most present-day scholars of Weber's PE see the relationship
between the protestant ethic and the spirit of capitalism as one of
elective affinity or of homologic structures and not of causality
(Fischoff 1968:81). The theorem of elective affinity (*Wahlverwandtschaft*)
originated in the natural sciences: The Swede Torbern Bergmann
wrote *De attractionibus electivis* in 1782, referring to the fact that in anor-
ganic chemistry elements may form combinations which can later be
dissolved in favour of others. Goethe, who had his own view of the
natural sciences, interpreted these phenomena of natural law
described by Bergmann as resulting from inclination, affection or
attraction, and he transferred these ideas and the German term
which described them (*Wahlverwandtschaft*) to the realm of interhuman
relationships.[2] Goethe's figurative use of the term was later adopted
by Weber in two different contexts and he attached to it two different
meanings. On the one hand, it is true that it is used by Weber to indicate meaningful adequacy (*Sinnadäquanz*) or affinity of meaning of religious concepts and motives in relation to each other and in relation to
the total construct of meaning to which they belong. For instance,
ethical (emissary) prophecy had, according to him, a profound elective affinity to the conception of a supra-mundane personal God
(Weber 1920:257), the dogma of predestination combined with the
doctrine of proof had an elective affinity with a systematic conduct of
life as opposed to single good deeds, and the protestant feeling of
being a tool and not a vessel of God fitted well into the whole
monotheistic world view although no causal relationships are implied

---

[1] A more complete definition would distinguish between the capitalistic enterprise
and the capitalistic system which can only develop under the rule of law and when
the administration of the monetary system has been monopolized by the State.

[2] See Benno von Wiese's Editorial Note on Goethe's novel 'Die Wahlver-
wandtschaften', in: *Goethes Werke*, Hamburger Ausgabe, Vol. VI, 1989, p. 675.

here. Similarly, the devout Hindu was accursed to remain within the structure of the karma doctrine (Weber 1921:121) which formed a meaningful whole resulting from the non-causal elective affinities of its parts.

On the other hand, Weber wished to place his methodology beyond the one-sided alternatives of materialism and idealism so that when he spoke, for instance, of an elective affinity between the spirit and the form of capitalism (Weber 1978b:171) or between calvinism and capitalism (ibid.:305), he wanted to reject any type of reductionism and he also wished to imply that any assertion about the manner and the general direction of causal relationships, while not excluding reciprocal influences, must be the result of further historical research, not just a methodological one.

It is in this second sense which does not exclude causal relationships if they can be established by historical research that Weber used the term *Wahlverwandtschaft* in the PE. He knew that for the historian the method of *Verstehen* provides no guarantee of empirical truth, if it is not complemented by a method which can establish causal relationships. Adequacy at the level of meaning, as he said, needs to be verified by causal adequacy.

This was achieved by Weber in "The Economic Ethics of World Religions" (EEWR), part of his *Collected Essays in the Sociology of Religion*, which were not intended as well-rounded monographs but rather emphasized those elements in the respective cultures in which they differed from Western civilization. While Weber's wife Marianne (1975:333) wrote that the essays on the EEWR contribute to the characterization of Western man and his culture, and while it may also be true that before the publication of his essays on India and China there lay Weber's discovery, as Schluchter (1989:45) puts it, that the whole of Western culture – not only its economic aspects, but also its law, its organizational aspects and even its music – is permeated by a specific mode of rationalism which needed to be characterized further by contrasting it with the different modes of rationalism in non-Western cultures, it should nevertheless not be forgotten that these essays also constituted an attempt to verify and to validate the PE-thesis within the context of a universal history of capitalism.[3] In fact, it was one of

---

[3] References to this 'Problematik' are too frequent to be ignored, e.g., Max Weber 1920, p. 12; p. 265; p. 373 sqq; p. 447; p. 512; Max Weber 1921, p. 110 sqq; p. 122; p. 203 sqq.

Weber's main historical and sociological interests, even in his studies on the 'Economic Ethics of World Religions', to establish the cause or the causes of those particular aspects of modern Western capitalism which distinguish it from all other forms and manifestations of capitalism.

As Weber talked of the causal imputation of the 'spirit' of modern Western capitalism to the religious ethic of Protestantism, or more generally of the attribution of a concrete effect to a concrete cause, it may not be superfluous to ask ourselves how he thought to achieve this causal imputation and what he meant by the terms cause or causation in a socio-historical context. For an answer, we shall go back to the work of the "distinguished physiologist" v. Kries (1888) on which Weber heavily relied (Weber 1949:162) and then to the essays on "The Economic Ethics of World Religions" which can serve to apply v. Kries' theory.

Adequate causation according to v. Kries

It is an axiom, says v. Kries, that every event which actually occurs, was necessarily produced by the totality of all previously existing circumstances many of which are often unknown to us. But if this is so, what do we mean when we attribute a concrete event to a single cause? In order to show this, we must first clarify the notion of objective possibility.

If we say that an event is objectively possible, we mean that we are uncertain about its occurrence or non-occurrence because we do not know all its conditions and all the surrounding circumstances, for under clearly defined conditions the notion of objective possibility cannot be applied. But the same notion imposes itself when the conditions and circumstances of an event are only partially or generally known and when we wish to consider the relationship of an effect to these general or partial conditions. For instance, it is indeed objectively possible that, while playing at dice, the six comes up ten times in a row, for there is nothing in the general conditions and circumstances of playing at dice which might necessarily prevent this particular outcome. But it is also objectively possible that the six never comes up.

We also say occasionally that a certain person could have done or known this or that. In such cases we abstract from the given particular thoughts and preoccupations which existed at the time of the event in question, as well as from the psychological make-up of the person under consideration, and refer only to that part of the circumstances which is of particular interest to us, namely the physical or intellectual capacities or the social position of that person. We thus assert the compatibility of a certain action with a part of the total conditions involved. It might be argued, for instance, that Chamberlain could have stopped Hitler by not accepting the Munich agreement, if one abstracts from the political situation in Europe at the time and from his personal characteristics and refers only to his position as prime minister of Britain. On the whole, therefore, we may talk of the objective possibility of an event under generally or partially defined conditions, if such determinations of the conditions are conceivable which would, according to our experience and nomological knowledge, produce the event.

This notion of objective possibility will now be used in the context of causal relationships. Without any doubt, only the total complex of all conditions which produced a result may be called its cause in the strict sense of the term. But sometimes another sense of the terms cause and causation plays an important role, and this was particularly so in German legal thought which in Weber's time was much concerned with the problem of causality. We might say, for instance, that certain generally defined conditions or circumstances represent a larger or smaller possibility of bringing about a given result (e.g.: driving under the influence of alcohol increases the possibility of an accident). The question is, then, how such general statements about causal relationships might influence the evaluation of concrete cases.

Before we return to this question, some preliminary remarks are necessary. According to v. Kries, the question regarding the causality of a certain circumstance or factor is equivalent to the question of what would have happened in a particular case if from the total context of conditions this circumstance or factor had been absent while all others had remained unchanged. Therefore, we shall say that a circumstance may be considered to have caused an effect if it can be shown that the same effect would probably not have occurred without it. But what do we mean when we talk about the *same* effect?

To be sure, we deny the causality of any factor not only if without it the effect would have occurred in the same way, but also if its absence would have produced only an unimportant modification of the effect. It is clear, therefore, that we are not interested in the effect with all its concrete details, but rather in a generalized idea of it. For instance, if we ask whether a certain medication has caused some-body's death, we want to know whether he would also have died without taking this medication but not whether he would have died in exactly the same position or in the same corner of his room.

Finally, the following distinction needs to be made: if a given factor has caused an effect, the causal nexus may be either general or a peculiarity of the given case. The following example taken from v. Kries will clarify this.

If a coachman who is driving a passenger is drunk or falls asleep and thus misses his way, and if then the passenger is killed by light-ning, it may be said that the sleep (or drunkenness) of the coachman has caused the death of the passenger. For if the coach had been on the right way, it would without a doubt have been at a different loca-tion at the time of the thunderstorm and the passenger would proba-bly not have been hurt. But one can perhaps say that there is here no general connection between the above-mentioned cause and the effect in all cases of drunkenness, although a causal connection is undeniable in this particular case. Moreover, in general, a traveller can also be hit by lightning, if the coachman is awake.

Matters are quite different if, in the same example, instead of being hit by lightning, the coach had been overturned and the traveller had in this way been hurt or killed. In this case one would have to assume not only an individual but a general causal relationship between the sleeping of the coachman and the accident; one might say that in our experience the sleeping of a coachman, although it does not necessar-ily always cause an accident, generally does increase the possibility and probability of an accident.

The purpose of these reflections will become clear with the help of the notion of objective possibility as it permits a general or abstract consideration of a causal relationship between a single factor and an effect. A theory which knows of no other causal relationship than that B always is the effect of A and which thus asserts the regularity of an effect without any exception, often appears to be fruitless, for the rela-tionship between a single factor and an effect often is not of such nature. But, as opposed to a causal theory which assumes an absolute regularity of the causal relationship, it is often possible to say that a causal element augments the objective possibility of an effect or that the presence of a causal element produces a certain effect in a much larger variety of circumstances.

In order to have short terms to designate the two variations in the

example of the sleeping coachman, v. Kries talks of adequate and of
'chance' causation. A is called the adequate cause of B, and B the
adequate effect of A, if generally (in the large majority of possible circumstances) A may be seen to favour B; in the opposite case he talks
of 'chance' causation. In the above example the drunkenness of the
coachman was the 'chance' cause of the effect that the traveller was
killed by lightning; it would, however, have to be considered as the
adequate cause in the modified example where the overturn of the
coach resulted in the death of the traveller.

It is perhaps useful to point to a frequently occurring confusion
which tends to result from the misunderstanding of the fact that there
is a basic difference between an event which is considered to be the
'chance' cause of an effect and an insignificant event. Weber
(1949:185) used the example of the two shots fired in Berlin in March
1848 which were, according to him, causally insignificant.[4] One
would speak of 'chance' causation and impute the March Revolution
to those two shots only if it could be argued convincingly that without
them the social and political circumstances would not have produced
a revolution. In fact, though, it is only conceivable that the two shots
have had an influence on the precise moment of the outbreak.

It must be stressed that the distinction between an adequate cause
and a 'chance' cause does not refer to the manner in which in a concrete case a causal factor produces an effect, but that it has an
abstract meaning. It is assumed that the causal factor is a behaviour
or an event which can be added in the scientist's mind to a manifold
variety of circumstances. Equally, the effect which may or may not
have been favoured by the cause, remains generally defined and not
described in all its details. The distinction between adequate and
'chance' causation is always based on a generalized consideration of a
particular case, the result of mental manipulations and comparisons,
by which the degree of objective possibility is intended to be grasped,
not, however, on the objective causality of the events.

It should also be noted that in v. Kries' theory of causality, which, as
has been seen, is based on the notion of objective possibility, a clear
dividing line between adequate and 'chance' causality cannot be

---

[4] Julien Freund (1968, p. 66) erroneously believed that the two shots were, in
Weber's thought, the 'chance' cause of the revolution of 1848. He did not distinguish
between insignificant events and such events which can be considered to be the
'chance' cause of other events.

drawn. The steady transition follows from the fact that the general causal conditions for any effect may take any value between 0 and 1. If, for instance, a train accident forces a traveller to spend a few hours at an unexpected location where he catches an infectious disease and dies, we might say that the train accident was a chance cause of his death. We would, however, be inclined to consider the death to be slightly more adequately caused, if the accident had happened in an area which is known to be disease-ridden. In fact, in this particular case the increase in the risk may be great though the resultant probability is still small. It should perhaps be mentioned in passing here that, as Hart & Honoré (1985:493) have noted, there is a standing danger of confusion, if adequacy theory is misunderstood, between the notion of a substantial increase of a risk and that of increasing the risk to a substantial one.

If one wanted to characterize the theory of adequate causation, one would have to view it at some distance from many modern scientific outlooks. Platonic thinking is nowadays rather rare, and yet one misunderstands the term 'adequate causation' if one thinks of it in any but a Platonic sense – i.e. that 'true' adequate causation is an ideal to which real life situations approximate more or less. Weber (1949:181) said that it admits gradations but that one cannot arrive at numerical estimates. When Turner & Factor (1981:25) who have tried to fit adequate causation theory into the Procrustean bed of modern probability theory criticize the concept by suggesting that its only requirement for a claim of causal connection was a plausible claim of a relationship of conditionality and a dependent probability of greater than zero – and that it is difficult to see what 'proof' means here, they think in the more modern terms of true/false which apply to propositions, rather than in the terms of less true/more true which apply to types or ideal types of reality itself.

The distinction between an adequate cause and a 'chance' cause can, according to v. Kries, easily be used in criminal law where it has to be decided whether someone is responsible for a criminal act. Our sense of justice seems to suggest that a person is responsible only for the adequate consequences of his actions. If, for instance, someone who in a street fight was slightly injured by a knife later died of tetanus, one would normally say that the fight was the 'chance' cause and not the adequate cause of his death, because in general experience superficial knife wounds do not result in death. In a legal system which accepts the notion of adequate causation, the opponent would then not be held responsible for the death.

Weber's use of the concept of adequate causation

Max Weber had been trained as a lawyer and was quite familiar with legal theory. Having seen the fruitfulness of v. Kries' work in German legal theory, especially in the work of Gustav Radbruch, he applied it to the historical and cultural sciences. Like v. Kries, Weber thought that reality is a 'heterogeneous continuum', a stream of immeasurable events which, because of the interdependence of all events, is infinitely complex. But scientific investigation can only grasp a finite and ever changing portion of this infinite reality and of the causal connections within it by concentrating on those aspects which acquire meaning and cultural significance for us or for the historian, i.e., which become "historical individuals". Weber went beyond v. Kries in concentrating on those aspects of "the infinite web of reality" which acquire meaning and cultural significance for us, i.e., which become "historical individuals", and then in perceiving these historical individuals as genetic ideal types which the scientist constructs in order to clarify reality and in the expectation of a possible causal relationship, and which he then uses as hypotheses for causal imputations.

It seemed to Max Weber that – apart from the question of subjective guilt – the legal expert and the historian or social scientist ask exactly the same question : under what circumstances and in what sense can it be asserted that an event or a person has caused a certain effect – and therefore that the ideas developed by v. Kries can and should be applied to the study of universal history. Both the judge and the historian do not explain causally the total course of events as that would be impossible and meaningless. While the judge's deliberations take into account those components of the events which are pertinent for the subsumption under the legal norms, the historian is exclusively concerned with the causal explanation of those elements of the events in question which are of "general significance" and hence of historical interest (Weber 1949:170).

The battle of Marathon serves as an example. By the end of the nineteenth century, the Greek victory in the battle of Marathon of 490 BC between the Athenian army under Miltiades and the Persian army of King Darios the Great was considered to have been of such importance for the subsequent development not only of Greek culture but of Western culture in general that the Baron de Coubertin did not hesitate to add the Marathon run of approximately 42 km to the list of Olympic competitions, in memory of the Athenian soldier who had run the same distance from Marathon to Athens in order to announce the victory – and had then died of exhaustion. If the Persians had been victorious – so it was thought – they would probably have imposed a theocratic regime in Greece as they had done in Israel and Egypt a few decades earlier; the providers of oracles and mystery cults would have dominated the *polis*, and Greek culture with its philosophy, tragedy, sculpture, etc., the seedbed of Western civilization, would never have blossomed.

In Weber's words, the battle "decided" between the independence of Greek culture and a Persian-dominated theocracy which, in the case of a Persian victory, would have been objectively possible (although we cannot state the degree, between 0 and 1, of this objective possibility), for, according to our general knowledge of the Persians, the course of events would have been different in its general outlines and in those features – the cultural values which depended on the Athenian victory – which are significant for Western man. (It should be added in passing that this is the reason why Western man, according to Weber, rates Marathon higher than a battle between two African tribes). Weber concludes that it is not the case that a Persian victory *must* have led to a quite different development of Hellenic culture – but a different development would have been the adequate effect of a Persian victory.

Adequate Causation and 'The Economic Ethics of World Religions'

The notions of objective possibility and of adequate and 'chance' causation are equally useful in the interpretation of Weber's investigation of the causes of the spirit of modern capitalism. The thesis of the causal relevance of the Protestant ethic meant for him that modern capitalism, with its unchanged general characteristics, and quite apart from all its concrete details, probably would not have appeared without this causal element.

This thesis, namely that the Protestant ethic is an adequate cause – and not simply a cause and definitely not the only cause and probably not even the only adequate cause and perhaps not the most important adequate cause – of the modern capitalist spirit, is at the centre of Weber's comparative sociology of religions. Within the field of the cultural sciences, according to Weber, we can only have knowledge of adequate causes, and to say that an event was necessarily caused by previous conditions, would be a pure *a priori*. A thesis about adequate causation presupposes, as has been shown, a judgement of objective possibility; in Weber's case it presupposes a judgement on what we can imagine to be the effect, according to the rules of experience, if in the total complex of the historical conditions of modern capitalism we assume the Protestant ethic to be either absent or modified. A judgement about what might have happened under different circumstances would at first sight perhaps be called irrational, but Weber does not simply rely on the imagination of what might have happened.

In order to be able to arrive at a reasoned judgement, Weber turns towards historical analogies of the most different time periods and cultural areas. Ideally he would like to find a historical course of events which coincides with the development towards modern capitalism in all economically relevant respects except for the protestant ethic. Weber does not find this logical ideal but he can show that, in spite of conditions in India and especially China which were at times and as a rule favourable for the development of capitalism (high esteem for wealth, significant technological knowledge, wars between competing states, etc.), capitalism of the modern occidental kind was not born there (although political capitalism did exist), while in the occidental cultural area, wherever the Protestant ethic took root, modern capitalism developed, even sometimes under the most unfavourable and miserable conditions, for example among the Puritans of New England. Weber, therefore, draws the conclusion that the objective possibility of the independent emergence of modern capitalism, when the Protestant ethic is absent, must be considered as small, for, in the absence of this causal factor, the other existing conditions and circumstances lead us to expect a high degree of possibility of another development.

It is possible to go one step beyond this argument. Weber was not only able to show, by means of intercultural comparison that, when the Protestant ethic was absent, modern capitalism as a rule did not arise (although, obviously, it could be imported from outside), but he also indicated that similar rational-ethical influences among certain other sects in other cultural areas (e.g. some Russian Old-Believers and sects or the Jains and Vallabhacarins of India), although they did not produce capitalism of the modern western kind, nevertheless resulted in economic rationalization and success (Weber 1958a:197 fn 12; v. Schelting 1934:305) compared with the surrounding population of the same cultural area. This seems to indicate an adequate causal relationship between the ethics of certain kinds of sects and a generalized concept of capitalism. It is the paradox of all rational-ethical asceticism – as can be seen in the history of many monasteries – that it itself produces the wealth which it rejects. Not only ascetic Protestantism but also certain other religious communities characterized by a religiously oriented asceticism and rationalism of the conduct of life have had a revolutionizing effect on economic activity and pushed it in the same direction – and the realization of this fact in turn strengthens the Protestant ethic thesis, if one wishes to interpret it not only as a thesis about elective affinity, as most scholars who know only the *PE* and not the *EEWR* do, but also as a thesis about adequate causation. It is true, though, that the religious communities in question (some ascetic sects before the Reformation, some monastic orders, some Russian sects) have not been closely studied by Weber – with the partial exception perhaps of the Jains, about whom he wrote a few pages in his essay on India. The preceding chapter on the Russian Old Believers and Sects was intended to remedy the situation with regard to Russia.

Some other possible explanations of the development of modern capitalism were rejected by Weber. Technical advances, for instance, can certainly favour capitalist growth, but historical experience teaches that they alone are not generally able to overcome traditionalism and to contribute to the formation of a new economic structure. In ancient Rome the capitalistic development was highest when the technological development had ended and the technical knowledge of the Chinese remained without practical applications (Weber 1924a:451 and Weber 1964:243). Similarly, the increase of the reserves of precious metal can accelerate an already existing economic development, but historical experience (e.g. in Ptolemaic Egypt) shows that precious metals alone do not create a new economic structure. It should also be remembered that after the discovery of America, the flow of gold and silver to Spain produced a recession and not an increase of capitalistic development (Weber 1924b:17 sq., 185 sqq.; Weber 1981:353). And, finally, the existence of rational law cannot generally, out of itself, change the prevailing circumstances in the direction of more modern capitalism. In Rome, for instance, the highest degree of rationality in the legal system was attained only after the conclusion of the capitalistic development (v. Schelting 1934:113).

Technical advances, precious metal-resources and rational law, therefore, although not irrelevant, cannot be held to be adequate causes of modern capitalism. Other possible causes mentioned by Weber, e.g. population increase, the development of autonomous cities or commercial routes, etc., would perhaps merit some consideration but have not been studied comparatively as causes of capitalism by Weber.

The low degree of the objective possibility of the independent development of modern capitalism without the Protestant ethic, the development of modern capitalism even under otherwise unfavourable circumstances where the Protestant ethic predominated, further the high degree of objective possibility of rational economic activity within the sphere of influence of rational-ethical sects in non-western cultural areas, and finally his rejection of other, though less investigated, possible causes of modern capitalism have led Weber to the conclusion that the causal influence of the Protestant ethic was very high (Weber 1978b:325), that it was the adequate cause of modern capitalism, although, obviously, it is never possible, in the historical imputation of an effect to a cause, to arrive at a numerical ratio.

It has thus perhaps been shown that "The Economic Ethics of World Religions" must not only be interpreted in relation to Weber's discovery of a specific mode of rationalism in Western culture, but also as the methodologically necessary consequence of his discovery in the PE that there is an elective affinity between certain aspects of protestantism and the spirit of capitalism. In the EEWR Weber proceeded to establish a relationship of adequate causation – assuming the precise understanding of this delicate notion as formulated by v. Kries – between certain idealtypically refined phenomena, while in the PE he had, to a large extent, only established elective affinity. Weber had perhaps referred to a yet undefined plan of this kind in the sibylline remark, made in 1908 in response to one of his critics, that the *Gegenprobe* (Weber 1978b:54) of his PE, although promised, was still lacking.

The interpretation of the term *Gegenprobe*, apparently used by Weber only once, is not without difficulties, but it probably refers to what in the anglosaxon literature on Weber is termed 'control-test' and what the French interpreters call, much more clearly, 'validation causale indirecte'.

This leads to a final point. When H. Tyrell (1990:132) sums up the premises and intentions of the PE-essay and then declares that Weber never plausibly or systematically explicated the power and efficacy of

religion which he rather took, in the wake of Nietzsche, to be self-evident, he simply ignores all the *Gegenproben* of the EEWR which Weber
had undertaken in his later years. By revealing relationships of adequate causation, Weber indeed also established the efficacy of religion, at least the 'adequate' efficacy. At least in this respect, the unity
of his theory of science (*Wissenschaftstheorie*) of which Henrich (1952)
spoke cannot be questioned.

GLOSSARY

adiaphoron	Neither good nor bad; indifferent.
affinity (elective)	Term used by Max Weber in two different senses: 1. affinity of meaning 2. a relationship in regard to which an assertion about the causal direction is not made and reciprocal influences are not excluded.
anatta	unreality of the self (atman) in Buddhism
apokatastasis	Restitution to a previous state; return to the original position.
ascetism	1. World-rejecting : entails withdrawal from the "world", from social ties, from political, economic or erotic activities; 2. Inner-worldly: although it rejects indulgence in epicurean satisfaction and the enjoyment of worldly pleasures, it requires participation within the "world" and its institutions and the obligation to transform and dominate the world.
asrama	The theory of the asramas divides the life of an orthodox Indian bramin into four stages.
auctoritas	(Priestly) authority.
auri sacra fames	The cursed hunger for gold.
bhakti	Ardent devotion to a particular deity in India.
Bildung	Personal cultivation, self-cultivation in Germany.
boutade	Amusing and paradoxical turn of words.
brahmins	Members of the priestly caste in India.
certitudo salutis	Certainty of salvation.
charisma, pl. charismata	Divinely conferred gifts or talents.
chin	Social rank.
connubium	The practice or right of intermarriage.
consensus ecclesiae	Consensus within the Church.
consilia evangelica	Proposals for a Christian life which surpass the obligations imposed on all Christians and are generally followed only by monks.
contemptus mundi	Contempt for the World.
defensor fidei	Defender of the faith.
deo placere vix potest	(The acquisition of wealth) can hardly please God.

disciplina arcani	Obligation not to divulge religious beliefs or achievements to outsiders.
dominant	The fifth note of the scale of any key
domovoi, vodianoi	House or water spirit
dvorianstvo	Service nobility in traditional Russia.
ecloga	A compilation of Byzantine laws (8th century)
economic rationalism	Methodical economic activity in the context of impersonal relationships.
Eigengesetzlichkeit	Inner logic; subjection of a societal sphere of action to its own inner laws. Not to be confused with autonomy.
eisagoge	Introduction to a planned collection of Byzantine laws (9th century).
ekklesia	Church
electi	The elect or chosen.
equus	Horse
expressis verbis	Expressly
extra ecclesiam nulla salus	There is no salvation outside the Church.
filioque	Formula added to the *credo* by the Catholic Church; it contributed to the split from the Orthodox Church.
Geisteswissenschaft	Humanities and letters, including philosophy.
Gemeinschaft	Traditionally grown social community (Tönnies).
Gesellschaft	Voluntary and purposive organization based on the rational pursuit of self-interest within an individualistic society.
hierarchy	To be distinguished from power or command; an order resulting from the consideration of value; the elementary hierarchical relation is that between a whole and an element of that whole or else that between two parts with reference to the whole (Dumont).
historical individual	Elements of historical reality which are united into a conceptual whole of unique and individual character from the standpoint of their cultural significance (Max Weber).
holism	An ideology that valorizes the social whole and neglects or subordinates the human individual; the opposite of individualism.
homo duplex	Dual man.

idealtype	It does not reproduce reality, but is a coherent construct of ideas, formed by the one-sided accentuation of a chosen pont of view according to which a multitude of historical phenomena are linked.
ideology	The set of ideas and values, the representations that are common in a society. The term refers to the global ideology and implies a rejection of the usage which is limited to social classes, thus discrediting ideas and representations.
imperium	(Universal) empire, based on personal loyalties; to be distinguished from the modern state within defined borders and oriented toward formal law and a legally established impersonal order.
individual	One needs to distinguish: a) the empirical individual, the sample of the human species, as encountered in all societies, b) the independent and autonomous moral being as encountered in the modern ideology of man and society.
individualism	The modern ideology which valorizes the individual as an independent and autonomous being and neglects or subordinates the social whole.
individuality	(=*Qualitative individualism*) interior individualism which underscores the concept of the unique individual, but leaves the holistic community intact.
infima species	The lowest or humblest species.
inner-worldly	In Weberian sociology an attitude which is world-negating but turned towards the world: ascetic world-domination or contemplative-mystic world-resignation.
inworldly / outworldly individual	The modern independent and autonomous individual, if "non-social" in thought, lives in society, he is in fact social; in contrast, in some cultures those who leave society (e.g. the Indian *samnyasin* or the Christian anchorite) become autonomous individuals. They are outworldly individuals (Dumont).
ius circa sacra	The ruler's right to intervene in exterior church matters (e.g. property administration); opposed to *ius in sacra* (e.g. sacraments) (Pufendorf).
ius utendi	The right to use.
Kautilya	Author of the Arthasastra, an ancient Indian treatise on the art of politics.
knout	In ancient Russia a kind of scourge for flogging criminals.

koinobion	The joining of individuals at a higher level of community.
ksatriyas	Members of the warrior caste in India.
Kürwille	A will based on individual choice (Tönnies).
lichnost'	Individuality – the unique features of an individual, resulting from self-fashioning.
megaloskhimi	Orthodox monks who have taken a higher vow of a purely contemplative life (*makroskhima*).
mestnichestvo	The attribution of government office to the Russian nobility (service precedence) according to hereditary criteria.
Methodenstreit	A dispute between economists of two schools (historical and theoretical) at the end of the nineteenth century.
mir	Village council.
modernity	The conquest of life by means of science and technology; the ethos of world domination, rooted in religious ideas; a social structure based on rational law and administration; and, as a precondition and concomitant of these characteristics, the individualistic ideology (please see *individualism*).
modes	(=*modi* or *echoi*) ; ancient Greek scales for diatonic style music, also used in medieval church music.
modus vivendi	Manner of living.
narod	People; may refer to ethnicity, nationality or the common people.
narodnichestvo	Populist movement in nineteenth century Russia which idealized the self-sufficient peasant community and the peasants.
Naturwissenschaft	Natural sciences.
neume	Sign used in ancient song to indicate notes to be sung.
obshchina	Peasant community, village commune.
oprichnina	Government, administration and special troops under the tsar Ivan IV.
opus supererogationis	Action exceeding what (religious) duty requires.
ora et labora	Pray and work (formula attributed to the Benedictine monks).
paideia	Education.

patria potestas	Sovereignty over the family customarily attributed to the father.
patrimonialism	Traditional form of political rule with an administration based on personal relationships to the ruler and not on formally defined tasks.
pax terrae	Peace on earth
persona	In early Christianity, the persona is a manifestation of a nature, to be distinguished from that nature or essence itself.
persona ficta	Artificially created social unit.
personality	It implies the exit from natural or creaturely life and the constancy of inner relations to certain ultimate values and meanings.
pneuma	Wind, divine inspiration, spirit.
politeia	Polity; Constitution of a state.
polyphony	The simultaneous combination of two or more melodies harmonizing with each other.
pontifex maximus	The highest priest in ancient Rome.
potestas	Power
Protestant ethic	The term refers to the rational and ascetic conduct of life of members of certain Protestant churches (Calvinists, Baptists, Quakers). Please see *rationalism*, part c.
Pythagorean comma	A minute interval (ratio of 81/80) corresponding to the difference between twelve perfect fifths and seven octaves.
radenie	Temporary possession of the Holy Spirit among certain Russian sects, achieved by means of ecstatic dancing.
raskol	Great schism of the Russian Church in the 17th century.
rationalism	In Max Weber's writings one finds three kinds of rationalism: a.) scientific-technical rationalism (referring to man's capacity and will to dominate the world by calculation) b.) metaphysical rationalism (systemizing the structures of meaning in order to comprehend the world as a meaningful cosmos); c.) practical rationalism, referring to a methodical and value-related conduct of life.
regnum	Office and dignity of the king.
rex-sacerdos	King-priest

sacerdotium	Priesthood
saeculum	In Christian tradition the socio-political order which precedes the return of Christ.
samnyasin	The monkish renouncer of life within Indian society.
sangha	The order of Buddhist monks.
Scheinkonstitutionalismus	Pseudo- (or: illusory) constitutionalism.
sit venia verbo	Be it permitted to say
skit (pl. skity)	Hermitage
slavophiles	They rejected foreign influences and proposed a return to Russia's own Orthodox sources.
sobornost'	Organic togetherness of people united by faith and love.
sola fide	Luther's thesis that man can only be saved by his faith (as opposed to his deeds).
Sonderweg	Special path
tat tvam asi	"Thou art that" – formula from the Chandogya Upanishad, equating the brahman and the atman, or the universe and the self .
temperament (equal floating)	Adjustment of the intervals of a scale to make them available in different keys (the octave divided into twelve equal semitones).
tertium quid	Third entity.
theoria	Vision, contemplation.
theosis	Deification, participation in God.
tonic	Keynote
ukaz	A decree (of the tsar).
uterque ordo	Both categories; *uterque potestas* both powers
Verfassungspatriotismus	A patriotism which is limited to an attachment to the Constitution of a country.
Volk, pl. Völker	A people as a collective cultural individual (Herder).
Wesenswille	Natural or essential will (Tönnies).

BIBLIOGRAPHY

Ahrweiler, H. (1975), *L'idéologie politique de l'empire byzantin*, Paris: PUF.

Arro, Elmar (1962), 'Hauptprobleme der osteuropäischen Musikgeschichte' in: *Musik des Ostens* I, pp. 9-48.

Avvakum (1965), *Das Leben des Protopopen Avvakum* (transl. by G. Hildebrandt), Göttingen, Vandenhoeck & Ruprecht.

Barker, Ernest (1957), *Social and Political Thought in Byzantium*, Oxford, Clarendon.

Baron, S.H. (1970), 'The Weber Thesis and the Failure of Capitalist Development in "Early Modern" Russia'. *Jahrbücher für Geschichte Osteuropas* 18: pp. 321-36.

Beck, H.-G. (1975), 'Res Publica Romana' in: H. Hunger (ed.) *Das byzantinische Herrscherbild*, Darmstadt.

—. H.-G. (1959), *Kirche und theologische Literatur im byzantinischen Reich*, Munich: C. H. Beck.

Beliaev, A.S. (1988), 'Staroobriadtsy i ikh otnoshenie k bogatstvu', in Panzer, B. (ed.), *Sprache, Literatur und Geschichte der Altgläubigen*. Heidelberg: Carl Winter.

Bell, Daniel (1973), *The Coming of Post-Industrial Society: A Venture in Social Forecasting*, New York: Basic Books.

Bellah, Robert (1970), 'Religious Evolution' in: *Beyond Belief*, New York: Harper and Row.

Benz, Ernst (1971), *Geist und Leben der Ostkirche*. Munich: Wilhelm Fink Verlag.

Berdiaev, Nikolai (1955), *Istok i smysl russkogo kommunizma*, Paris: YMCA.

Berger, Peter et al. (1973), *The Homeless Mind*. New York: Random House.

Berger, Peter (1980), *The Heretical Imperative*. London: Collins.

Berlin, Isaiah (1953), *The Hedgehog and the Fox, An Essay on Tolstoy's View of History*, New York: Schuster & Schuster.

—. (1974), The Divorce Between the Sciences and the Humanities, *Salmagundi*, No. 27, Summer/ Fall, pp. 9-39.

—. (1979), *Russian Thinkers*, Harmondsworth: Penguin.

Berman, Harold (1983), *Law and Revolution*, Cambridge, Mass.: Harvard University Press.

Besançon, Alain (1977), *Les origines intellectuelles du Léninisme*. Paris, Calmann-Lévy.

—. (1994), *L'image interdite*, Paris: Fayard.

Bevan, Edwyn (1913), *Stoics and Sceptics*, Oxford : Clarendon Press.

Billington, J.H. (1958), *Mikhailovsky and Russian Populism*, Oxford: Clarendon Press.

—. (1966), *The Icon and the Axe*. London: Weidenfeld and Nicolson.

Blackwell, W.L. (1968), *The Beginnings of Russian Industrialization 1800-1860.* Princeton: Princeton University Press.

Bloch, Marc (1968), *La société féodale.* Paris: Albin Michel.

Bonch-Bruevich, V.D. (1959), *Izbrannye sochineniia*, Vol. I. Moscow.

Braun, Christoph (1992), *Max Webers Musiksoziologie*, Laaber: Laaber Verlag.

Brown, Peter (1978), *The Making of Late Antiquity*, Cambridge, Mass.: Harvard University Press.

Bruford, Walter H. (1975), *The German Tradition of Self-Cultivation. "Bildung" from Humboldt to Thomas Mann.* Cambridge University Press.

Brym, Robert (1996), "The Ethic of Self-Reliance and the Spirit of Capitalism in Russia" in: *International Sociology*, Vol 11, No. 4.

Bulgakov, Sergei (1911), *Dva grada*, Vol. 1-2, Moscow, 1911.

Bultot, Robert (1963), *La doctrine du mépris du monde. Le XIe siècle.* Louvain.

Buss, Andreas (1978), *Société, Politique, Individu. Les formes élémentaires de la vie sociale en Inde ancienne*, Assen: Van Gorcum.

—. (1985), *Max Weber and Asia, Contributions to the Sociology of Development*, London/Munich: Weltforum.

Carrithers, M. (1985), 'An alternative social history of the self' in : M. Carrithers, S. Collins, S. Lukes (eds) : *The Category of the Person*, Cambridge University Press, pp. 234-256.

Caspary, Gerard (1979), *Politics and Exegesis : Origen and the Two Swords*, Berkeley: University of California Press.

Cherniavsky, Michael (1966), 'The Old Believers and the New Religion' in: *Slavic Review*, No. 25, pp. 1-39.

Chrysostomus, P. Johannes O.S.B. (1957), *Die 'Pomorskie Otvety' als Denkmal der russischen Altgläubigen gegen Ende des 1. Viertels des XVIII. Jahrhunderts.* Rome: Pont. Institutum Orientalium Studiorum.

Conybeare, F.C. (1921), *Russian Dissenters.* Cambridge: Harvard University Press.

Crummey, R.O. (1970), *The Old Believers and the World of Antichrist.* Madison: University of Wisconsin Press.

Dagron, Gilbert (1996), *Empereur et prêtre. Étude sur le "césaropapisme" byzantin.* Paris: Gallimard.

Danilevsky, N. (1869), *Rossiia i Evropa*, St. Petersburg.

Daraki, Maria (1981), 'L'émergence du sujet singulier dans les Confessions d'Augustin' in: *Esprit* No 50 (fév.), pp. 95-115.

Davydov J. & P. Gaidenko (1995), *Russland und der Westen*, Frankfurt, Suhrkamp.

Descombes, V. (1999), 'Louis Dumont et les outils de la tolérance' in: *Esprit*, no. 253 (June), pp. 65-82.

Deveau, Alphonse (1987), *Les Acadiens – de paria à partenaire?.* Church Point, N.S.: Presses de l'Université Sainte-Anne.

Diedrich, H.-C. (1985), *Ursprünge und Anfänge des russischen Freikirchentums* (Vol. 21, Oikonomia). Erlangen: Lehrstuhl für Geschichte und Theologie des christlichen Ostens.

Donskis, L. (1994/5), 'Louis Dumont on the National Variants of the Modern Ideology I and II' in: *Comparative Civilization Review*, pp. 2-25.

Duchesne, E. (1910), *Le Domostroi. Ménagier russe du XVIe siècle* (translation and commentary). Paris: Alphonse Picard.

Dumont, Louis (1966), *Homo hierarchicus. Essai sur le système des castes*. Paris : Gallimard.

—. (1970), *Religion/Politics and History in India*. Paris: Mouton.

—. (1975), 'On the Comparative Understanding of Non-Modern Civilizations' in: *Daedalus* V. 104, pp. 153-172.

—. (1977), *From Mandeville to Marx*, University of Chicago Press, Chicago.

—. (1982), 'A modified view of our origins: the Christian beginnings of modern individualism' in: *Religion*, 12, pp. 1-27.

—. (1983), *Essais sur l'individualisme*. Paris: Seuil.

—. (1986), *Essays on Individualism*, University of Chicago Press.

—. (1991), *L'idéologie allemande*. Paris : Gallimard.

Durkheim, E. (1898), "L'individualisme et les intellectuels" in: *Revue bleue*, 4e série, No 10, pp. 7-13.

Eisenstadt, S.N. (1983), 'Transcendental Visions – Otherworldliness and its Transformations. Some more Comments on Louis Dumont.' in : *Religion* 13, pp. 1-17.

—. (1986), *The Origins and Diversity of Axial Age Civilizations*. New York : State University of New York Press.

Esser, Ambrosius (1963), 'Die Lehre der Epanagoge – eine oströmische Reichstheorie' in: *Freiburger Zeitschrift für Philosophie und Theologie*, 10 (1-2) pp. 61-85.

Fedorenko, F. (1965), *Sekty, ikh vera i dela*. Moscow.

Feldbrugge, F. (2000), 'The Rule of Law in the European CIS States' in: *Review of Central and East European Law*, Vol. 26, No. 3, pp. 213-230.

Festinger, L., Riecken, H. and Schachter, S. (1956), *When Prophecy Fails*. Minneapolis: University of Minnesota Press.

Figes, Orlando (1996), *A People's Tragedy*, Penguin Books.

Figgis, J.N. (1956), *Studies in Political Thought from Gerson to Grotius 1414-1625*. Cambridge: Cambridge University Press.

Fischoff, E. (1968), 'The Protestant Ethic and the Spirit of Capitalism: The History of a Controversy' in: Eisenstadt, S.N. (ed.) *The Protestant Ethic and Modernization*. New York: Basic Books.

Freund, Julien (1968), *Sociologie de Max Weber* 2e éd. Paris: PUF.

Fuhrmann, Horst (ed.), (1968), *Das Constitutum Constantini* (Fontes Iuris Germanici Antiqui X). Hannover : Hahnsche Buchhandlung.

Gardner, J. von (1976), *System und Wesen des russischen Kirchengesanges*. Wiesbaden: Otto Harrassowitz.

Geanakoplos, D.J. (1966), *Byzantine East and Latin West: Two Worlds of Christendom in Middle Ages and Renaissance*. New York: Harper.

Geertz, C. (1973), *The Interpretation of Cultures*, New York: Basic Books.

Gershenkron, A. (1966), *Economic Backwardness in Historical Perspective*. Cambridge, Mass.: Harvard University Press.

—. (1970), *Europe in the Russian Mirror*. Cambridge University Press.

Gershenzon, M. (1913), *Sochineniya i Pisma Chaadaeva*, Moscow.

—. (1909), 'Preface' to *Vekhi* (collective publication), Moscow.

Gierke, Otto (1913), *Political Theories of the Middle Age*, Cambridge University Press.

—. (1958), *Natural Law and the Theory of Society 1500-1800*. Transl. by E. Barker, Cambridge University Press.

—. (1977), *Associations and Law*. Toronto: University of Toronto Press.

Giterman, V. (1945/1965), *Geschichte Russlands*, Vols. 1-3. Frankfurt: Europäische Verlagsanstalt.

Goehrke, C. (1964), *Theorien über Entstehung und Entwicklung des 'Mir'*. Wiesbaden: Otto Harrassowitz.

Goldfrank, D.M. (1983), *The Monastic Rule of Josif Volotsky*, Kalamazoo, Michigan, Cistercian Publications.

Goldman, H. (1988), *Max Weber and Thomas Mann*. Berkeley: University of California Press.

Gomez, H. (1949), *Las sectas rusas*. Madrid.

Goodenough, Erwin (1940), *An Introduction to Philo Judaeus*, New Haven: Yale University Press.

Grass, K. (1907/1914), *Die russischen Sekten*, Vols. 1-2. Leipzig (reprint 1966).

—. (1908), 'Die Bedeutung der russischen Sektenkunde für die Beurteilung von russischer Religiosität und Kultur' in: *Religion und Geisteskultur*, p. 161 sqq.

Gunkel (1912), 'Individualismus und Sozialismus im AT' in: *Religion in Geschichte und Gegenwart*, Bd. III, Spalte 493-501, Tübingen: Siebeck.

Harnack, Adolf von (1889), *Dogmengeschichte*, Tübingen, Mohr (1991).

—. (1913), 'Der Geist der morgenländischen Kirche im Unterschied von der abendländischen'. *Sitzungsberichte der königlich-preussischen Akademie der Wissenschaften* I: pp. 157-183. Berlin.

Hart, H.L.A. & T. Honoré (1985), *Causation in the Law*. Oxford: Clarendon.

Heiler, Friedrich (1971), *Die Ostkirchen*. Munich: Ernst Reinhard Verlag.

Heinzer, Felix (1980), *Gottes Sohn als Mensch*, (Paradosis XXVI), Freiburg (Schweiz).

Henrich, Dieter (1952), *Die Einheit der Wissenschaftslehre Max Webers*. Tübingen: Mohr (Siebeck).

Herder, Johann G. (1978), 'Auch eine Philosophie der Geschichte zur Bildung der Menschheit' (1774), in: *Herders Werke*, Vol. 1-5. Berlin: Aufbau-Verlag.

Herzen, Alexandr (1919), *Sobranie Sochinenii*. 20 vols. Petrograd

——. (1967), *My Past and Thoughts*. New York: Russell & Russell.

Hildermeier, M. (1987), 'Das Privileg der Rückständigkeit' in: *Historische Zeitschrift*, Bd. 244, pp. 557-603.

Holl, Karl (1898), *Enthusiasmus und Bussgewalt beim griechischen Mönchtum*, Leipzig: Hinrichs'sche Buchhandlung.

Jaspers, Karl (1949), *Vom Ursprung und Ziel der Geschichte*. München : Piper.

Jellinek, Georg (1919), *Die Erklärung der Menschen – und Bürgerrechte*. München : Duncker & Humblot (1895).

Kästner, Erhart (1956), *Die Stundentrommel vom heiligen Berg Athos*, Frankfurt: Insel.

Kaiser, D.H. (1980), *The Growth of Law in Medieval Russia*. Princeton, N.J.: Princeton University Press.

Kalberg, Stephen (1994), *Max Weber's Comparative-Historical Sociology*. The University of Chicago Press.

Kandinsky, W. (1989), *Du spirituel dans l'art*, Paris: Denoël.

Kane, P.V. (1974), *History of Dharmasastra*, Poona (1941).

Kantorowicz, E. (1957), *The King's Two Bodies*. Princeton University Press.

Kapterev, N.F. (1909-12), *Patriarkh Nikon i Tsar Aleksei Mikhailovich*, Vol. 1-2, Sergiev Posad.

Kartashov, A. (1925), 'Smysl staroobryadchestva' in: *Mélanges Pierre Struve*, Prague.

Kaufmann-Rochard, J. (1969), *Origines d'une bourgeoisie russe*. Paris: Flammarion.

Kharkhordin, Oleg (1994), "The Corporate Ethic, the Ethic of Samostoiatel-nost' and the Spirit of Capitalism" in: *International Sociology* 9, no. 4, pp. 405-429

——. (1999), *The Collective and the Individual in Russia*. Berkeley: The University of California Press.

Khomiakov, A.S. (1900-1904), *Polnoe Sobranie Sochinenii*. Moscow.

——. (1867), *The Church is One*, Berlin.

Kingston-Mann, E. (1999), *In Search of the True West*, Princeton University Press.

Kireevsky, I. (1911), *Polnoe Sobranie Sochinenii*, 2 vols., Moscow.

Klibanov, A.J. 1982. *History of Religious Sectarianism in Russia (1860s-1917)*. Oxford: Pergamon Press. (1965. Moscow: Nauka).

Kolakowski, L. (1977), 'The Persistence of the Sein-Sollen Dilemma' in: *Man and World* 10, No 2, pp. 194-233.

Kolarz, W. (1963), *Die Religionen in der Sowjetunion*. Freiburg: Herder. (*Religion in the Soviet Union*. London: Macmillan, 1962).

Kovalevsky, P. (1957), 'Le "rascol" et son rôle dans le développement indus- triel de la Russie'. *Archives de sociologie des religions* No 3: pp. 37-55.

Kries, J. von (1888), *Über den Begriff der objektiven Möglichkeit*. Leipzig: Fues's.

Kulischer, J. (1931), 'Die kapitalistischen Unternehmer in Russland (ins- besondere die Bauern als Unternehmer) in den Anfangsstadien des Kapi- talismus'. *Archiv für Sozialwissenschaft und Sozialpolitik* 65.2: 309-55.

Lagarde, G. de (1934-1946), *Naissance de l'esprit laïque au déclin du Moyen Age*, Vol. 1-6, Paris: Béatrice-Nauwelaer.

Leitsch, W. (1973), 'Die Stadtbevölkerung im Moskauer Staat in der zweiten Hälfte des 17. Jahrhunderts'. *Forschungen zur osteuropäischen Geschichte* 18 : 221-48.

Leroy-Beaulieu, A. (1893-97), *L'empire des tsars et les Russes* (Vol. I: 4th edn. 1897; Vol. 2: 3rd edn. 1893; Vol. 3: 2nd edn. 1896). Paris: Librairie Hachette.

Louth, Andrew (1996), *Maximus the Confessor*. London: Routledge.

Magdelain, A. (1947), *Auctoritas principis*, Paris: Société d'Édition "Les Belles Lettres".

Maine, Sir Henry Sumner (1887), *Ancient Law*. London.

Malraux, André (1965), *Le musée imaginaire*, Paris: Gallimard (idées/arts).

Mann, Thomas (1983), *Betrachtungen eines Unpolitischen*. Frankfurt: Fischer.

Mannheim, Karl (1936), *Ideology and Utopia*, New York: Harcourt.

Mantzaridis, G. (1981), *Soziologie des Christentums*. Berlin : Duncker & Hum- blot.

Mar'ianovskii, V. (1997), 'The Russian Economic Mentality' in: *Russian Social Science Review*, vol. 38, no. 4, pp. 34-37.

Martin, L. (1994), "The Anti-Individualistic Ideology of Hellenistic Culture" in: *Numen*, Vol. 41, p. 117 sqq.

Mauss, M. (1938), 'Une catégorie de l'esprit humain : la notion de personne, celle de "moi" '. *Journal of the Royal Anthropological Institute*, Vol. 68, pp. 333-361.

Medlin, William (1952), *Moscow and East Rome*. Genève: Droz.

Mehnert, Klaus (1981), *Der Sowjetmensch*. Berlin: Ullstein

Metzger, Thomas (1977), *Escape from Predicament. Neo-Confucianism and China's Evolving Political Culture*. New York: Columbia University Press.

Meyendorff, John (1979), *Byzantine Theology*, New York: Fordham University Press.

—. (1981), *Byzantium and the Rise of Russia*, Cambridge University Press.

—. (1982), *The Byzantine Legacy in the Orthodox Church*, Crestwood, N.Y.: St. Vladimir's Seminary Press.

Meyerson, I. (ed.) (1973), *Problèmes de la personne*. Paris : Mouton.

Mikhailovsky, N.K. (1896), *Sochineniya Mikhailovskogo*, St. Peterburg.

Miliukov, P. (1948), *Outlines of Russian Culture*. Philadelphia: University of Pennsylvania Press. (Original Russian 2nd edn. 1899, Vol. 2, St. Petersburg).

Mitzmann, A. (1970), *The Iron Cage. An Historical Interpretation of Max Weber*, New York.

Mommsen, W. (1965), Max Weber's Political Sociology and his Philosophy of World History, *International Social Science Journal*, Vol. 17, pp. 23-45.

Morris, Colin (1972), *The Discovery of the Individual 1050-1200*. New York : Harper & Row.

Moulin, Léo (1964), *Le monde vivant des religieux*, Paris : Calmann – Lévy.

Mühlmann, Wilhelm (1961), *Chiliasmus und Nativismus*, Berlin: Dietrich Reimer.

Müller-Armack, A. (1959), *Religion und Wirtschaft: Geistesgeschichtliche Hintergründe unserer europäischen Lebensform*. Stuttgart: Kohlhammer.

Nestle, Wilhelm (1941), 'Die Haupteinwände des antiken Denkens gegen das Christentum' in: *Archiv für Religionswissenschaften*, No. 37, pp. 51-100.

Neusykhin, A. (1974), *Problemy evropeiskogo feodalizma. Izbrannye trudy*. Moscow.

Niebuhr, B.G., ed. (1828), *Corpus Scriptorum Historiae Byzantinae*, Pars XI, Bonn.

Nikol'skii, N.M. (1983), *Istoriia russkoi tserkvi*. Moscow.

Nitsche, Peter (1991), *Nicht an die Griechen glaube ich, sondern an Christus. Russen und Griechen im Selbstverständnis des Moskauer Staates*, Düsseldorf: Droste.

Nolte, H.-H. (1975), 'Sozialgeschichtliche Zusammenhänge der russischen Kirchenspaltung'. *Jahrbücher für Geschichte Osteuropas* 23, pp. 321-43.

Ostrogorsky, G. (1931), 'Otnoshenie tserkvi i gosudarstva v Vizantii' in: *Seminarium Kondakovianum*, pp. 121-134.

—. (1940/1965), *Geschichte des byzantinischen Staates*. Munich: C.H. Beck.

—. (1968), *History of the Byzantine State*, Oxford, Blackwell (1940).

Ouspensky, Leonid & V. Lossky (1983), *The Meaning of Icons*, Crestwood, New York: St. Vladimir's Seminary Press.

Palmer, William (1871), *The Patriarch and the Tsar*, London, Trübner.

Pasternak, Boris (1958), *Doctor Zhivago*, London: Collins and Harvill Press

Pipes, Richard (1974), *Russia under the Old Regime*. New York: Scribner's.

Pleyer, V. (1961), *Das russische Altgläubigentum*. Munich: Otto Sagner.

Pohlenz, Max (1948), *Die Stoa*, Göttingen: Vandenhoeck & Ruprecht.

Portal, Roger (1961), 'Origines d'une bourgeoisie industrielle en Russie' in: *Revue d'histoire moderne et contemporaine*, tome 8, pp. 35-60.

Prestige, G.L. (1936), *God in Patristic Thought*, London: William Heinemann.

Rasputin, V. (1989), *Siberia on Fire*. Northern Illinois University Press.

Rheinfelder, Hans (1928), *Das Wort "Persona"* (Beiheft LXVII, *Zeitschrift für romanische Philologie*) Halle : Max Niemeyer.

Riesemann, O. von (1926), *Geschichte der russischen Musik*. Leipzig: Breitkopf & Härtel.

Roth, G. & Schluchter, W. (1979), *Max Weber's Vision of History*, Berkeley: University of California Press.

Rousseau, J.J. (1971), *Discours sur les sciences et les arts*, Paris: Garnier (1750).

Runciman, Steven (1957), 'Byzantium, Russia and Caesaropapism' in: *Canadian Slavonic Papers II*, pp. 1-10.

Ryndziunskii, P.G. (1950), 'Staroobriadcheskaia organizatsiia v usloviiakh razvitiia promyshlennogo kapitalizma'. *Voprosy istorii religii i ateizma* pp. 188-248. Moscow.

Sabine, George (1963), *A History of Political Theory*. New York: Holt, Rinehart & Winston.

Sachs, Jeffrey D. & K. Pistor, eds (1997), *The Rule of Law and Economic Reform in Russia*. Boulder: Westview Press.

Sarkisyanz, Emanuel (1955), *Russland und der Messianismus des Orients*, Mohr (Siebeck), Tübingen.

Savramis, D. (1966), '"Ora et labora" bei Basilios dem Grossen' in: *Kyrios*, VI, pp. 129-149.

—. (1982), *Zwischen Himmel und Erde. Die orthodoxe Kirche heute*. Stuttgart: Seewald.

Scharf, J. (1959), "Quellenstudien zum Prooimion der Epanagoge" in: *Byzantinische Zeitschrift*, Vol. 52, pp. 68-81.

Schelting, A. von (1934), *Max Webers Wissenschaftslehre*. Tübingen: Mohr (Siebeck).

—. (1948), *Russland und Europa im russischen Geschichtsdenken*. Bern: A. Francke.

Schlossmann, Siegmund (1906), *Persona und Prosopon im Recht und im christlichen Dogma*, Kiel: Festschrift der Universität Kiel.

Schluchter, W. (1971), *Wertfreiheit und Verantwortungsethik*, Tübingen: Mohr (Siebeck).

—. (1976), Die Paradoxie der Rationalisierung, *Zeitschrift für Soziologie*, Jg. 5, Heft 3, Juli, pp. 256-284.

—. (1981), *The Rise of Western Rationalism*. Berkeley: University of California Press.

—. (1984), 'Max Webers Religionssoziologie' in: *Kölner Zeitschrift für Soziologie und Sozialpsychologie* No. 2, pp. 342-365.

—. (1988), *Religion und Lebensführung*, Vol 1 & 2. Frankfurt a.M.: Suhrkamp.

—. (1989), *Rationalism, Religion and Domination*. Berkeley: University of California Press.

—. (1996), *Paradoxes of Modernity*, Stanford: Stanford University Press.

Schmalenbach, H. (1919), 'Individualität und Individualismus' in : *Kantstudien* 24, pp. 365-388.

Schminck, A. (1986), *Studien zu mittelbyzantinischen Rechtsbüchern*, Frankfurt a.M.: Löwenklau Gesellschaft.

Schneckenburger, M. (1855), Vergleichende Darstellung des lutherischen und reformirten Lehrbegriffs. Stuttgart: Metzler.

Schönborn, Ch. von (1976), *L'icône du Christ*. Fribourg : Editions Universitaires.

Simmel, G. (1912), "Goethes Individualismus" in : *Logos*, Vol. 3, pp. 251-274.

Smith, W. Cantwell (1984), "Philosophia, as one of the religious traditions of humankind" in: J.-C. Galey (ed) : *Différences, valeurs, hiérarchie. Textes offerts à Louis Dumont.* (pp. 253-279) Paris : École des Hautes Études en Sciences Sociales.

Smolitsch, I. (1953), *Russisches Mönchtum*. Würzburg: Augustinus Verlag.

Sokolov, N.S. (1888), *Raskol v Saratovskom krae*. Saratov.

Soloviev, V. (1947), *Crise de la philosophie occidentale*. Introduction et traduction par M. Herman. Paris: Aubier.

—. (1968), *Kurze Erzählung vom Antichrist*. Munich. Wewel.

Solzhenitsyn, A. et al. (1974), *From Under the Rubble*. Paris: YMCA Press.

Straub, J. (1957), Kaiser Konstantin als ἐπίσκοπος των ἐκτός *Studia Patristica*, Vol. 1, pp. 678-695.

Strauss, L. (1953), *Natural Law and History*, Chicago.

Svoronos, N.G. (1951), 'Le serment de fidélité à l'empereur byzantin', *Revue d'Études Byzantines*, Vol. 9, pp. 106-142.

Symeon der Theologe (1951), *Licht vom Licht*. Munich: Kösel Verlag.

Tenbruck, F. (1974a), Max Weber and the Sociology of Science. A Case Reopened, *Zeitschrift für Soziologie*, Jg. 3, Heft 3, pp. 312-20.

—. (1974b), 'Science as a Vocation' – Revisited, in: *Standorte im Zeitstrom* (Festschrift für Arnold Gehlen), edited by: E. Forsthoff and R. Hörstel, Frankfurt a. M., pp. 351-365.

—. (1980). 'The Problem of Thematic Unity in the Works of Max Weber'. *British Journal of Sociology* 31 (3): 316-51.

Thiel, Andreas (ed.), (1867), *Epistolae Romanorum Pontificum Genuinae*, Braunsberg (Reprint 1974).

Tocqueville, Alexis de (1968), *De la démocratie en Amérique*. Paris: Gallimard (Collection Idées).

Tolstoy, Leo (1930), *What is Art?*, London: Oxford University Press (1898).

—. (1934), *What Then Must We Do?* in: Tolstoy Centenary Edition, Oxford U. Press, Vol. 14.

Troeltsch, Ernst (1915), *Augustin, die christliche Antike und das Mittelalter*, München: Oldenbourg (Reprint Aalen: Scientia 1963).

—. (1925), *Aufsätze zur Geistesgeschichte und Religionssoziologie. (Gesammelte Schriften* Bd. 4) Tübingen: J.C.B. Mohr (Siebeck).

—. (1960), *The Social Teaching of the Christian Churches*, (trans. by Olive Wyon), New York: Harper.

—. (1977), *Die Soziallehren der christlichen Kirchen und Gruppen. (Gesammelte Schriften* Bd. 1, Aalen : Scientia (Tübingen 1911).

Tsakni, N. (1888), *La Russie sectaire*. Paris: Plon.

Tugan-Baranowsky, M. (1900), *Geschichte der russischen Fabrik*. Berlin: Emil Felber.

Turner, S. & Factor, R. (1981), "Objective Possibility and Adequate Causation in Weber's Methodological Writings" in: *Sociological Review*, Vol 29, No 1, pp. 5-28.

Tyrell, H. (1990), 'Worum geht es in der 'Protestantischen Ethik'?' in: *Saeculum*, No 41, Vol. 2, pp. 130-177.

Vernant, J.-P. (1989), *L'individu, la mort, l'amour. Soi-même et l'autre en Grèce ancienne*. Paris : Gallimard.

Vietsch, Eberhard von (1950), *Die Tradition der grossen Mächte*, Stuttgart: Union Deutsche Verlagsgesellschaft.

Villey, Michel (1975), *La formation de la pensée juridique moderne*. Paris : Montchrétien.

Vinogradov, V.V. (1994), *Istoriia slov*, Moscow: Tolk.

Walicki, A. (1963), 'Personality and Society in the Ideology of Russian Slavophiles' in: *California Slavic Studies*, Vol. II, pp. 1-20.

—. (1975), *The Slavophile Controversy*, Oxford: Clarendon.

—. (1979), *A History of Russian Thought*, Stanford: Stanford University Press.

Weber, Marianne (1975), *Max Weber: A Biography*. New York: John Wiley.

Weber, Max (1905), 'Die protestantische Ethik und der 'Geist' des Kapitalismus' in: *Archiv für Sozialwissenschaft und Sozialpolitik*, Vol. 20, pp. 1-54 & Vol. 21, pp. 1-110.

—. (1906a), 'Zur Lage der bürgerlichen Demokratie in Russland'. *Archiv für Sozialwissenchaft und Sozialpolitik* (ASS) 22: pp. 234-353.

—. (1906b), 'Russlands Übergang zum Scheinkonstitutionalismus'. *Archiv für Sozialwissenschaft und Sozialpolitik* (ASS) 23: pp. 165-401.

—. (1920/21), *Gesammelte Aufsätze zur Religionssoziologie* (GAzRS), Vols. 1-3. Tübingen: J.C.B. Mohr (Siebeck).

—. (1924a), *Gesammelte Aufsätze zur Soziologie und Sozialpolitik*. Tübingen: Mohr (Siebeck).

—. (1924b), *Gesammelte Aufsätze zur Sozial- und Wirtschaftsgeschichte*. Tübingen: Mohr (Siebeck).

—. (1949), *The Methodology of the Social Sciences*. New York: Free Press.

—. (1954), *Max Weber on Law in Economy and Society*, ed. Max Rheinstein, New York: Simon and Schuster

—. (1958a), *The Protestant Ethic and the Spirit of Capitalism*. Translated by T. Parsons. New York: Scribner's.

—. (1958b), *The Religion of India. The Sociology of Hinduism and Buddhism*. Glencoe: Free Press.

—. (1958c), *From Max Weber. Essays in Sociology*, New York: Oxford University Press.

—. (1958d), *The Rational and Social Foundations of Music*, Carbondale: Southern Illinois University Press.

—. (1964a), *The Religion of China*. Glencoe: The Free Press.

—. (1964b), *The Sociology of Religion*, Boston: Beacon Press.

—. (1968), *Gesammelte Aufsätze zur Wissenschaftslehre*. Tübingen: Mohr.

—. (1971), *Gesammelte Politische Schriften*, Tübingen: Mohr (Siebeck).

—. (1972), *Wirtschaft und Gesellschaft*. Tübingen: Mohr (Siebeck), (1921/22).

—. (1978a), *Economy and Society*, Vol. I & II. Berkeley: University of California Press.

—. (1978b), *Die protestantische Ethik II. Kritiken und Antikritiken*. Gütersloh: Mohn.

—. (1981), *General Economic History*. New Brunswick: Transaction Books (Original German Edition 1923).

Webster, Charles (1975), *The Great Instauration: Science, Medicine and Reform*, London.

Weintraub, K.J. (1978), *The Value of the Individual. Self and Circumstance in Autobiography*. Chicago: University of Chicago Press.

Wilson, B.R. ed. (1979), *Rationality*. Oxford: Blackwell

Windelband, W. (1893), *A History of Philosophy*. New York : MacMillan.

Zenkovsky, Serge A. (1957), 'The Ideological World of the Denisov Brothers' in: *Harvard Slavic Studies*, No. 3, pp. 49-66.

—. (1970), *Russkoe Staroobriadchestvo*. Munich: Wilhelm Fink.

Zenkovsky, V.V. (1953), *A History of Russian Philosophy*, 2 vols. London: Routledge and Kegan Paul.

Zepos, J. & P. (1962), *Jus Graecoromanum*, Aalen : Scientia.

Zimin, A.A. and Lure, Ia.S. (1959), *Poslaniia Iosifa Volotskogo*. Moscow.

INDEX OF NAMES

STUDIES IN THE HISTORY OF RELIGIONS
NUMEN BOOK SERIES

8 K.W. Bolle. *The Persistence of Religion*. An Essay on Tantrism and Sri Auro-
bindo's Philosophy. Repr. 1971. ISBN 90 04 03307 6

17 *Liber Amicorum*. Studies in honour of Professor Dr. C.J. Bleeker. Published on
the occasion of his retirement from the Chair of the History of Religions
and the Phenomenology of Religion at the University of Amsterdam.
1969. ISBN 90 04 03092 1

19 U. Bianchi, C.J. Bleeker & A. Bausani (eds.). *Problems and Methods of the
History of Religions*. Proceedings of the Study Conference organized by the
Italian Society for the History of Religions on the Occasion of the Tenth
Anniversary of the Death of Raffaele Pettazzoni, Rome 6th to 8th
December 1969. Papers and discussions. 1972. ISBN 90 04 02640 1

31 C.J. Bleeker, G. Widengren & E.J. Sharpe (eds.). *Proceedings of the 12th International Congress, Stockholm 1970*. 1975. ISBN 90 04 04318 7

34 V.L. Oliver, *Caodai Spiritism*. A Study of Religion in Vietnamese Society.
With a preface by P. Rondot. 1976. ISBN 90 04 04547 3

41 B. Layton (ed.). *The Rediscovery of Gnosticism*. Proceedings of the International Conference on Gnosticism at Yale, New Haven, Conn., March 28-31,
1978. Two vols.
1. *The School of Valentinus*. 1980. ISBN 90 04 06177 0   *Out of print*
2. *Sethian Gnosticism*. 1981. ISBN 90 04 06178 9

43 M. Heerma van Voss, D.J. Hoens, G. Mussies, D. van der Plas & H. te Velde
(eds.). *Studies in Egyptian Religion, dedicated to Professor Jan Zandee. 1982*.
ISBN 90 04 06728 0

44 P.J. Awn. *Satan's Tragedy and Redemption*. Iblīs in Sufi Psychology. With a fore-
word by A. Schimmel. 1983. ISBN 90 04 06906 2

45 R. Kloppenborg (ed.). *Selected Studies on Ritual in the Indian Religions*.
Essays to D.J. Hoens. 1983. ISBN 90 04 07129 6

50 S. Shaked, D. Shulman & G.G. Stroumsa (eds.). *Gilgul*. Essays on Transformation, Revolution and Permanence in the History of Religions,
dedicated to R.J. Zwi Werblowsky. 1987. ISBN 90 04 08509 2

52 J.G. Griffiths. *The Divine Verdict*. A Study of Divine Judgement in the Ancient
Religions. 1991. ISBN 90 04 09231 5

53 K. Rudolph. *Geschichte und Probleme der Religionswissenschaft*. 1992.
ISBN 90 04 09503 9

54 A.N. Balslev & J.N. Mohanty (eds.). Religion and Time. 1993.
ISBN 90 04 09583 7

55 E. Jacobson. *The Deer Goddess of Ancient Siberia*. A Study in the Ecology of
Belief. 1993. ISBN 90 04 09628 0

56 B. Saler. *Conceptualizing Religion*. Immanent Anthropologists, Transcendent
Natives, and Unbounded Categories. 1993. ISBN 90 04 09585 3

57 C. Knox. *Changing Christian Paradigms*. And their Implications for Modern
Thought. 1993. ISBN 90 04 09670 1

58 J. Cohen. *The Origins and Evolution of the Moses Nativity Story*. 1993.
ISBN 90 04 09652 3

59 S. Benko. *The Virgin Goddess.* Studies in the Pagan and Christian Roots of Mariology. 1993. ISBN 90 04 09747 3

60 Z.P. Thundy. *Buddha and Christ.* Nativity Stories and Indian Traditions. 1993. ISBN 90 04 09741 4

61 S. Hjelde. *Die Religionswissenschaft und das Christentum.* Eine historische Untersuchung über das Verhältnis von Religionswissenschaft und Theologie. 1994. ISBN 90 04 09922 0

62 Th.A. Idinopulos & E.A. Yonan (eds.). *Religion and Reductionism.* Essays on Eliade, Segal, and the Challenge of the Social Sciences for the Study of Religion. 1994. ISBN 90 04 09870 4

63 S. Khalil Samir & J.S. Nielsen (eds.). *Christian Arabic Apologetics during the Abbasid Period (750-1258).* 1994. ISBN 90 04 09568 3

64 S.N. Balagangadhara. *'The Heathen in His Blindness...'* Asia, the West and the Dynamic of Religion. 1994. ISBN 90 04 09943 3

65 H.G. Kippenberg & G.G. Stroumsa (eds.). *Secrecy and Concealment.* Studies in the History of Mediterranean and Near Eastern Religions. 1995. ISBN 90 04 10235 3

66 R. Kloppenborg & W.J. Hanegraaff (eds.). *Female Stereotypes in Religious Traditions.* 1995. ISBN 90 04 10290 6

67 J. Platvoet & K. van der Toorn (eds.). *Pluralism and Identity.* Studies on Ritual Behaviour. 1995. ISBN 90 04 10373 2

68 G. Jonker. *The Topography of Remembrance.* The Dead, Tradition and Collective Memory in Mesopotamia. 1995. ISBN 90 04 10162 4

69 S. Biderman. *Scripture and Knowledge.* An Essay on Religious Epistemology. 1995. ISBN 90 04 10154 3

70 G.G. Stroumsa. *Hidden Wisdom.* Esoteric Traditions and the Roots of Christian Mysticism. 1996. ISBN 90 04 10504 2

71 J.G. Katz. *Dreams, Sufism and Sainthood.* The Visionary Career of Muhammad al-Zawâwî. 1996. ISBN 90 04 10599 9

72 W.J. Hanegraaff. *New Age Religion and Western Culture.* Esotericism in the Mirror of Secular Thought. 1996. ISBN 90 04 10695 2

73 T.A. Idinopulos & E.A. Yonan (eds.). *The Sacred and its Scholars.* Comparative Methodologies for the Study of Primary Religious Data. 1996. ISBN 90 04 10623 5

74 K. Evans. *Epic Narratives in the Hoysaḷa Temples.* The Rāmāyaṇa, Mahābhārata and Bhāgavata Purāṇa in Haḷebīd, Belūr and Amṛtapura. 1997. ISBN 90 04 10575 1

75 P. Schäfer & H.G. Kippenberg (eds.). *Envisioning Magic.* A Princeton Seminar and Symposium. 1997. ISBN 90 04 10777 0

77 P. Schäfer & M.R. Cohen (eds.). *Toward the Millennium.* Messianic Expectations from the Bible to Waco. 1998. ISBN 90 04 11037 2

78 A.I. Baumgarten, with J. Assmann & G.G. Stroumsa (eds.). *Self, Soul and Body in Religious Experience.* 1998. ISBN 90 04 10943 9

79 M. Houseman & C. Severi. *Naven or the Other Self.* A Relational Approach to Ritual Action. 1998. ISBN 90 04 11220 0

80 A.L. Molendijk & P. Pels (eds.). *Religion in the Making.* The Emergence of the Sciences of Religion. 1998. ISBN 90 04 11239 1

81 Th.A. Idinopulos & B.C. Wilson (eds.). *What is Religion?* Origins, Definitions, & Explanations. 1998. ISBN 90 04 11022 4

82 A. van der Kooij & K. van der Toorn (eds.). *Canonization & Decanonization.* Papers presented to the International Conference of the Leiden Institute for the Study of Religions (LISOR) held at Leiden 9-10 January 1997. 1999. ISBN 90 04 11246 4

83 J. Assmann & G.G. Stroumsa (eds.). *Transformations of the Inner Self in Ancient Religions.* 1999. ISBN 90 04 11356 8

84 J.G. Platvoet & A.L. Molendijk (eds.). *The Pragmatics of Defining Religion.* Contexts, Concepts & Contests. 1999. ISBN 90 04 11544 7

85 B.J. Malkovsky (ed.). *New Perspectives on Advaita Vedānta.* Essays in Commemoration of Professor Richard De Smet, sj. 2000. ISBN 90 04 11666 4

86 A.I. Baumgarten (ed.). *Apocalyptic Time.* 2000. ISBN 90 04 11879 9

87 S. Hjelde (ed.). *Man, Meaning, and Mystery.* Hundred Years of History of Religions in Norway. The Heritage of W. Brede Kristensen. 2000. ISBN 90 04 11497 1

88 A. Korte (ed.). *Women and Miracle Stories.* A Multidisciplinary Exploration. 2000. ISBN 90 04 11681 8

89 J. Assmann & A.I. Baumgarten (eds.). *Representation in Religion.* Studies in Honor of Moshe Barasch. 2001. ISBN 90 04 11939 6

90 O. Hammer. *Claiming Knowledge.* Strategies of Epistemology from Theosophy to the New Age. 2001. ISBN 90 04 12016 5

91 B.J. Malkovsky. *The Role of Divine Grace in the Soteriology of Śaṃkarācārya.* 2001. ISBN 90 04 12044 0

92 T.A. Idinopulos & B.C. Wilson (eds.). *Reappraising Durkheim for the Study and Teaching of Religion Today.* 2002. ISBN 90 04 12339 3.

93 A.I. Baumgarten (eds.). *Sacrifice in Religious Experience.* 2002. ISBN 90 04 12483 7

94 L.P. van den Bosch. *F.M. Müller. A Life Devoted to the Humanities.* 2002. ISBN 90 04 12505 1

95 G. Wiegers. *Modern Societies & the Science of Religions.* Studies in Honour of Lammert Leertouwer. 2002. ISBN 90 04 11665 6

96 D. Zeidan. *The Resurgence of Religion.* A Comparative Study of Selected Themes in Christian and Islamic Fundamentalist Discourses. 2003. ISBN 90 04 12877 8

97 S. Meyer (ed.). *Egypt — Temple of the Whole World / Ägypten — Tempel der Gesamten Welt.* Studies in Honour of Jan Assmann. 2003. ISBN 90 04 13240 6

98 I. Strenski. *Theology and the First Theory of Sacrifice.* 2003. ISBN 90 04 13559 6

99 T. Light & B.C. Wilson (eds.). *Religion as a Human Capacity.* A Festschrift in Honor of E. Thomas Lawson. 2003. ISBN 90 04 12676 7

100 A.E. Buss. *The Russian-Orthodox Tradition and Modernity.* 2003. ISBN 90 04 13324 0

101 K.A. Jacobsen & P.P. Kumar (eds.). South Asians in the Diaspora. Histories and Religious Traditions. 2004. ISBN 90 04 12488 8

102 M. Stausberg. *Zoroastrian Rituals in Context.* 2003. ISBN 90 04 13131 0

ISSN 0169-8834